The Passion of

ABBY HEMENWAY

*Memory, Spirit, and
the Making of
History*

DEBORAH PICKMAN CLIFFORD

HISTORICAL
· SOCIETY ·

109 State Street, Montpelier, Vermont 05609

Distributed by
University Press of New England
HANOVER & LONDON

Vermont Historical Society, 109 State Street, Montpelier, Vermont 05609

Design by Suzanne Church

Library of Congress Cataloging-in-Publication Data

Clifford, Deborah Pickman.
The Passion of Abby Hemenway : memory, spirit, and the making of history / Deborah Pickman Clifford.
p. cm.
Includes bibliographical references (p.) and index.
ISBN 0-934720-46-0 (cloth : alk. paper) -- ISBN 0-934720-47-9 (pbk. : alk. paper)
1. Hemenway, Abby Maria, 1828-1890. 2. Women historians--Vermont--Biography. 3. Women historians--United States--Biography. 4. Historians--Vermont--Biography. 5. Historians--United States--Biography. 6. Vermont historical gazetteer. 7. Vermont--Historiography. 8. United States--Historiography. I. Vermont Historical Society. II. Title.

E175.5.H38 C58 2001
974.3'041'092--dc21
[B]

Printed in the United States of America
01 00 99 98 1 2 3 4 5

Contents

Acknowledgments

In the early 1990s, when I began researching the life of Abby Hemenway, I knew of only a few dozen letters of hers scattered in various Vermont archives. These letters, together with Hemenway's published works (many of which were edited, not written, by her), and an M.A. thesis from the 1930s, constituted the principal resource material on her life. Since then, with the help of numerous individuals both in Vermont and elsewhere, I have uncovered several dozen more letters and other documents that have helped to enrich this biography.

I would like to start by thanking David Hemenway (a descendant of Abby's through her brother Charles) for letting me see and use his collection of family papers, including letters and photographs. The late Barbara Chiolino, a descendant of Abby's mother's family, the Bartons, was particularly helpful as a source of family lore. The Reverend John R. McSweeney kindly let me spend many hours perusing his extensive collection of Abby Hemenway memorabilia. Other individuals who let me use materials in their private collections include Ruth Cozzens, Donald P. Johnstone, Florence Plumb, and Mary Torrey.

Most of my research was done right here in Vermont. I owe special thanks to librarians at the Vermont Historical Society, at Special Collections at the Bailey/Howe Library of the University of Vermont, to Georgia Brehm at the Black River Academy Museum in Ludlow, and most of all to Polly Darnell and Nancy Rucker, Henry Sheldon Museum librarians, who were unfailingly patient and helpful in meeting my many requests.

Three archives in the Midwest contain small collections of Hemenway letters. These proved invaluable in shedding light on Hemenway's last years and her struggles to keep the *Vermont Historical Gazetteer* alive. My thanks go to the Chicago Historical Society, to Charles Lamb at the University Archives, University of Notre Dame, and to Jacqueline Dougherty of the Province Archives Center of the Indiana Province of the Congregation of the Holy Cross at Notre Dame.

A number of individuals, including Kevin Graffagnino and Dennis O'Brien, were helpful in leading me to resources that I might otherwise have overlooked. Others to whom I owe thanks include Elizabeth Dow, Bob Ferm, Kate Sonderegger, Julia Alvarez, Jane Beck, David Blow, Dennis Devereux, Jere Daniell, Mary Kelley, and the late Tom Bassett and William Goss.

When it came time to begin writing I solicited guidance of all sorts. First are the members of my old writing group. My thanks go to Barbara Bloom, Ann Cooper, Kathy Harris, and Libby Van Buskirk for their unfailing support, also to the members of Sally Brady's writers' workshop who provided welcome criticism and encouragement.

Lyn Blackwell, Upton Brady, Bill Catton, Dick Hathaway, and Michael Sherman all read the manuscript and gave helpful critiques. My deepest thanks, however, go to my husband, Nicholas, who not only read and critiqued the manuscript at various stages but provided essential computer assistance, helped with the formatting and printing of several drafts, and above all was a tireless supporter of my work.

Finally, I would like to thank my editor at the Vermont Historical Society, Alan Berolzheimer, for his help in readying this book for publication.

Introduction

"Not a suitable work for a woman" Abby Hemenway was told in 1859 when she first embarked on her life's work as editor of the *Vermont Historical Gazetteer*.[1] Yet nearly a century and a half later, as other early American histories gather dust in secondhand bookshops, well-thumbed copies of these five hefty volumes in their faded brown bindings grace the shelves of most public libraries in the Green Mountain State. Each book contains more than one thousand two-columned pages, packed with information about the early history of most Vermont towns.

In the years since her death in 1890, neither Abby Hemenway nor her work have received the respect they deserve. As recently as the 1970s, a critic of the *Gazetteer* dismissed it as a hodgepodge of "indigestible gleanings, crammed into five sausage-like volumes in white-hot haste."[2] Hemenway herself, meanwhile, has been remembered, if at all, as an eccentric spinster who died in poverty in Chicago while on the run from her creditors. Yet the continuing importance of her *Gazetteer* has not gone unrecognized. In 1950 the historian Ralph Nading Hill wrote that "there will never be a book of Vermont history written that will not owe a profound debt to these bulky volumes."[3]

When a friend first suggested, back in 1991, that I write a biography of Abby Hemenway, I realized immediately that she was exactly the kind of subject I'd been looking for: a Vermont woman who had profoundly influenced her state and whose life had assumed legendary, even epic proportions. I was familiar with Hemenway from my own work in Vermont history and knew that I would have a hard time finding a more stimulating and engaging person to write about. Beyond that I knew little.

As I began my research I quickly discovered how few sources of a personal nature survive. Apart from a handful of family stories passed down through the generations and a smattering of facts about Hemenway's childhood in her published writings, little is known of her early years. The sources of her ambition and extraordinary self-confidence are largely matters of conjecture. Also slimly documented is the path that led Hemenway from the Baptist faith of her childhood into the Roman Catholic Church, which she joined in 1864. What deep spiritual craving did this religion satisfy? What is the connection between the appeal of Catholicism and Abby Hemenway's calling as a historian?

While the fruits of her historical labors are preserved for posterity in the five fat volumes of the *Gazetteer* still in active use today, many of Hemenway's personal papers were destroyed in a fire that occurred in 1911, twenty-one years after her death. Also destroyed were the manuscripts for a final volume that would have covered the history of Windsor County. Apart from a hundred or so of her letters scattered in various archives both in and outside Vermont, all that remains is an eclectic assortment of published works. These include (in addition to the *Gazetteer*) a book of Vermont poetry, an autobiography of sorts describing her early editorial experiences, three volumes of not very good religious poetry, and a play about Fanny Allen, Ethan Allen's daughter.[4]

The lack of personal papers presents a further challenge. Of the more than one hundred of Hemenway's letters that I have managed to uncover, only eight are addressed to women. The rest of her surviving correspondence pertains largely to her editorship of the *Gazetteer*. Thus Hemenway's life as a woman must be pieced together from her extant papers and published writings and from a scattering of secondary sources. Whatever intimate letters she may have written to her mother, her sisters, and close women friends, with a few notable exceptions, no longer exist. It is, therefore, Abby Hemenway in her role as editor of the *Vermont Historical Gazetteer*, who forms the centerpiece of this book.

As far as we know, no one else in the whole country attempted to do what Hemenway did, single-handedly collecting and publishing the history of every community in her state. And while each of the United States by the late nineteenth century had produced its own crop of dedicated historians, none of their work surpassed the *Gazetteer* as an achievement in the field of state and local history.[5]

Over the course of her years as editor of the *Vermont Historical Gazetteer*, Hemenway engaged hundreds of men and women to write the histories of their towns, their churches, their businesses, and their schools. Hundreds more contributed memoirs of the early days of white settlement or provided sketches of forebears who had braved the terrors of the wilderness to build the first log cabins in their communities.

For a man to have embarked on such a vast historical enterprise would have seemed ambitious enough, but for a woman to manage such a multifaceted project on her own was unprecedented. It helped, of course, that Abby Hemenway never married. Even so, her story is a remarkable one. Given the limited career choices available to women in nineteenth-century America, what likelihood was there that the daughter of a hill country farmer might compose a challenging professional life for herself, much less succeed at it? Yet Abby Hemenway not only dreamed ambitious, unwomanly dreams of creating an important work of history, but she also lived to see the greater part of those dreams realized. It must be added, too, that she accomplished all this despite the innumerable obstacles placed in her path, from money and legal troubles to floods and conflagrations. According to Hemenway family tradition, at one time in Abby's life she was engaged in no less than eleven separate lawsuits.[6]

As George Eliot wrote of Saint Teresa of Avila, a woman with such a "passionate and ideal nature demanded an epic life." While no one would claim for a moment that this northern New England woman was another Saint Teresa, like that sixteenth-century Spanish mystic the ardor of Abby Hemenway's ambition "soared after some illimitable satisfaction, some object which would never justify weariness."[7]

Hemenway was thirty-one years old when she embarked on this work of gathering up and preserving the history of every Vermont village and town. The year was 1859, a time when regional and local identities were competing with an emerging national identity. Moreover, those with memories of the state's founding and its early years had mostly passed away, and Hemenway came to see her mission as one that preserved the heritage of even the smallest village in the state. Her high purpose was to unite her fellow Vermonters through their shared recollections of the past, to give them a pride in their town and state, and in themselves as a people. As we would say today, she was seeking to enshrine a cultural memory.

But Abby Hemenway's sway extended beyond the borders of Vermont. David Russo has called her "the most influential antiquarian in New England between the Civil War and the Great Depression."[8] Today the word "antiquarian" is too often used pejoratively, and early local historians such as Hemenway tend to be dismissed by modern scholars as amateurish. The truth is that most of the historical writing in this country before 1900 came not from such popular historians as Francis Parkman and John Lothrop Motley or the professionals of the American Historical Association, but from local amateurs. Furthermore, the history written by these amateurs was in many ways more comprehensive in scope than the heavily political history produced by such men or their more academic successors. It was, as Hemenway's *Gazetteer* amply demonstrates, social, cultural, intellectual, and economic history.

Fortunately, time has narrowed the gap between the amateur local historians of the nineteenth century and the professional analytical scholars of the twentieth. Not only are social and cultural histories once more in vogue, but since the 1960s local history has also enjoyed a comeback among academics. Modern "community studies" of New England towns range from Charles Grant's groundbreaking *Democracy in the Connecticut Frontier Town of Kent,* published in 1961, to Laurel Thatcher Ulrich's *A Midwife's Tale* (1990) with its superb blending of the narrative and analytical approaches to writing local history. Because Hemenway's histories are filled with useful information about Vermont's early heritage, they are once again appreciated for the rich sources they contain and as an early example of the inscription of cultural memory.

"Let them be sea captains if they will," wrote Margaret Fuller in the 1840s, challenging her sisters to take charge of their own lives. Abby Hemenway, for one, heeded that call, and in her last years proudly called herself a pioneer who had launched the boat of local history in Vermont.[9] It is the story of this indomitable, unwavering editor of the *Vermont Historical Gazetteer* that this book seeks to tell.

In our little mountain town, away up among the Green Mountains, we have no great history to write of, no mighty deeds of valiant men to chronicle, no biography of some brilliant person who has gone from here and startled the world with his history . . . but simply a story of hardy men and brave women seeking and making their homes among these hills.

Historical Address by Z.S. Stanton delivered at Roxbury, Vermont, 22 August 1876,
in
Abby M. Hemenway, ed.,
Vermont Historical Gazetteer, Vol. IV, p. 784

1

Hill Country Childhood

———•◦◊○◊◦•———

The child that has an intellectual mother
is twice mothered.

Abby Hemenway [1]

V ermont was less than forty years old when Abby
Hemenway was born on October 7, 1828. Admitted to the
Union in 1791, the state's early history had been shaped, not
by the colonial experience, but by the Revolution and the per-
ceived triumph of democratic republicanism over aristocratic
tyranny and corruption. The post-Revolutionary years had seen
a steady influx of settlers from southern New England seeking
prosperous farms and shops for themselves and their children.
Between 1790 and 1800 the population of the state nearly doubled, rising from 85,341 to 154,465, making Vermont the fastest
growing of the new United States.

All four of Abby Hemenway's grandparents had been part of this flood of emigrants to Vermont, moving north from Massachusetts in the last years of the eighteenth century. Her mother's family, the Bartons, came first in the late 1780s, choosing Andover, a Vermont frontier settlement on the western edge of the Connecticut River Valley. The Hemenways followed a few years later, settling in the nearby town of Ludlow.

Both Ludlow and Andover are mountain towns in southwestern Windsor County that enjoy long, cold winters and short, bracing summers. Okemo Mountain, known today for its trails and ski lifts, looms immediately to the west of Ludlow and operates as a huge snow fence, causing the drifts on its west side to blow over the ridge and down into the Black River Valley below where it can lie from September until May. Of these two Windsor County towns Ludlow is the newer. Organized in 1792, it then had a population of just under two hundred. Today it numbers more than two thousand.[2]

Abby Hemenway's forebears, like most of Vermont's early white settlers, all came of old Yankee stock. Their story mirrors those of countless other families who emigrated north to the Green Mountains in the last decades of the eighteenth century and is one that, with minor variations, would later be told and retold by Hemenway's town historians in the pages of the *Vermont Historical Gazetteer.* Like other narratives of early Vermont settlers, the family record that follows has been pieced together from scattered and limited sources. Made up of local and family lore as well as hard fact, such a historical account demands an imaginative reconstruction of the past, drawing on the kind of storytelling that had been so important for the historians of the *Gazetteer.*

Ralph Hemenway was the first of his family to come to the American colonies. He had joined the Great Migration from England in 1634 and settled in Roxbury, Massachusetts. Some of his descendants moved first to Salem and later to Framingham. From there, in 1794 or 1795, Jacob and Sarah

Hemenway, Abby's great-grandparents, moved north to Ludlow, Vermont, taking their son, also named Jacob, and his wife, Hannah. The younger Jacob, Abby's grandfather, was in his early twenties at the time. Upon arriving in Ludlow, the family acquired land south of town high up on Bear Hill near the Andover line, where they first built a log house and some-time later a frame house. There Jacob and Hannah raised their children, including Abby's father, Daniel.[3]

Although Abby never knew her Hemenway grandmother, young Jacob's wife, Hannah, was considered the aristocrat in the family. She was descended on her father's side from Lord Edmund Sheffield, one of the grantors of Plymouth Colony. It has been suggested that the life annuity Hannah received from her ancestor's English estate helped to pay for the Hemenways' move north to Vermont.[4]

The first member of Abby's mother's family, the Bartons, to settle in the New World was Samuel. He, too, lived in Salem, where at the time of the witchcraft persecutions two of his wife's aunts, Rebecca Nurse and Mary Estey, were among the accused, and they were hanged on Salem Hill in 1692. Fearing perhaps for his own wife's safety, Samuel carried his family out of Salem. Like the Hemenways, the Bartons also settled first in Framingham and in the early eighteenth century moved to North Oxford.

Sometime before 1790, Rufus Barton, Abby Hemenway's grandfather, journeyed northward to the Vermont frontier, together with his brother Jerry and his elderly parents, John and Abigail. John Barton was a vigorous old gentleman who had enlisted as a Revolutionary soldier while in his fifties. He later claimed that the hardships of the war had aged him, but he then lived to be eighty, longer than most of his contemporaries. His wife, Abigail Dana, a descendant of Richard Dana of Cambridge, was equally hardy. Only fourteen years old when she married, she gave birth to fourteen children. Her grandson Asa Barton (Abby's uncle) remembered her as a kind and pious woman who never evinced anger or manifested "the least resentment" during a long and hard life. Abigail Barton lived to the age of ninety-four.[5]

The four Bartons made the trip from North Oxford to Vermont in winter when it was easier to travel over the hard, snow-covered ground. After piling their possessions on an ox sled, the elderly couple and their two sons spent nine cold, tedious days on the road before reaching the tiny settlement of Andover. There Rufus purchased one hundred acres in the northwest part of town near the Ludlow line. His daughter, Abby's mother—who was also named Abigail Dana—used to boast that the Bartons had been only the fifth family to settle in Andover.[6]

Having purchased land and built a house, Rufus Barton also found himself a wife, marrying Lydia Washer in 1798. A native of Amherst, New Hampshire, Abby's grandmother had been living with her sister and husband who were tavern keepers in Chester, a flourishing market town just southeast of Ludlow. There she became accomplished at cooking for "those fine old style balls, to which the young elite for forty miles around came."[7] Lydia would always pride herself on her culinary skills. After the wedding in Chester, Rufus brought his bride back to the Andover farm to share the privations and hardships of pioneer life and together they raised a family of four children. Many years later their eldest daughter, Abigail Dana, romanticized this "forest home" of her childhood in a poem:

> My birth and early home was where
>> The wildflowers sweetly bloomed
> And through the opening forest glade
>> The radiant morn perfumed.
>
> No glittering spires or lofty domes
>> E'er met my youthful eye,

But the Green Mountain's archy brow
   And blue transparent sky.

. . . .

And I have never found a home
   So sweetly free from care,
As that dear forest home of mine,
   So lovely and so fair.[8]

Abigail Dana's brother Asa described their father, Rufus, as "a man of clear and vigorous mind . . . quick of perception" and "keen in repartee." An eager debater, Rufus was so passionately fond of religious disputation that he would often play the devil's advocate, simply to test the skill and ingenuity of his companion in an argument. Some people in Andover believed he was opposed to the leading principles of Christianity. But, apart from his outspoken hatred of Calvinist theology, Rufus kept his private beliefs to himself. Asa remembered once overhearing an exchange between his father and Thomas Weatherby, an elderly Ludlow clergyman. The latter claimed that twenty-one of the infants born during his tenure as pastor were now in hell because they had died before being baptized. In reply, Barton assured Weatherby that he had "one consolation left . . . if they are orphans and now in Hell they will soon have a father to protect them."[9]

At least three of Rufus' four children inherited his independent, argumentative spirit. According to family lore, Abigail Dana and her two younger brothers, Asa and Rufus, honed their sharp wits during many heated family debates on religious, political, and social issues. When, years later, a noted visitor to Ludlow remarked that Abigail Dana was the most intelligent woman he had ever met, the compliment was welcomed by the Bartons as a "contribution to family pride."[10]

Intelligence and independence were characteristics cherished by other Barton women. A distant cousin of Abby's, Clara

Barton, would prove her strong-mindedness as a nurse on the battlefields of the Civil War. This valiant woman had little difficulty taking on the male establishment single-handedly, and would later overcome governmental and public apathy to found the American Red Cross.[11]

In the years preceding her marriage, Abigail Dana Barton put her intellectual skills to use as a teacher in the district schools. The demand for instructors in the fast-growing towns of Vermont would peak in the second decade of the nineteenth century, as population growth filled to overflowing the hundreds of one-room schoolhouses scattered throughout the hill country. Thanks in part to this increased demand, young New England women like Abigail Barton began entering the teaching force in significant numbers. While few of them taught for a long period, this paid employment was the only one open to women that presented them with any degree of intellectual challenge.

We don't know where Abigail Dana Barton taught or for how many terms. But it is not hard to imagine this energetic, resourceful, and sharp-witted young woman holding the attention of the forty to as many as ninety boys and girls of all ages who crowded the benches of her Vermont rural classroom.

Abigail Dana may have been teaching the winter term in a school some distance from home and boarding, as was the custom, with the family of one of her students, when, in late January 1822, she received a letter from her future husband, Daniel Hemenway. Perhaps the two were already engaged, for Daniel himself had delivered Abby's mother to her new post, and, concerned for her welfare, had penned a few awkwardly shaped lines expressing his dismay at leaving her "with strangers on that lonesome hill," and evincing concern about her health. A week later he sent off another letter claiming "pen and paper cant tell you how disagreeable I feel to have you so far from home," and urging her not "to stay enelonger than the first ingagement"—meaning presumably the term that

From the Gazetteer

∗ ∗ ∗

Clarendon Springs

by H.B. Spofford

About 1797 there were eight families residing in the
immediate vicinity of the springs, who had 113 children,
99 of whom were living and attended the same school.
These families are and always have been well known in
town, and I give, in the following table, the names of the
heads of the families, being the husband and maiden
name of the wife, and the number of children born to
them, and the number alive who attended school at one
and the same time.

	Born	Scholars
James Harrington and Polly Bates	12	10
Theophilus Harrington and Betsey Buck	12	11
William Harrington and Amy Briggs	17	13
George Round and Martha Hopkins	12	12
John Simonds and Sarah Wescott	12	12
Charles Simonds and Mehitable Esborn	16	16
Richard Weaver and Judith Reynolds	13	11
Jonathan Eddy and Temperance Pratt	19	14
	113	99

In these families no one [father] of the 8 ever had more
than one wife, and there was but one pair of twins in the
lot; and the extreme differences between the first-born of
all these families was 16 years.

[Volume III, page 570]

she'd been hired to teach. In any case, before the end of that
year Abigail Dana Barton returned home and on December 5,
1822, she and Daniel Hemenway were married.[12]

Daniel Hemenway, Abby's father, 1860s.
(Permission David Hemenway.)

Daniel was a kind, hardworking man. While still in his teens he had enlisted, along with six other men from Ludlow, as a soldier in the War of 1812. At the war's end, having fought in two battles, he stayed for a time in Brownville, New York,

Abigail Dana Hemenway, Abby's mother, 1860s.
(Permission David Hemenway.)

before returning to Ludlow. Once back home he acquired land south of town on the road to Weston, where in 1820 he built a log cabin. It was to this house that he brought his new bride.[13]

The marriage had taken place on Thanksgiving Day

(which occurred that year in December) at Jacob and Hannah Hemenway's farm. The ceremony was followed by one of Lydia Barton's traditional Thanksgiving breakfasts consisting of hot wheat bread, buttered toast, chickens stewed in butter, and a huge oblong, plum-stuffed mince pie. When all had eaten their fill the whole wedding party went to meeting at the neighboring schoolhouse where a Methodist elder, Benjamin Shaw, preached a Thanksgiving sermon.[14]

The first years of Daniel and Abigail's marriage were spent in his log cabin. Here on August 9, 1823, their first child, named Rufus Nelson, was born. He was followed quickly by an infant who died, then by a daughter, the first Abigail. "Too pretty for this world" the neighbors had said of this flaxen-haired child. True to their predictions, the little girl, her mother's favorite, lived for only two-and-a-half years.[15]

Meanwhile, in 1827 Daniel and Abigail moved in with his parents, sharing the frame house Jacob Hemenway had built on Bear Hill in 1805. With its two square rooms, its kitchen and buttery, large attic, and cellar, even half of this dwelling probably had more room for a growing family than Daniel's small log cabin. In any case, father and son divided the house in two, Jacob taking the west half and Daniel the east, and it was here that the second Abigail was born on October 7, 1828. While the arrival of another daughter doubtless eased the sorrows of the young Hemenway parents over the loss of their first, the pain associated with the name Abigail had proved too much. The new arrival, whose middle name was Maria, would henceforth be known simply as Abby.[16]

At the time of Abby's birth her father was thirty-two years old and her mother thirty. Her only sibling, Rufus, was five. In the ensuing twelve years, however, six more Hemenway children would be born, five of whom survived infancy: Lydia Washer in 1830, Charles Wesley in 1832, Carrie Elizabeth in

1834, Horace Cushman in 1837, and Daniel Dana in 1840. Large families were common then in New England, and the Hemenways were luckier than most in seeing the majority of their offspring live into adulthood.

The growing family, however, did not remain for long with the Jacob Hemenways. By the time Abby's sister Lydia was born in 1830, her parents had moved yet again, to a farm that Daniel had acquired on the corner of Andover and Old County Roads. The house he built there for his family would be home for Abby for the remainder of her childhood.

None of these moves had carried the Daniel Hemenways very far. All three dwellings were in what is called the Barton District, located in the hills south of town adjacent to the Andover line. By the time Abby was seven years old, the neighborhood contained nearly a dozen separate Barton and Hemenway households. Closest by were Abigail Dana's three brothers and their families. Grandfather Jacob Hemenway's farm was several miles distant, but just to their south was a newly erected frame house belonging to Elijah Hemenway, whose precise relationship to Daniel is not known.[17]

With Ludlow village several miles distant down a twisty mountain road, this collection of family farms comprised Abby's whole childhood world. This was especially true in winter, because these Barton and Hemenway holdings were all in the snowiest part of the valley. In times of severe blizzards the Elijah Hemenway house was so deeply buried that a sleigh could pass easily over it. Daniel Hemenway's farm adjoined Elijah's, so similar conditions would have prevailed there.[18]

But long snowy winters were not the only hardships endured by hill country families like the Bartons and Hemenways. When Abby was a small child in the early 1830s, few of the modern conveniences that were introduced over the course of the nineteenth century, such as kitchen stoves, kerosene lamps, and sewing machines, had yet made their appearance. Cooking, for example, was still done over an open fire, and Abby never forgot the day her father brought home the family's first stove. Its arrival, she later remembered, marked

> the inauguration of a new era in the culinary kingdom—the pleasant old fire-place with the swinging crane of well-filled pots and kettles, hearth-spiders with legs and bake-kettles and tin-bakers to stand before the blazing logs and bake custard pies in—all went down at once and disappeared before the first stove, without so much as a passing struggle.[19]

Farming equipment was equally primitive. By 1830 wagons were in general use, but mowing machines did not arrive in Ludlow until Wesley Barton, Abby's cousin, bought the first one, known as a "Kirby machine," in 1858.[20]

Like his parents and grandparents before him, Daniel Hemenway struggled to make a living from his rocky hillside and money was never plentiful. One surviving family anecdote provides a rare glimpse of the unruly Hemenway brood and the degree to which Daniel's children sometimes took advantage of his good nature.

As the story goes, one Sunday afternoon, while his wife was calling on a sick neighbor, Daniel was left in charge of the younger children. His attempt to "preserve the Sabbath calm," however, was soon interrupted by an attack of suppressed giggles from Charles, the family mischief maker. The father, threatening punishment if his son did not behave, was in the act of taking the switch down from its resting place on the wall when he spied the doctor returning from the sick neighbor's house. Anxious for news he put down the switch and stepped outside for a word with the doctor. No sooner was Daniel out the door than Charles seized the stick. After carefully removing the bark in one piece he cut the wood into small segments and put these back inside the bark. When Daniel came back into the house his three youngest sons greeted him with "particularly offensive snickers." As expected, the angry father picked up the switch and raised it to strike one of the boys, whereupon it collapsed, along with his parental dignity. Everyone, father and children, laughed together.[21]

This story illustrates the easing of family discipline in New England during the early decades of the nineteenth century. While Daniel Hemenway was not averse to using corporal punishment when his children got out of hand, he was equally willing to let good humor outweigh his sternest intentions. What would have seemed shamefully indulgent a generation or two earlier was now an accepted mode of child rearing. As Philip Greven has pointed out, the children "who grew up in these families began their lives with a sense of self-worth, self-love, and self-confidence that set them apart from those reared in different ways. They also began their lives with a sense of inner security, a security that was missing from many of their contemporaries . . ."[22]

Abby's own later memories of Daniel Hemenway were happy ones. She remembered him as a "kind old father," yet she does not appear to have been particularly close to him.[23] By contrast, her relationship with her mother was intimate. Perhaps Abigail Dana Hemenway recognized much of herself in her eldest daughter, for Abby Maria had not only inherited her energy, intelligence, and resourcefulness but her literary bent as well. By the time young Abby was grown her mother had acquired a solid reputation as a local poet, having, by her daughter's accounting, published more verses in the county newspapers than any other Ludlow resident of her day.[24]

But Abigail Dana Hemenway was first and foremost a wife and mother, not a poet. Duty, not literary ambitions, guided her actions, and the cares of raising a large family eventually took their toll on the Ludlow farm wife. The only surviving portrait of Abby's mother shows a woman of sad-eyed strength whose expression reflects a life of hardship and sorrow endured with patient, God-fearing equanimity. Some of the sadness and resignation seen in this portrait are conveyed as well in this representative sample of her bittersweet verses:

Autumn

The Summer's golden days are past,
    Its blooming tints are fled,
And Autumn's frost o'er hill and dale
    A withering blight has spread.

The chilling blast sweeps wailing by,
    And calls, Oh, man! to thee,—
Go, read upon the fading leaf
    Thy future destiny.

As fairest blossoms withered lie,
    Sad emblems of decay,
So time's rude frost will fade thy cheek,
    And thou must pass away.[25]

Unlike her husband, Daniel, who was a Methodist, or her brother Asa, who belonged to no church and made little secret of his marked dislike for Calvinist theology, Abigail Dana had gone her own way. Sometime during the early years of her marriage she joined the Ludlow Baptist Church, the stronghold of local orthodoxy.[26]

From the time she was small Abby shared both her mother's piety and her love of literature. As a child, one of her favorite pastimes had been to memorize the verses from a stout little hymnal treasured by her mother. According to Abby's later recollection, "Village Hymns" included selections from such English literary lights as Addison and Steele. One contributor to the volume, David Lamb, she remembered confusing with the English poet William Lamb only to find out later that David was a Vermont farmer living in Whitingham. The following lines of this "fine old hymn writer" were among her favorites:

> Lord give me strength to die to sin
> To run the Christian race:
> To live to God and Glorify
> The riches of his grace.[27]

But if young Abby shared many of Abigail Dana's tastes and convictions, she was not much help to her mother around the house. While little Carrie Hemenway by the age of six could knit a whole stocking by herself, family tradition credits her older sister Abby with no such accomplishment. When it was her turn to dry the dishes, likely as not she would wander, dishcloth in hand, out of the house and through the woods to her favorite retreat on the banks of Jewell Brook. There, removed from the noise and bustle of family life, and, as she wrote later, "unwistful of the silent flow of time / Lost in the vista of a revery sublime," she was free to dream or read her favorite books.[28]

Abby's interests, quite simply, were very different from those of her brothers and sisters. While she loved all kinds of games and enjoyed exploring the woods and fields, her bent, like her mother's, was chiefly literary. She was a great devourer of books, and particularly loved reading about the past. By the age of ten she had already consumed several hefty volumes of English, Greek, and Roman history.[29]

For a nineteenth-century girl living on a remote hill farm to have access to such sophisticated reading material was not unusual. By the third decade of the nineteenth century, thanks to the freedom and unprecedented cheapness of the press, printed matter of all kinds from newspapers, Bibles, and almanacs to books of theology, history, and science were available even in the Connecticut River Valley's most remote hamlets. If individual families could afford to own few books, they happily lent the ones they had. In addition, a circulating library in Chester, founded in 1829, and a small lending library in Andover, were two local sources of reading matter that Abby's family may have used.[30]

Abby's easy access to books is less remarkable than her choice of those she wished to read. Her favorites seem to have been volumes filled with facts and action, with accounts of purposeful men of indomitable will whose deeds had changed the course of history, and thus helped to feed her ambitions. One relative who openly encouraged her intellectual precociousness was her uncle Asa Barton, whose library proved a likely source of reading material for his niece. An an avid reader and a frequent contributor of essays and reviews to local periodicals, in the late 1840s Asa briefly shared with his brother Rufus the editorship of Ludlow's first newspaper, the *Genius of Liberty.*

Abby did not have to go far to borrow books from her uncle's library since Asa Barton's farm adjoined Daniel Hemenway's. Two of Asa's children, Wesley and Ralph, were closer to Abby in age than anyone in her own family, and all five cousins treated her like a sister. Abby returned their affection, feeling perhaps more at home in the Barton household than in her own. There the lively intellectual and literary atmosphere encouraged by Uncle Asa precisely suited her own tastes. Asa Barton, like his father before him, enjoyed nothing so much as a heated debate on the great issues of the day, and Abby and her mother, when they could be spared from domestic duties at home, would walk over to the Barton farmhouse and join in.

It is not hard to imagine what subjects of discussion were enjoyed by the Barton family. By 1840, when Abby was twelve, many Vermonters had lost their earlier optimism about their state's future. The previous decades had shown a number of disturbing trends, including the rising number of young men and women leaving the state to seek their fortunes elsewhere, together with reports of growing disorder and unruly behavior in the hill towns. By the late 1830s, confidence in continued growth and prosperity had eroded further, thanks to a nationwide recession that severely reduced the demand for Vermont crops and manufactured goods.

Beginning in 1828 a season of growing religious enthusiasm was drawing upon the widespread belief that indifference to God was responsible for this threatening disorder. Well into the next decade wave after wave of revivals broke across Vermont, sweeping thousands of converts into its churches. Quite possibly, one of these outbursts of religious fervor had carried Abigail Dana Hemenway out of the Methodist and into the Baptist Church.

Not everyone, however, was pleased with this surge of evangelicalism. When the renowned itinerant preacher, Jedediah Burchard, made his stormy tour of Vermont in the fall of 1834, holding boisterous revivals in towns across the state, some questioned the extreme "new measures" this eloquent evangelist employed to gain converts. Middlebury College, which had enjoyed great success after its founding in 1800, was almost brought to its knees by one of Burchard's "protracted" meetings.

The only Windsor County town to experience one of Burchard's revivals was Woodstock. The meeting there lasted twenty-six days, during which time sinners were urged to come forward and take the empty pews at the front of the church known as "anxious seats." There they were given fifteen minutes to repent or be assured of certain damnation. These fervent revivals brought dozens of new members and a renewed and welcome vitality to many Vermont congregations. Abigail Dana Hemenway may have welcomed this season of religious renewal, but her brother Asa, who was in Woodstock the day after Burchard left town, denounced all the "commotion and excitement," as a "disgrace to the common sense of the place." Other more pious critics doubted the durability of the conversions obtained by such means.[31]

Meanwhile, secular as well as religious reform was the object of much impassioned discussion in Vermont. No other state in the Union could match the eagerness with which its citizens rallied to the antislavery and antimasonic crusades, two reforms that questioned the social and political status quo. Anti-Masons, for one, were obsessed by what they saw as an elitist conspiracy by members of the fraternal order of Freemasons—many of whom were prosperous lawyers, farmers, and tradesmen—against equality and religious liberty. In West Windsor and South Woodstock, both struggling Windsor County farming communities, antimasonic leaders expressed their resentment of the prosperity and political dominance of towns such as Windsor and Woodstock, denouncing them as seats of privilege and corruption. By 1833 the Anti-Masonic party could boast a majority of the voters in the Connecticut River Valley.[32]

Reformist fervor, like religious fervor, could thus divide Vermonters as much as it united them. Yet, while Asa Barton and his sister Abigail might disagree about the kind of evangelical Christianity preached by Burchard, they shared a horror of the institution of slavery. Abigail wrote at least one poem, "The Slave's Lament," denouncing the "Peculiar Institution," while Asa regularly contributed antislavery articles to reformist journals.[33]

It is not hard to imagine young Abby entering eagerly into whatever subject was under discussion. She later described frequent debates with this favorite uncle over religious matters.

Like his father before him, Asa nursed a lifelong horror of Calvinist theology, dismissing it as "a medley of errors and contradictions." The concept of original sin made no sense to him. "It is a moral impossibility," he wrote a friend in his last years, "for any one to feel condemned for an event which occurred six thousand years ago." Because Abigail Dana was a committed Baptist, she was unlikely to have shared her brother's rationalistic views, but that only made the arguments around the Barton kitchen table livelier.[34]

As a grown woman Abby would exhibit a remarkable gift both for winning people over to her point of view and for persuading them to do her bidding. If most nineteenth-century American girls were discouraged by their families and society from developing such assertiveness, this was not the case either for Abby or her cousin Lucia, Uncle Asa's only daughter. As one Barton descendant has pointed out, neither of these young women "were about to take back seats for men."[35]

Besides her own mother, Uncle Asa was the family member who gave young Abby the most encouragement to pursue her bookish aspirations. Asa Barton supported the budding writers in his own family and next to his second son, Ralph, he apparently saw the most literary promise in his favorite niece, Abby. Asa undoubtedly lent her many of the books she read as a child, and he certainly later spurred her on to write and edit the *Gazetteer*. Indeed, uncle and niece, despite many differences of opinion, would remain close for the rest of their lives.[36]

Before Abby Hemenway even learned to read or write, however, she developed a passion for stories. Even as a small child her principal contribution to the Hemenway family was as a raconteur. If this oldest Hemenway daughter was not much help to her mother in the kitchen, she willingly spent hours amusing her younger brothers and sisters with tales of all sorts. The stories Abby loved best were about the past. "When old men talk we love to listen," she later wrote, perhaps recalling with nostalgia the cold winter evenings when her family had gathered around the warmth of the fireplace and listened to the elder members reminisce about earlier times.[37]

Most of the surviving family lore that nurtured Abby's life-long love for homely stories concerns the Bartons. Two feature her great-grandfather John Barton, a figure of almost mythic proportions. Quick and wiry as a young man, John had loved to boast how he once threw the most powerful wrestler in Worcester. More admirable, perhaps, had been his enlistment as a Revolutionary soldier while in his fifties—a decision prompted, so the story went, by the sight of a much younger man, who, when drafted, had turned pale and entreated to be let off.[38]

There is the story, too, of John Barton's wife, Abigail, who was very superstitious and a firm believer in witches. Three of her grandsons, Abby's uncles Asa, Rufus, and Eben, were terrible teases, and they decided to give their grandmother a good scare. One Sunday, while the rest of the family was at church and Abigail Barton was alone in her log house, the boys climbed up onto the roof and into the chimney. One by one they slid down into the fireplace hoping to appear before their startled grandmother as if by magic. What the story does not reveal is whether Abigail Barton even for a moment believed these soot-covered pranksters were witches.[39]

More serious is the tale told of Abby's grandfather Rufus Barton. The incident occurred at the end of 1816, the terrible year of no summer, when crops froze and starvation threatened. At the time Rufus was farming his Andover land and calling himself a Methodist. No lover of orthodoxy, his independent line of thinking got him into trouble one Sunday in December. For some weeks Rufus had been constructing a log barn. It was only half built and there were as yet no stanchions to hold the cattle. On this particular Sunday morning he awoke to driving snow from a severe northeaster. Fearing for the safety of his beasts, Rufus stayed away from Methodist meeting and spent the day hammering the necessary stakes into the barn floor. By evening the cattle were indoors safely tied up, but Rufus was in trouble with the Methodist elder, Joseph Manning, who stopped by the next morning to demand why Barton had been absent from meeting. Rufus explained that he "considered it his duty to remain at home and shelter his cattle from the storm." When Manning accused him of having "more regard for your cattle, than you do for the worship of God Almighty" and threatened him with expulsion from the society, Rufus merely repeated that he considered it "necessary labor, and would do the same again under similar circumstances." He might have added that Jesus himself had sanctioned his behavior by condoning the man who saved his ox on the Sabbath by pulling it out of a well.[40]

From the Gazetteer

*   *   *

Wilmington

by Rev. Volney Forbes

[This story is typical of many in the *Gazetteer* that emphasize the prodigious strength of the early settlers. Here, however, the hero is a woman. After describing the early settlers of Windham as "hardy, resolute and perservering; and the women fully their equals," Forbes provides an anecdote "told of Mrs. Titus which shows the spirit of those days." Titus had carried on the farm for her husband, Ephriam, while he was away fighting for independence.]

Mr. Nye at the house of Mrs. Titus was boasting that no man in town could throw him. She sat weaving at her loom till tired of hearing him bragg, she left her seat and seizing him by the collar threw him upon the floor, telling him that if there was no man in town who could throw him, there was one woman who had done it.

[Volume V (Wilmington), page 5]

The following Sunday a "rising" vote was called during meeting to expel Barton. But the sympathy of the congregation was with the farmer and only Manning stood up in support of the measure. The orthodox elder, however, refused to give up. The next week the sermon from a circuit preacher dwelt pointedly on the sanctity of the Sabbath. Again a "rising" vote was taken and again only Manning favored Barton's expulsion. In disgust the preacher took the list of the members of the society and hurled it into the blazing fire on the hearth, announcing that "this class is broken up." Methodism in Andover, so the account goes, "was never the same again."[41]

This story, illustrating a lack of respect for traditional authority, together with the other tales Abby listened to around the fireside, told her much about the world into which she had been born, its customs, values, and traditions. While such storytelling was an important part of the upbringing of most children of the time, it was particularly influential in Abby's case, for this rootedness in an oral tradition helped to shape her view of Vermont's past, and would later influence her editing of the *Gazetteer*. Maybe, too, it was from this grandfather that Abby inherited her own single-mindedness and dogged determination.

In addition to the learning Abby eagerly absorbed through such oral sources and the many books she borrowed and read, she also went to school. Her grandfather Jacob Hemenway had been instrumental in erecting the first log schoolhouse in the Barton district. This original structure was later moved to the edge of Uncle Rufus Barton's farm, where Abby together with the other children in her neighborhood attended district school.[42]

Abby left no recollections of this earliest phase of her schooling. But until reforms were instituted at the state level in the mid-1840s, the one-room schoolhouses of the sort she attended were notoriously primitive affairs. Most lacked such basic pedagogical amenities as blackboards, maps, or

𝔉𝔯𝔬𝔪 𝔱𝔥𝔢 𝔊𝔞𝔷𝔢𝔱𝔱𝔢𝔢𝔯

* * *

Brookfield

by E. P. Wild

[This story reflects the antiaristocratic predelictions shared by many of the early settlers. The Prince of Wales in question was George IV (1762–1830), who became King of Great Britain and Ireland in 1820.]

During the visit of the Prince of Wales to this country, not many years after the Revolution, that bigoted scion of royalty passed through Vermont, on his way to Canada. In the northern part of Brookfield resided Abner Pride, a shoemaker by trade, and, as his house was a long way from any other, it was frequently made a stopping-place by travelers. The Prince called here for refreshment, on his journey, and when about to take his leave, stepped up to Mrs. Pride, with saucy freedom, and kissed her. Observing that she showed signs of resentment, he remarked "soothingly," "O, never mind; you can now tell your people that you have had the honor of being kissed by an English Prince." Mr. Pride, from his work at his bench, had witnessed the scene and, hearing these words, rose indignantly, and, with a kick, more forcible than graceful, ejected the impertinent prince from the door, sending him this mocking farewell, "O, never mind; you can now go home and tell your people that you have had the honor of being kicked out of doors by an American cobbler."

[Volume II, page 865]

---

dictionaries. The subjects taught rarely extended beyond the three Rs and a daily Scripture reading. Most of the teaching was by rote.[43]

Abby was no longer a pupil in 1843 when her cousin, the younger Rufus Barton, taught the winter term in this same schoolhouse. His experience gives some idea of the challenge nineteenth-century rural schoolteachers faced. Among the pupils was a hefty young man named Joseph Gould who believed he could run the school better than Barton. Rufus thought differently and reprimanded Gould with the help of a large wooden ruler. Upon returning to his seat Gould spat on his hand and crowed to his neighbors that the teacher hadn't even raised a blister. Barton, overhearing this boast, called Gould up to the front of the room a second time and proceeded to raise the required blister. As one historian of Ludlow has noted, in those days "it required much pluck and perseverance on the part of the teachers to keep order."[44]

In 1843 when this incident occurred, Abby, aged fourteen, had already begun her own career as a district schoolteacher.

2

𝔄cademy 𝔖tudent

———•◦⚬◦•———

There are some ambitious spirits who
cannot be confined in the household and who need
a theatre in which to act.

Emma Willard[1]

Abby Hemenway's teaching career began in an eighteen-by-twenty-foot schoolhouse in Ludlow's West Hill. Originally known as the Mountain School District, it included all the hilly terrain to the west of town up to the Mount Holly line. Hemenway was only fourteen years old and had just finished district school herself when she was hired in 1843. Her gender, youthfulness, and lack of experience meant that she was put in charge of the summer session. In most rural districts this ran from May to September and was attended chiefly by small children—some as young as two or three—whose parents wanted them out of the way during the busiest agricultural season.

Since her classroom was too far from the Barton district for her to walk to school, like other rural teachers Hemenway "boarded around," taking turns living with the families of her pupils.

When Hemenway greeted her first district school class, the old adage, that a woman could no more run a schoolroom than she could mow or chop wood, had been refuted, and teaching was increasingly viewed as ideally suited to the female sex. By 1844 nearly two-thirds of all teaching positions in Vermont were held by women, most of whom were young and single. Their employment, especially for the instruction of small children, was seen by educators of the time as stemming directly from their natural function as nurturers. In towns and cities across America child care had become a mother's principal occupation. Anticipating this future role as the teachers of their own children, young unmarried women's work in the classroom was seen as a suitable, if temporary occupation. In the words of the Vermont state superintendent of schools, writing in 1864, such employment made full use of a woman's "moral and intellectual qualifications, her devotion, her unselfishness, her calm and quiet resolution, her love of children and natural aptitude to teach."[2]

But an even stronger argument in favor of hiring women was economic: They could be paid much less than men. When Hemenway began her teaching career she probably earned, in addition to room and board, no more than a dollar a week. At a time when a simple cotton shawl cost $7.00 this was hardly enough even to keep her properly dressed.[3]

By today's standards the difficulties facing the nineteenth-century rural schoolmistress seem daunting. To keep control of the dozens of pupils of all ages who crowded onto the rural schoolroom's narrow benches, much less teach them anything, was a challenge for even the most experienced instructors. Fortunately, by the time Hemenway had charge of her own classroom she was not only skilled at keeping her younger brothers and sisters entertained and out of mischief, but also equally adept at holding her own in the company of sharp-tongued adolescent boys like her Barton cousins. If Abby Hemenway was not equipped to take charge of a district school-room, it would be hard to imagine what hill country girl was.

Might Hemenway have considered other forms of employment? By 1840 industrialization and urbanization had transformed women's work in New England, carrying young girls by the thousands away from their isolated hillside farms to cities such as Lowell and Boston where they found jobs as domestics, in factories, or in the needle trades. The most lucrative of these employments was mill work and the average Lowell textile operative could expect to earn more than $140 a year, in addition to room and board. In contrast, the rural female school mistress accounted herself lucky if she took home more than $50 annually. Hemenway, whose employment during her first years of teaching was restricted to the summer term, would have earned far less.

Compared to other paid work, however, teaching held a distinct advantage for literary-minded girls. Back in the early 1830s Emily Chubbuck of New Hampshire—a young woman who, like Abby Hemenway, cherished hopes of a literary career—had refused better-paid manual employment in favor of teaching.[4] Presiding over a classroom, though demanding, was at least intellectually stimulating, and anyone who knew Abby Hemenway would have singled her out as promising teacher material. A prolific reader with an excellent memory, she had a wide-ranging knowledge matched by a love of games and a gift for storytelling. She also had considerable experience minding her younger siblings. Many years later one of Hemenway's former students remembered her as "a kindly but exacting teacher."[5]

One of Hemenway's motives for hiring herself out as a teacher was to earn enough money to pay the tuition at Black River Academy, Ludlow's only institution of higher learning.

Before the advent of normal schools it was common for young women to spend a few years at a private academy to train themselves for teaching, the only paid employment that offered them a semblance of a career.

Nothing is known of Hemenway's early years as a teacher. Did she continue in charge of the West Hill school? Or, as seems more likely, did she move around from district to district, returning home during the winter months when older, more experienced teachers were hired? The only precise information we have about this period of Hemenway's life is that on April 2, 1843, only a few weeks before she would have left home to teach the summer session in the West Hill School District, she joined the Baptist Church of Ludlow.[6]

Hemenway's mother had been a founding member of this second Ludlow Baptist society. Eight years earlier, during the height of what Vermonters called the Great Revival, seventy-eight members, including Abigail Dana Hemenway, had separated from the first church over the issue of temperance. This followed more than a decade of divisiveness that had paralyzed church work and discipline. The reformist society young Abby joined in 1843, known officially as the Baptist Church of Ludlow, was pledged to "use no ardent spirits except for medicinal purposes." The members also shared the beliefs of other Calvinist churches in the Connecticut River Valley. On the one hand they acknowledged human depravity and the need for God's grace to achieve salvation; on the other hand they believed in free will and the part human effort played in the soul's redemption. Abby thus followed in her mother's footsteps when she joined the Baptist Church of Ludlow in 1843, and, according to the church record books, she was the only one of her brothers and sisters to do so. The rest of the Hemenway children are said to have remained Methodists like their father.[7]

Abby's particular intimacy with her mother probably helped

to dictate her choice of a church. Was she perhaps also, like her mother, signaling her independence from the rest of the family in church matters? In Abby's case, such religious independence would manifest itself even more dramatically twenty years later when she became a Roman Catholic.

Abby Hemenway was fourteen when she joined the Ludlow Baptist Church, a common age in the waning years of the Great Revival for young people to undergo a conversion experience and become full members of a church. Such potent, deeply felt, coming-of-age events were prevalent reflections of contemporary Protestant religious life.

The actual circumstances of Hemenway's conversion are nowhere precisely documented, but she does provide a description of such a moment of rebirth in a work she began writing about this time but which would not be published for many years. When it appeared in 1865, it carried the title *The Mystical Rose* and was nothing less than a poetic biography of the Virgin Mary.[8]

The subject of this poem was surely extraordinary, because Mary was hardly a popular object of devotion among New England Protestants, who regarded her as symbolic of the idolatrous excesses of the Roman Catholic Church. But in the context of Hemenway's life writing such a poem made sense. By her own account the inspiration was prompted by a series of visions near her favorite retreat on the banks of Jewell Brook. While she doesn't say exactly when these apparitions occurred, a poem (also published in 1865) tells us that throughout her childhood she had wandered "guideless through the wilderness till weary." Then "Mary Mother," "a vision, sweet as angel" had visited her in her "enchanted dell" and led her gently out of that wilderness and "toward the Garden of her Son."[9]

What prompted this unusual apparition, Hemenway does not say. This motherly figure may at first simply have represented a celestial substitute for her own mother whom she loved deeply and whom she would be leaving in a few weeks time. Then, perhaps, as she sought to identify these recurring visions more precisely, Hemenway began associating them with the Virgin Mary. Her own middle name, Maria, could easily have led her to feel a special bond with Jesus' mother. When in later life Abby recalled these visions on the banks of Jewell Brook, she linked them with her conversion to Roman Catholicism in 1864. How far back she was reading all this through spectacles colored by this later conversion we will never know. But a careful perusal of the poem she composed in 1865 shows that these apparitions began much earlier, "almost," as she obliquely suggests, "from her very childhood." Thus they are also tied to her first conversion, the one that marked her entry into the Ludlow Baptist Church in 1843.[10]

Apparitions themselves, while hardly commonplace, were not unknown and were welcomed by evangelical Christians in the Green Mountains, who regarded such intense religious experiences as visions, voices, and speaking in tongues as symbols of the saving grace of redemption. In 1785, for example, sixteen-year-old Elias Young of Woodstock claimed to have been carried up to heaven in a shaft of light where, under the very throne of God, he felt his past sinfulness fall away and he was filled with the certainty of salvation. Solomon Mack, grandfather of the Mormon founder, Joseph Smith, saw visions of light in Sharon and heard voices summoning him to salvation, while Lucy Mack, Joseph's aunt, at one point glimpsed her Savior through a veil, calling on her to warn the people of their imminent death. In 1843, the year Hemenway joined the Baptist Church, in a vision probably connected to the apocalyptic beliefs of the Millerites, the Father, the Son, and the Holy Spirit appeared to Melissa Warner near her house in Bristol. And in 1838, John Weeks of Danville managed to replicate Dante's earlier journey when he traveled through the realms of hell and heaven in the footsteps of an angelic guide.[11]

Hemenway's baptism and entry into the Ludlow church coincided with the concluding months of the Great Revival. Though in 1834 Jedediah Burchard had swept through the towns and villages of Vermont, swelling their evangelical churches with new converts, within three years a reaction against his extremist measures had set in. Meanwhile, critics' fears of religious zealotry were further compounded by an upsurge of "fanatick" movements. These included the followers of William Miller, a Baptist preacher who spoke to the sufferings of many in the Connecticut River Valley who were struggling to make a living for themselves and their children. Promising eternal happiness to all who freely accepted God's grace, he assured those who gathered in the Valley's churches to hear him preach that the end was near for sinner and saint alike. The world as they knew it would vanish on March 21, 1843, he predicted, and many chose to believe him. When the day came the Millerites gathered on hillsides to await Christ's coming. A few sold their farms and other property. Others fabricated wings to hasten their journey to paradise.[12]

The predicted end never came, of course. But two weeks later Abby Hemenway joined the Ludlow Baptist Church. This may simply be a coincidence, since there is no evidence that any Barton or Hemenway sympathized with the Millerites. Asa Barton, as a confirmed rationalist, proved an outspoken opponent and published a pamphlet denouncing the movement. But fourteen-year-old Abby's religious views were more heartfelt than rational. Imbued with what Karen Hansen calls the "culture of the countryside," an earthy emotionalism that embraced fatalism, mysticism, and superstition, Hemenway was far more susceptible than her uncle to warnings of an imminent Judgment Day.[13]

Such spiritual fervor had drawn many into the Baptist Church where they welcomed apparitions and other personal encounters with the Divine as redemptive symbols. A close reading of the early chapters of Abby Hemenway's *Mystical Rose* uncovers just such a conversion narrative. We find it hidden away in her description of the Annunciation, that transcendent moment when the angel Gabriel appeared to Mary with the news that she was to be the mother of the Savior.

By Hemenway's account, this and other early scenes in *The Mystical Rose* were written before she had any knowledge of Mary apart from the Gospel stories. "In the quiet of Sabbaths it grew, in the calm of holy eves," she tells us in the preface to the printed book, piously recalling the few hours of writing she had enjoyed on those distant Sundays. She remembered, too, her ecstasy as she wrote the verses, how she lost herself in a "labyrinth of beauty, pious allegory, ancient and mystic, luminous legend, lovingly warm with words that burn, shedding odors as incense from a censer."[14]

A careful perusal of the early chapters of *The Mystical Rose* shows that Hemenway relied largely on her youthful imagination—often drawing from her own experience—to amplify and enrich her life of Mary. The Annunciation, for example, takes place in a private retreat, which, except for the presence of a cypress tree, sounds remarkably like Abby's favorite hideaway on the banks of Jewell Brook.

> . . . a little garden grotto where
> Gray jutting rock and tree and
> floweret fair,
> The quaintest alcove form.
> . . . .
> Where gradual slopes the banklet
> drapery bright
> Down to a rill that glides from
> sound and sight,
> Beneath the cypress shade
> Unwistful of the silent flow of time,

Lost in the vista of a revery sublime,
    Reclines a soul-rapt maid.

In Mary's hands is a "blurred and ancient scroll." She has, like Hemenway, escaped to this quiet retreat to read and think. But on this occasion Mary's reveries are expectant. Much as the anxious convert awaits a sign of redemption, Mary asks, "When will the Peace-Prince her salvation bring? . . . When . . . will / The Swift Deliverer come, this to fulfill / And save from sin and damnation?"

Then, suddenly, the angel Gabriel stands before Mary, and "the meek maid feels the revelation clasp / And hold her soul astonished great."[15]

One way to read the Annunciation, in Christian terms, is as the great conversion narrative. Mary, like the nineteenth-century evangelical convert, by accepting Jesus has accepted God's will for herself. She has been transformed, reborn. Similarly, Abby Hemenway's salvation, her rebirth as a member of the Baptist Church, would come through accepting Jesus as her savior.

As a new member of Ludlow's Baptist Church, Hemenway committed herself to a lifetime of purposeful struggle and was expected to take an active part in church affairs.[16] For the women of the parish these included the Ladies' Benevolent Society, an association that traced its origins to a time early in the century when the young men and women of the village had joined together to raise funds to build a fence around the Ludlow cemetery. By the time Hemenway was old enough to join, the organization had evolved into a Baptist women's missionary society that raised money to send a young clergyman to the Sandwich Islands.[17]

Whether or not Hemenway was a member of this active circle of Ludlow Baptist women, by the spring of 1847, after four years of sporadic teaching in mountain schoolrooms, she had

From the Gazetteer

* * *

Rutland

by Marion Hooker Roe
a contributor to
Poets and Poetry of Vermont

"Sewing Circle Song"

Sisters there is work to do
    Sew, sisters, sew!
Press the shining needle through,
    Sew, sisters, sew!
Wintry winds are howling round;
Snow-wrapt lies the frozen ground,
Hunger has its victims found;
    Sew, sisters, sew!

'Tis no time for idling now
    Sew, sisters, sew!
We must brighten many a brow;
    Sew, sisters, sew!
Pain and care imploring stand;
Starving children stretch the hand
To our friendly sister-band;
    Sew, sisters, sew!

Not in vain, we labor thus;
    Sew, sisters, sew!
There's a rich reward for us;
    Sew, sisters, sew!
Garret high and dungeon dread,
Basement dim and dying bed
Pour their blessings on our head;
    Sew, sisters, sew!

[Volume III, page 1008]

put aside enough money to pay the required $3.00 tuition and enrolled in the English course at Black River Academy.

Most of the other young women who enrolled in this course were training to become teachers. But Hemenway's dreams were not only about visions; they were also literary dreams, and her wide reading had introduced her to the growing number of American women writers, including Catharine Sedgwick, Lydia Sigourney, and Caroline Gilman, who were making successful careers for themselves as poets and novelists. Filled as she was with youthful ambition, Hemenway may simply have regarded teaching as a way station on the route to fulfilling higher aspirations.[18]

Black River Academy had been founded in 1835 by prominent Baptists with the help of the leading members of other denominations in and around Ludlow. At the time, formal education in Windsor County was limited to district schools. If further learning was required, young men and women had to travel long distances at considerable expense to attend academies and seminaries as far away as Randolph, Middlebury, or Burlington. Thus, in an era of expanding population and a growing demand for schoolteachers, the need for an institution of higher education where the youth of Windsor County could be prepared for teaching and for college was evident.[19]

Unlike the modern high school, Black River Academy enrolled few who did not wish to be there. All, or nearly all, studies were elective and discipline was relatively lax. Austin Adams, who was vice principal of Black River while Hemenway was a student, later described the free atmosphere of the school and its mixed student body containing boys and girls of widely differing ages and attainments. According to Adams, the relaxed atmosphere of New England academies like Black River suited rural communities where the inhabitants shared "a correct and elevated ambition, born of puritan blood and puritan habits." Pupils who attended these schools, in other words, were both disciplined and ready to work hard at their studies.[20]

While the students ranged widely in age and their educational attainments varied, the faculty consisted mostly of young men and women who taught for a year or two before moving on to better positions. The turnover among academy principals was also high. Although most were recent college graduates, the pay at $400 a year was hardly more than a day laborer would have earned and few stayed longer than two years.[21]

Abby Hemenway was thus fortunate in attending Black River during the prosperous years when Claudius B. Smith served as principal. A Middlebury College graduate, Smith was in his late twenties when he arrived in Ludlow in February 1847. He remained for five years and during his popular and able tenure the academy flourished, its total enrollment rising from three hundred students to more than four hundred. Years later, recalling his experience at Black River, Smith remembered "a class of young people of more than usual intelligence, desirous of learning and remarkably free of improper habits."[22]

Smith, known affectionately among his pupils as "C.B. the Mighty," taught classics. Early each morning during term he would march into the classroom, where the girls as well as the boys were waiting for recitation to begin, calling out *"perge modo,"* Latin for, roughly, "Fire away." "What good times we used to have!" one of the young women later wrote recalling these classes. She also remembered gatherings known as Lyceums where students and a few villagers met to hear the girls read "bright papers" and the boys debate "grave and weighty questions." This student might have added that in permitting its female students to speak from a public platform Black River Academy was refreshingly modern; most educators of the time would have considered such exposure unwomanly.[23]

Black River was also exceptional in that boys and girls

studied together rather than in separate classrooms, as was the rule in many other coeducational academies. While the existence of mixed classes may simply have been the consequence of limited space, they also conveyed an important message to young women like Abby Hemenway who were training to be teachers. Together with the young men sharing their classroom they learned that teaching was an important career that would enable them to influence others and assist in shaping society. It was not regarded simply as a job that would occupy them until they married.[24]

In 1844, three years before Hemenway enrolled, the original school building had burned down. The academy then took over the ground floor of the brick Union Meetinghouse, which stood at the west end of the Ludlow village green. At the front was an assembly room large enough for the entire student body to gather for morning exercises. Two classrooms at the back completed the available teaching space, and all three rooms were in constant use throughout the day. The school remained in these crowded quarters until 1889 when the present building, now the Black River Academy Museum, was built.[25]

Hemenway was eighteen years old when she entered Black River. Short of stature and a striking, if not handsome, woman, she would be remembered for her intense blue eyes, straight brown hair, and long slender hands, and, most particularly, for her beautiful speaking voice. This young woman's energy, her wide learning, and her considerable teaching experience would have made her a welcome presence in any classroom, and it comes as no surprise that her fellow students later remembered her as "an active, earnest scholar, foremost in her classes and eager to make practical use of knowledge when acquired."[26]

During her first few terms at Black River, Hemenway studied such basic subjects as English, arithmetic, geography, and history, the standard course load carried by those preparing to teach district school.[27] But she soon moved up to the classical department, to study Latin, Greek, history, and mathematics. Here her fellow students included young men preparing for college, and others of both sexes who, according to the school's catalogue, could be furnished with the equivalent of a college education.[28] While it seems unlikely that Hemenway's studies at Black River were on a par with those at liberal arts institutions such as Middlebury or Dartmouth, she did acquire a proficiency in Latin and other advanced subjects that later proved invaluable in her future career as a teacher, writer, and historian.

An examination of the school catalogues shows that by 1848 Abby Hemenway had a heavier course schedule than most of her fellow students. That summer term she added to her regular studies in classics and English a teacher-training class taught by Claudius Smith, a French class with Monsieur Buteau, and a course in drawing and painting.

Among the books assigned in Monsieur Buteau's French class was Germaine de Stael's *Corinne,* an idealistic and passionate novel that was eagerly perused by nineteenth-century schoolgirls who dreamed of literary distinction. Published in 1807, it tells the story of a famous woman poet, half-English and half-Italian, who lives in Rome. Corinne falls in love with a British lord, Oswald Nevil, but refuses to marry him, preferring to continue her unconventional life in Italy. When she later learns Nevil has returned home and taken an English wife, Corinne dies of grief. For bright, ambitious young women such as Hemenway, *Corinne,* despite its tragic ending, offered encouragement for their own half-formed ambitions for literary glory.

Corinne, however, seems an unlikely book for a teacher in a sedate Baptist academy to have assigned, especially since many American educators of the time were opposed to novel reading on principle. Fiction, they believed, encouraged "base" passions at the expense of "acceptable" emotions. Presumably Monsieur Buteau admired his countrywoman's intellect and thus considered her writings suitable reading for his students. Presumably, too, he was not a Baptist.[29]

We don't know if Mme. de Stael's writings and the power of this Frenchwoman's intellect moved Hemenway as deeply as they did other aspiring woman writers of her day. Given this Ludlow schoolgirl's ambitions and faith in her own abilities, they doubtless did. But the single surviving reference to her early taste in women writers makes no mention of Germaine de Stael. We are told simply that two of Hemenway's favorite authors were Margaret Fuller and Elizabeth Barrett Browning.[30]

Knowing Hemenway's love of verse, it is hardly surprising that she admired Browning, that renowned English poet who, in the 1850s, would produce her own epic of the literary woman, *Aurora Leigh*. But Margaret Fuller's influence on Hemenway may have been the most profound of all. A well-known intellectual, and the author of *Woman in the Nineteenth Century*, a feminist tract published in 1844, Fuller urged American women to claim their right to individualism, self-fulfillment, and self-reliance, attributes not commonly assigned to the female sex. While Hemenway's extant writings show no sympathy for the woman's rights movement, her life story exemplifies Fuller's conviction that women must take charge of their own lives and not simply rely on men to tell them what to do. Just as Fuller in *Woman in the Nineteenth Century* declares that every career should be as open to women as to men, Hemenway felt free to fashion a life on her own terms.

Even as a student at Black River, Abby Hemenway gave no hint that she shared the domestic dreams of most of her fellow female students. If she had beaux there is no mention of them. And while she was certainly no recluse, it is hard to imagine Abby standing around with a group of other schoolgirls discussing their marriage prospects.

Hemenway's reading tastes were also wider than the recollection of her erstwhile schoolmates might suggest. If her own memory is to be credited, her love of history equaled her love of poetry and more than matched her interest in fiction or tracts on women's rights. She later remembered that while still in her teens she developed a great admiration for Napoleon and his battles. She moved from there to the history of Poland and then to William Parry's lengthy (and for some, rather tedious) account of his voyages in the Arctic.[31]

Educators of the time, who regarded the study of the past as particularly well suited to young women, warmly applauded such a strong appetite for history. Unlike novels that encouraged youthful feminine imaginations to run wild, history, by teaching its readers the virtues of their ancestors, helped women to develop into responsible beings and responsible members of civic society. Emma Willard, a leading educator of women who became famous for her history textbooks, wrote in 1819 that "in those great republics, which have fallen of themselves, the loss of republican manners and virtues, has been the invariable precursor of their loss of republican forms of government." Willard's statement was by no means unusual for the time and reflected a common belief that Americans, while prizing their individualism, also owed a debt to the society of which they formed a part. To help preserve public virtue in the then youthful United States, Willard proposed that women, as the principal educators of future citizens, should study history.[32]

The adult Abby Hemenway would have agreed with Emma Willard that the study of history makes good citizens. But as a child and later as a young woman she would have loved reading about the past, not so much for the lessons it had to teach as for the rich pleasures it provided in allowing her to escape the all-too-familiar confines of her rural Vermont home and enter an exotic world filled with strange and wonderful people, places, and events.

As an academy student Hemenway plunged eagerly into the life of Ludlow village. In the catalogue for 1847 she, along with

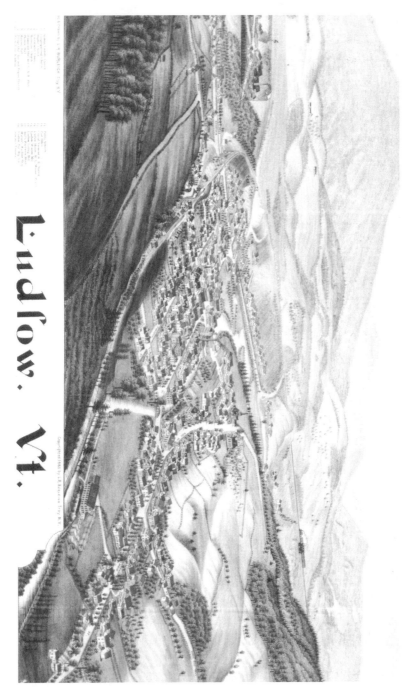

Birdseye view of Ludlow, Vermont in 1859.
H.P. Moore, Concord, N.H.

other students who lived too far away to walk to school, is listed as boarding with local families. Hemenway stayed in the home of Reuben Washburn, a founder and trustee of Black River, and a prominent Vermont lawyer. But she only lived there during her first term or so. The following year she is listed as living with Daniel Hemenway, suggesting that in the interim her family had left their farm in the Barton district and moved into town. Abby's father sustained a crippling injury sometime in middle life that prevented his doing farm work, so this may explain the Hemenways' change of residence.[33]

With this move into Ludlow village the geographic center of Abby's existence was no longer the cluster of Hemenway and Barton farms on Brook Road, or the district school neighborhoods where she had taught, but rather this small, bustling market town, which by 1850 had a population of 1,619. A woolen mill was Ludlow's principal industry. But there were also smaller factories and shops manufacturing such necessities as combs and bowls, tubs and tinware, harnesses and leather goods. Most recently, Ludlow's steady, if not spectacular, growth had been augmented by the building of the Rutland division of the Central Vermont Railroad. The first train passed through town in the fall of 1849, raising expectations, as it did in the other villages along its path, of a coming boost in Ludlow's fortunes.[34]

During her years at Black River Academy, Abby Hemenway took an active part in Ludlow's cultural life. Together with a group of other literary-minded women in town, she belonged to a society known as the Ladies' Association for Mental and Other Improvement. The wife of Judge Reuben Washburn, in whose house Hemenway boarded during her first term at the academy, was one of the founding members. Known about town as "a real blue stocking club," its book-loving members were discouraged from paying too careful attention to their appearance. Little else is known of this particular female reading circle, but it may have resembled similar organizations that flourished in towns and cities across the Northeast in these years. The noted teacher, Elizabeth Palmer Peabody, was a member of one in Boston that in 1823 comprised sixteen members who met weekly in the evenings to read and sew for the poor. While this, too, was dubbed a "blue stocking club," literary discussion ended at half past eight, at which time young men were admitted to the circle and the gathering took on a more frivolous tone.[35]

Whether men ever attended the meetings of the Ludlow Ladies' Association is not known. But it would be intriguing to learn if the books these women selected were as unconventional as their careless attitude toward dress. In addition to the writings of Great Men, did they include the works of Margaret Fuller and other advocates of women's rights?[36]

If the reading enjoyed by the Ladies' Association for Mental and Other Improvement is lost to history, its theatrical productions are not. On at least three occasions the members put on dramatic performances to raise money for the purchase of books for the town library. According to Frances Babb, the November 1850 "Original Exhibition" featured Hemenway as the author of an ambitious classical drama entitled "Colloquy—The Seasons," in which she played the role of "Summer." The play's classical theme is reflected in the names of the two dozen or so characters, including such deities as Jupiter and Apollo, Diana and Iris, with the "three Graces" and "four nymphs" added for good measure.[37]

A surviving program for the "Exhibition" of 1851 does not name the authors of the eight musical and dramatic pieces performed on September 9 in the Ludlow Town Hall, but it does list A. M. Hemenway as playing three separate roles: Lady Alice in "Mary of England," Tocalco, Queen of Montezuma, in "Marina, or Scenes from the Conquest of Mexico," and finally "Miss Bustle" in "A Peep at the Follies of the Day."[38] Since all the performers in these pieces are listed as "Miss" on the program, we can presume a good number were students at Black River Academy.

Hemenway herself remained at the Academy until sometime in 1852, by which time she had probably learned everything the school had to teach her. Later, in the pages of her *Gazetteer*, she made occasional mention of teachers and students she had known there. They included Adaline Cobb, her first preceptress, whom she recalled with particular fondness; also Mary and Ellen Bennett, who were fellow students as well as friends. Hemenway described their mother, Maria Bennett Cudworth, the wife of the Reverend Nathanial Cudworth, pastor of the Ludlow Baptist Church, as "one of the women whom we always remember preciously."[39]

There is little question that Hemenway's years at Black River Academy were of critical importance in determining her subsequent career. Kathryn Kerns, writing about Alfred Academy in New York State, where similar conditions prevailed, suggests that such coeducational academies served the same role for young women that the antebellum college did for young men, aiding the former in making the transition from rural to urban life and helping them to move from their families' hillside farms into the careers—principally teaching—that awaited them in the nation's fast-growing towns and cities.[40]

We know that Hemenway herself went on to teach, to dream of a literary career, and finally to take on the immense task of compiling the *Vermont Historical Gazetteer*. In one way or another the education she obtained at Black River, the family support and encouragement she received from her mother and her uncle Asa Barton, and the reading she did on her own led Hemenway to imagine that the pursuit of a career was not only appealing, but also within her reach.

3

"Western Fever"

———•◦✦◦✦◦•———

Ah! other bright scenes may entice us away:
   In other lands oft we may roam;
Yet still will the heart ever beat with delight
   At the name of its own mountain home.

Mary Cutts, "Green Mountain Song"[1]

If the education Abby Hemenway received at Black River Academy helped to feed her literary ambitions, the years that immediately followed gave little indication of how she might fulfill those dreams. While she seems to have accepted teaching as her chosen profession until something better came along, a certain restlessness marks this period in her life as she moved first from one Vermont schoolroom to the next, later repeating this pattern when she headed west to the newly settled state of Michigan. Was she searching, perhaps, for that powerful sense of place that would inform her life's work, and that, in the end, she could only find by leaving Vermont?

For the moment, however, there was little alternative to the life of a local schoolteacher. During the five years that Abby Hemenway was enrolled at Black River Academy, she, like other students who were paying their own way, mixed terms of teaching with terms as a student. One such teaching interlude for which Hemenway left an unusually detailed record occurred in the late 1840s. On the recommendation of Claudius Smith, she received an offer to take charge of the summer session at the Mount Holly North Village school high in the hills west of Ludlow.[2]

In later life Hemenway recalled with particular nostalgia the nine months she spent in Mount Holly. Her schoolhouse, a small, brown, weather-beaten structure on the edge of the North Village, probably resembled most of the others she had taught in since she was a girl of fourteen. In contrast "the Ives mansion on the hill," where she boarded that summer, was large and luxurious by local standards. Hemenway made no mention of Mr. Ives, but she described "Madame Ives" as harboring delusions of grandeur, while nonetheless treating her boarder with kindly consideration. The Ives had two children. The elder, a daughter named Amarillas, was married and lived away from home. But Jewett, a precocious and spoiled fourteen year old and the darling of his elderly parents, was very much in evidence. Hemenway quickly grew fond of Jewett, who charmed her with his "more than tolerable verses and blank poetry." She called him her "philosopher boy."[3]

Hemenway was charmed as well by what she described as the "delightful quietude" of the Ives' farm surrounded by the gently rolling spring-green Mount Holly meadows. She never forgot "the pleasure of coming in from a heated, hungry school-room" to the cool house where meals were conveniently timed for her arrival and she was fed such delicacies as tender chicken or fresh mountain trout cooked in "fragrant June butter," served with "cream biscuit to melt in the mouth." For dessert a pyramid of strawberries was accompanied by "a cut-glass pitcher filled to the beak with thick fresh cream." Such luxury, a rare commodity in the rugged Vermont hills, made Hemenway feel "very comfortable and contented." Because the family was small and the house was large she probably also had a room of her own, a coveted privacy for the rural schoolteacher.

In pleasant weather Hemenway walked the mile or so along the winding North Village roads lined with newly leafed sugar maples to her schoolhouse. If it rained she was driven there in a buggy, and if it was still raining when school let out at four o'clock, the buggy would be waiting outside the schoolhouse to take her home.[4]

Hemenway's summer term in the North Village school proved successful enough that she was asked to stay on and teach a select school that fall. Such informal, privately sponsored classes—the rural substitute for academies—were attended by older students taking advantage of a teacher's knowledge of more advanced subjects to continue their education. Select schools were temporary arrangements, often held in private parlors and lasting only for a term. Because Jewett would be attending district school and not Hemenway's classes, his tutor probably left the Ives' to board elsewhere.

Among Hemenway's pupils that autumn were two young men in their early twenties, whom she described as good looking, well mannered, and "of advanced scholarship." But she would look back on one with particular fondness. Ryland Ackley was a farmer's son who had taught the winter school the previous year. He enrolled in Hemenway's select school to study Latin and geometry, and later she could recall no other student of hers who had matched Ackley's brilliance and intellectual power. Certain that he was "one of the handsomest young men in our State," she conjured up with sentimental fondness his "fair lifted brow, softly lit with conscious power, his dark eyes now deep with penetration, now rich with humor." Had Abby Hemenway perhaps fallen in love with Ryland Ackley?[5]

Perhaps she had, but, apart from a proposal of marriage much later in her career that she rejected out of hand, this is the only hint that Hemenway enjoyed any romantic attachments. Judging from her surviving correspondence and other writings, love affairs were not central to her life.

Hemenway's skill at handling the pupils in her select school brought her an offer from Mr. Pierce, the Ives' son-in-law and a member of the school committee, to teach the winter term at the North Village school. She was probably flattered to be asked, but she also knew from her own years in the district school classroom that teaching the winter term was not a job for sissies. This was the session attended by the largest number of students, including older boys who could be spared from farm work only in the coldest months. The teacher's task was further hampered by the frequent presence of a few unruly and restless youths (some as old as twenty-two) determined to make trouble.

According to Hemenway's account, the North Village school had been having difficulties with its winter term for more than a decade, so Pierce must have had considerable faith in her skills as a disciplinarian to offer her the job. Hemenway took it "nothing doubting," as she later ruefully recalled. "They that know nothing, fear nothing." The pay would have been a big inducement. Hemenway didn't mention her salary, but in 1858 when Mira Dickerman taught the winter term in the same school, her salary was $39.00. This is more than twice the amount the summer schoolteacher obtained that same year.[6]

"I had sixteen scholars old enough to go into company with me," Hemenway observed in her recounting of this experience, and she was certain there was no more sociable town in the state of Vermont than Mount Holly that winter. Where she boarded she does not say, but she did remember that balls and sleigh rides were the preferred form of entertainment among the older students. At least once every two weeks there was a party, and Hemenway claimed that it had "required some tact . . . to rule in the school-room all those young, daring, ingenious spirits," fresh from one party or "ready to plunge" into the next. "It was a hard spot" for a teacher, she admitted, trying to maintain order and sobriety, particularly when the teacher herself was the same age as some of her students. On one occasion Hemenway was forced to take a switch to two students whose father served on the school committee. Such corporal punishment was common enough in every district school, and doubtless considered necessary to keep order in a classroom filled with students of all ages, where the teacher was expected to teach every subject from the ABCs to Latin and geometry.[7]

A good "feruling" with a switch was one thing, but to expel a student was quite another, especially when that student was a promising poet and a school idol. Sometime during that winter term Hemenway was forced to dismiss Jewett Ives, her "philosopher boy," from her winter school. She later claimed that never again did she shed so many tears as over this one action. She does not specify Jewett's crime, but his bad character came through again later in life, when, according to Hemenway's account, he "swindled away his parents' property" and wasted their last dollar. When she wrote about this painful experience many years later she admitted that she "would sicken at such a task now as that school," but then she "took pride in it and survived."[8]

After nine months of teaching in Mount Holly, Hemenway returned to Black River Academy, remaining there until sometime in 1852. She turned twenty-four that October, and, with her education completed, continued teaching for another year or so in towns not far from home.[9]

As Abby Hemenway soon learned, the satisfactions of serving as schoolmistress in a succession of isolated rural villages such as Mount Holly were limited. Among other disadvantages

From the Gazetteer

* * *

Panton

"The Lone Indian," by Harriet Bishop

[This poem follows excerpts from the memoirs of
Harriet E. Bishop, *Floral Home; or, First Years of
Minnesota* (1857). A pioneer Minnesota teacher and missionary, Bishop was born in Panton. Her first Minnesota
school was in a primitive trading post and her pupils were
mostly Sioux Indians. The inspiration for this poem came
from watching a solitary Sioux warrior as he observed U.S.
troops erecting "a defense against the encroachment
of the Indian."]

> Not a word he spake, not a gesture made,
>   As he gazed on the passing scene;
> But he folded his arms across his breast
>   With proud and majestic mien.
> The warrior's plume is adorning his head,
>   The fire of the brave in his eye,
> His pallid lips are together pressed,
>   Nor kindred, nor friend is nigh.
>
> Closely with grace his blanket he drew
>   As he thought of the white man's skill;
> But he mastered each muscle of face and form
>   With an Indian's iron will;
> For surely no good was tokened to him
>   In the scene that was passing around;
> For the strong defense of the white man's walls
>   Would rest on his hunting ground.
>
> He looked on the graves where his fathers slept,
>   On the spot where his teepee had stood,
> On the stream where glided his light canoe,

And the wild deer coursed in the wood.
And never again to his vision would seem
  The sky so bright and fair,
Or earth be dressed in such beauty and green,
  Or so pure and serene the air.

The pale face come[s], so potent in skill!
  His own race were dwindling away;
The remnant doomed; how brief the hour
  They might on their hunting ground stay!
And sadly, oh, sadly, his spirit was stirred,
  For life was bereft of its charms,
Since these flower-clad plains and crested bluffs
  Were marked for the white man's farms.

More closely, more closely, his blanket he drew,
  More firmly his lips compressed;
And stronger he folded his brawny arms
  O'er his painfully heaving breast.
His eagle eye had divined the scene,
  The river and plain he has crossed;
And he climbs the bluff, and, westward away,
  He is soon in the distance lost.

[Volume I, pages 84–85]

was the lack of privacy. From the moment she arrived in a district school community to take up her teaching duties Hemenway's every move would have been noted and commented on. As Thomas Dublin has observed, "the common practice of boarding around among the families of students, the frequent classroom visits of parents and school committee members, the final public exams of the scholars at the end of the term—all continuously subjected rural school teachers to public scrutiny."[10]

Hemenway may also have found herself competing with a growing number of New England women for the available district school jobs. This kept salaries low and working conditions poor.[11] In 1854 the *Rutland Herald* described half the school buildings in Vermont as "black, rickety, ugly, boy-killing affairs where comfort never comes and where coughs, consumptions, fevers and crooked backs are manifested wholesale."[12] Given these Dickensian conditions and the limited employment opportunities available in small towns, women such as Abby Hemenway began questioning their future as district school-teachers and dreaming of adventures and employment opportunities elsewhere.

Nor was Hemenway alone in her desire to escape the narrow valleys and rocky hillsides of her native state. By the 1850s the number of Vermonters leaving the state for better opportunities elsewhere reached its peak. Even Ludlow, where the coming of the railroad in 1849 had promised prosperity, saw its population fall for the first time between 1850 and 1860. A history of this Black River Valley town published at the end of the century recalled that "Westward Ho!" had been the watchword of the decade and attributed Ludlow's declining fortunes to this epidemic of "western fever."[13]

Abby's cousins Ralph and Wesley Barton were among those infected. One day late in the winter of 1852 the two brothers boarded the train in Ludlow to begin the long journey west to California. There, like thousands before them, they hoped to better their fortunes by prospecting for gold. The first gold seekers had reached San Francisco three years earlier in February 1849. Most were young single men like Ralph and Wesley and shared their financial motives for making the dangerous journey by ship from New York, across the Isthmus of Panama by land and canoe, and then by ship again up the coast to San Francisco. "I am determined to go," Ralph wrote a friend, "as I have certain objects which I wish to carry out, but cannot under present circumstances." What these objects were or whether Wesley shared them he does not say, but neither planned to remain in the West for more than a few years. Ralph was twenty-two years old at the time, working as a blacksmith in Mount Holly. Wesley, two years his junior, may still have been at home. By September the two brothers had reached Canyon Creek, California, and were living in a canvas tent and prospecting for gold.[14]

Back home in Ludlow, Abigail Dana Hemenway wrote a poem depicting the lonely, dangerous life she imagined her nephews leading in California, which she described as a desolate land filled with "lurking" Indians and "ravenous" wolves. She hoped they were avoiding even more treacherous foes—gamblers and "vice in every form"—and made it clear that she thought this "effort to win the golden dust" a greedy and perilous venture.[15]

Abby and her cousin Lucia did not agree. Family lore tells us that the two had watched the young men's departure with considerable envy. Lucia, described by a relative as a "rather daring and impertinent young miss" of seventeen, was reputedly "the spoiled darling" of the Barton family. An aspiring poet, she was her parents' only daughter and, like her older cousin Abby, had spent several terms at Black River Academy. Since leaving school Lucia seems to have worked part of the time in Ludlow's woolen mill and may have done some teaching as well.[16]

At first the two cousins were determined to join Ralph and Wesley in California, until Ralph made it very clear in his letters home that mining towns were not suitable places for young ladies. His description of Sunday in Jacksonville, the closest town to Canyon Creek, would have been enough to give even Abby and Lucia second thoughts. "It is miner's market day," he wrote, "the day to get drunk, to fight, to gamble, to have a general row, a general holy day throughout the mines," he added facetiously. But then Ralph took pains to assure his family that he and Wesley, after buying their week's provisions, returned home "sober, honest men" to spend the rest of the day reading, cooking, and gathering wood.[17]

Dissuaded from going to California by Ralph's letters, and presumably by Abigail Dana as well, Abby and Lucia were nonetheless determined to head west. One newly settled region attracting restless Vermonters was southern Michigan. Already by 1850 eleven thousand natives of the Green Mountains were living in this northern state sprawled along the shores of four of the Great Lakes. According to one historian, "Heaven competed with Michigan as the promised land."[18]

In these decades just prior to the Civil War thousands of women traveled west as members of families. A far smaller number went alone. These were mostly young single women, many of them teachers, who ventured independently into this vast, sparsely settled territory. Most, spurred on by missionary zeal, dreamed of bringing education and Protestant evangelical religion to thriving towns as well as pioneer settlements. But some had other reasons prompting them to leave home. One Michigan-bound teacher who declared that she was going west "to do the Will of my Heavenly Father," also spoke of her desire to be independent "and not beholden to my friends for a livelihood."[19]

We will never know precisely what prompted Abby Hemenway to head west. A longing for independence and adventure combined with uncertainty regarding her future career as a Vermont district schoolteacher were all likely inducements. Also, as a committed Baptist, Hemenway would have shared the missionary zeal of other evangelical pioneer women teachers. But, above all, this zealous and ambitious young woman must have seen this move to Michigan as an empowerment, an irresistible opportunity to take charge of her own destiny.

Abby and Lucia chose the town of St. Clair, a bustling new community sixty miles north of Detroit. Why St. Clair and not some other town? Only because Lucia had an aunt and uncle named Hinkley living there with whom the two could board while looking for teaching positions.[20]

When Ralph Barton learned that his sister and cousin had left for Michigan he was not happy. In a letter home he called Lucia a "foolish girl," adding that "it is no place for her or Abby either out west."[21] Most parents of unmarried daughters eager to head for the newly settled states and territories agreed, and many refused to grant their approval.[22] But Abby, aged twenty-four, had been on her own for many years, and Daniel and Abigail Hemenway probably could have done little to prevent her from going even if they had wanted to. Lucia at seventeen was another matter. But she, too, was used to getting her own way and could claim her older cousin Abby as a suitable chaperone. Presumably also, the presence of relatives like the Hinkleys in St. Clair further eased the concerns of both families.[23]

What Daniel Hemenway thought of his daughter's Michigan plans can only be imagined. We know, however, that Abigail Dana Hemenway missed Abby sorely. In a poem she wrote following the cousins' departure she spoke of the "cloud of deepest gloom" that had shaded her heart on that bright September morning in 1853 as she watched her beloved eldest daughter board the train that would carry her so far from home. She mailed these verses to Michigan together with a blossom from Abby's rosebush, which had been left in her care.

Now thou art gone, how sad and lone
Is the deserted nest;
I long to see thy face again
And clasp thee to my breast.

I miss thee in the evening hours,
Thou hast so oft beguiled
Amid these pensive hours, my heart
Still yearns for thee, my child.

Abby replied to these verses with some sentimental lines of
her own in which the image of the rose Abigail Dana had cut
from her daughter's bush becomes symbolic of a greater separation:

Precious little treasure this!
Does the stalk its blossom miss?

. . . .

Did the parent stem, too, weep,
With a silent sorrow deep
For the bud it could not keep,
For this token sent to me,
Love's memento, sweet to be?[24]

Abby and Lucia's trip to Detroit, which only a decade earlier would have taken a month or more by wagon train, in 1853
could be accomplished in two weeks or less. The epic character
of the journey had vanished with the coming of the railroad. It
now began with a ride in the "cars"—as trains were called
then—via Rutland and Albany to Buffalo. From there the
quickest route was by steamer across Lake Erie to Detroit. For
travelers to the West this Lake Erie crossing was especially symbolic. Mary Arnold, a teacher from Monmouth, Maine, made
her first trip in 1852 and described her feelings. "It seemed like

being transported into a new clime and I suppose we were just then beginning to cross the *boundary line* which separates East from West."[25]

The few letters that survive from this western adventure tell us that by late September the two cousins had arrived safely in St. Clair and had found teaching positions. Lucia reported to her parents that she was boarding with Uncle Hinkley and his family, which included six rambunctious children. She had thirty pupils in her school but was disappointed that her salary was only $2.00 per week. Abby, who was not living with the Hinkleys, had joined up with a Mrs. Arnold and was running a select school in the village. She, too, had about thirty pupils, who paid a higher tuition; but, as Lucia pointed out, "there are two to divide the spoils."[26]

Compared to Ludlow, St. Clair, like other fast-growing towns in the West, was a booming, bustling new community. Incorporated as a village as recently as 1850, by 1858 it had grown into a small city. Hemenway's prosaic impressions of St. Clair echoed those of other women teachers, who found the tone of life in the West not only commercial but culturally impoverished. Delia Horsford, a Vermonter who taught for a time in Ottawa, Illinois, described "the greater part of the people" as "so engrossed in their business that they have no time for anything else." Mary Rogers of Champlain, New York, after arriving in Cassville, Missouri, declared in a letter home that there was "no congenial society in this place, not one." She had young women in her class as old as twenty-two who could hardly read and children whose parents could not read at all.[27] Nor was there much reverence for history in the West. As late as 1865 E. L. Godkin would write in the *North American Review* that "new communities are springing up in the West every month, on whom the past has but little hold. They have no history, and no traditions . . . The West, in short, had inherited nothing, and so far from regretting this, it glories in it."[28]

If Abby and Lucia expected teaching conditions in Michigan to be an improvement over those in Vermont they were disappointed. The design of most schools, like other public buildings, had traveled west with the settlers and ranged from one-room frame houses to two-story brick seminaries. The size of the schoolrooms may have been even smaller than they were back home, for Lucia reported that the meeting-houses in St. Clair were not half as large as the ones in Ludlow.[29]

Job security was even more precarious in the West than it had been in the Green Mountain State. Unlike the school system Abby and Lucia had known in Vermont, where towns were mandated by state law to support common schools, in western states such as Michigan no guarantee of public support for education existed. Yet, as two women teachers in Indiana discovered, many of the people in these new western towns did not "have the means or desire to send their children to school unless it is free." Thus, teachers whose schools were closed for lack of funds had to choose between finding a new position or taking the financial risk of opening a select school and collecting their own fees.[30]

Life as a schoolteacher in Michigan was also lonely. As single, unattached women Abby and Lucia would have been anomalies in a town like St. Clair. While it is true that Abby was accustomed to going out to work and bringing home a salary, she was also used to having the support of a wide network of family and friends. In St. Clair there was only Lucia and perhaps the Hinkleys.

By November 1853 both cousins were disheartened. The West had not measured up to their expectations, and Lucia already talked of returning to Vermont. She had yet to be paid properly, and the school committee in her district was thinking of hiring a man to teach the winter term. In a letter home Lucia told her parents she would have to find a position in a nearby district or leave. Abby, in a postscript to the same letter, tried to sound sanguine about Lucia's prospects, portraying her cousin as "easily discouraged and encouraged." But Abby, too, was homesick and didn't want her cousin to leave without her. She hoped they could both earn enough money to pay their way back to Vermont the following spring.[31]

By the fall of 1854 Lucia Barton was discouraged enough by life in St. Clair to return home to Ludlow. Abby, however, stayed on in Michigan for at least another two years. Thanks to her classical education and considerable teaching experience she probably earned better wages than her cousin and thus could save more. But unfortunately Hemenway left no record of these earnings. Nor, apart from the select school she taught that first autumn, do we know what other teaching jobs she held during her time in the West.

With Lucia gone, Abby lost her last link with the family in Ludlow. If she made any close friends in St. Clair there is no mention of them in the two letters that survive from this time. Like most women teachers in the West she probably changed jobs more than once, and without a network of support, Hemenway would have had to find these positions on her own. A long letter to Elvira Hemenway, the wife of her oldest brother, Nelson, written on October 8, 1854, painted a forlorn picture of her existence.

> No one knows the weight of multiplied cares and anx-
> ieties that press oftimes upon the weary schoolteacher
> in the Western world. . . . Morning after morning sees
> me in the same old beaten track plodding along to the
> schoolroom. Noon finds me hurrying home to dinner
> and hurrying back again and night witnesses the tired
> and somewhat discouraged Yankee girl returning to her
> boarding place to eat, drink and sleep and next morn-
> ing commences anew the same course.[52]

But Hemenway had been a teacher long enough to know how to obtain solace from the tedious days and lonely evenings. Working on *The Mystical Rose,* her life of the Virgin Mary, provided much-needed solace, comforting her in the absence of her own earthly mother.

Hemenway composed other poetry as well, enclosing a sample in her letter to Elvira. Though awkward and sentimental, its verses reveal Hemenway's use of pious daydreams to ease her discouragement. As she admitted to her sister-in-law, the lines were "more truthful than poetical." She was finding it hard to write poetry. "The muses sing not to me by night in this land of realities," she told her Uncle Asa.[33]

The sample she sent to Elvira describes three guardian angels who come to cheer Hemenway "on her tiresome way": Love, Hope, and Patience. Each imagined angel visits her in turn, shedding a "sweet perfume" on the hot, ill-smelling schoolroom, and makes the hours from nine to four bearable, even "blissful." "Sweet Patience," especially, delivers "a honied balm," her "hallowed accents" calming Hemenway's "tired and sinking heart." But all three of these symbolic angels succeed in making the long days both easier and more purposeful:

> Holy and high her task they paint
> Until her heart grows light
> They fan her with a radiant wing
> Until her smile is bright.[34]

The only other surviving letter of Hemenway's from these years was dated from Hopeville on July 20, 1855. No town of this name exists today, but the letter gave Centreville, situated some two hundred miles from St. Clair near the Indiana border, as her post office address, placing Hopeville presumably somewhere close by. What prompted Hemenway to make this move she didn't explain. The letter only revealed that she had

seventy-four students who monopolized her time. "I am growing thin and pale," she informed her unnamed correspondent.
The term would soon end, however, and Hemenway was certain that four weeks of rest would send her back to the classroom with renewed energy.[35]

The principal subject of this letter was friendship. It shows
something of Hemenway's passionate attachments as a young
woman, in this case her waning intimacy with a Miss Lathan,
whose first name she omitted. Nor are we told where the two
had known each other. Miss Lathan, who had once shared with
Hemenway all the feelings "brought to her heart," was now
neglecting her old friend by failing to write. To make matters
worse she didn't seem to care that their intimacy was a thing of
the past. Hemenway, who had learned all this from her correspondent, poured her anger and frustration with this erstwhile
friend's behavior into her reply.

> Have I lost the power to sympathize the will to bless,
> that now she denies me even the casual glance of recog-
> nition. So be It! There is a life within my soul that will
> not die out with the vanishing of *such a love*, a glory in
> my spirit that will not fade under the blighting influ-
> ence of *such a change*. This is the day *my heart foretold*.
> I *knew* it would come, it has come, and *I would* not lift
> my *finger*, even, to bid it back. Should she say to you
> again that on account of her *uncalled for neglect* she is
> *"ashamed to write,"* tell her, "I hope God will bless
> her!" *I forgive her!* I hope she will find among her *new
> friends* those who will *love* her so truly as I have done,
> and *forgive* her with as little bitterness at heart as I do.
> Say to her from me "I have bread that ye know not of."
> That is all. Tell her that I shall not regret the wasting
> of a love to[o] weak to endure through absence.

I love thee, yet I do not weep
    That thou are mine no more;
I mourn thee, but my feelings sleep
    In silence as before.

In the end her Christian faith, the bread that Miss Lathan knows not of, will console Hemenway for this loss. She concludes the letter by asking her correspondent, presumably also a close woman friend, to write more on the subject in her next letter. "I want to look down deeper, still deeper into your heart, and you are not afraid to trust me with the sight of its hidden things, I know. Restore the office of Confessor to me, that I may look down, down, deep into the hidden mysteries of the spirit. Let me read the oracles of the soul."[36]

This letter, which evokes so keenly Hemenway's longing for intimacy with other women, suggests the loneliness of her life in the West and the degree to which she depended on correspondence with close female friends to ease that loneliness. Such intimacy between women was common in the nineteenth century, an era when men and women inhabited different worlds, and relationships between them tended to be distant and awkward. As Carroll Smith-Rosenberg has written: "In sharp contrast to their distant relationship with boys, young women's relationships with one another were close, often frolicsome, and surprisingly long-lasting and devoted. They wrote secret missives to one another, spent long, solitary days with one another, curled up together in bed at night to whisper fantasies and secrets."[37]

While Hemenway's emotional language reveals a similar longing for intimacy with other women, it is not physical intimacy that she sought from these friends so much as spiritual closeness, a sharing of what was most heartfelt, most private. In *The Mystical Rose* Hemenway recounts the visit of Mary to her cousin Elizabeth. Mary has as yet told no one of her pregnancy, but upon her arrival at her cousin's house, Elizabeth's own unborn baby—the future John the Baptist—leaps in her womb in recognition of Jesus' presence. Over the course of the next three months the two mothers-to-be share many confidences, leading Hemenway to extol the intimacy of such friendships. In affecting language that, even for the day, was overwrought she writes: "O woman-sympathy / So priceless precious in its preciousness."[38]

By the summer of 1855 whatever dreams Hemenway may have brought with her to the West had long since faded. She was lonely and overworked, and there was a limit to how long her guardian angels and "Mother Mary" could keep her heart light and make her task seem holy. Eventually the drudgery and loneliness of school teaching in the West took its toll. As home and mother beckoned, Vermont may have seemed a more promising place than Michigan to satisfy her intellectual tastes and realize her literary ambitions.

4

Vermont Poets and Poetry

——•◦✿◦•——

Though cold our clime, and rude our mountain scenes,
Though snow-wreaths crown our hills of evergreens,
Yet here are cradled hearts that genius fires
And here are those whose spirit fame inspires,
Who cherish noble thoughts, whose bosoms glow
With all the warmth that love and friendship know.

Charles Linsley, "The Departed Year"[1]

Abby Hemenway's letter from Hopeville in July 1855 is the last record of her whereabouts until January 1858, by which time she was back home in Ludlow, living with her parents and collecting materials for a book of Vermont poetry.[2] Such a gap in the record is unfortunate, and this is not the only one; the problem is common enough for any biographer trying to work with lesser-known figures from the past.

The Hemenway house was emptier than when Abby had left for Michigan in the fall of 1853. Her two oldest brothers,

Rufus Nelson and Charles, still lived nearby, but they had married and had homes of their own. Horace may already have settled in the West, where he became a railroad conductor based in Council Bluffs, Iowa, and later St. Louis, Missouri. But the younger members of the family still living at home probably included the youngest, Daniel, who turned eighteen years old in May 1858, and Lydia and Carrie, both single and in their twenties. In the early 1860s Abby's two younger sisters would move to Brandon, a prosperous village north of Rutland, where they opened a small women's apparel shop. Both eventually found husbands in Brandon and ended up living on the same street.[3]

Regardless of how many family members were at the Ludlow house to welcome Abby back from the West, the reunion of mother and daughter would have been a particularly joyful one. Abby relives the delight of this moment in *The Mystical Rose* when she describes Mary's return home after visiting her cousin Elizabeth, and her pleasure in being "Home once again!" and enjoying her "mother's dear caress."[4]

But Abby's father, as the parent of three unmarried daughters in their twenties, may have felt less enthusiasm about his eldest daughter's return, particularly because she was not accompanied by a husband. In October 1858 Abby turned thirty—well past the age when most women married—and as long as she was single she remained legally her father's responsibility. Few unmarried women possessed sufficient income to live alone. Unless his eldest daughter found a husband soon, Daniel Hemenway could look forward to having Abby as a permanent member of his household.

For a hill country woman to escape being pulled back into the hardscrabble existence of the Vermont farm wife took courage and a strong dedication to a professional objective. In these years most young women who had left their families to

Abby, Lydia, and Carrie Hemenway, c. 1850.
(Permission David Hemenway.)

teach or secure other employment either found husbands in their new place of work or returned home, as Lucia Barton did, to settle down as wives and mothers. Yet, despite the risks and insecurities of remaining single, Abby, in common with a growing number of educated and ambitious American women, may have deliberately chosen this path. Of those who made this choice, some felt called to a vocation such as teaching or missionary work. Others desired a fuller intellectual life than was possible in most marriages.[5] Maria Mitchell, an astronomer who lived on the island of Nantucket, claimed that she remained single to be "more vigilant in her work." The Boston sculptor Harriet Hosmer went even further and declared that a woman artist had no business marrying. "For a man, it may be well enough," she wrote, but for a woman, on whom the matrimonial duties and cares weigh more heavily, it is a moral wrong, I think, for she must either neglect her profession or her family, becoming neither a good wife and mother nor a good artist. My ambition is to become the latter, so I wage eternal feud with the consolidating knot.

The historian Lee Chambers-Schiller has observed that such women "rejected marriage with a clear understanding both of what they were giving up and of what they were seeking."[6]

Whether Abby Hemenway deliberately chose the single state or not we don't know. Perhaps if exactly the right man had come along when she was younger she might have married. But in an era when wives were expected to be submissive and dependent, Hemenway's literary ambitions and lack of interest in domestic matters made her an unpromising candidate for matrimony. Few eligible young men would have been attracted by such independence of spirit. As Margaret Fuller—dubbed "the Corinne of New England"—once asked, "How can a woman of genius love and marry? A man of genius will not love her. He wants repose."[7]

Abby was also familiar with the realities of domestic life for married women both in the Vermont hill country and in the newly settled towns of the West. She had seen and experienced firsthand the heavy cares imposed on these women: the drudgery of housework, the dangers of childbearing, the isolation. Above all, she was aware that once married, most women had to forgo their personal dreams and pursuits. How little time had been spared her own mother for the writing of poetry!

Abby's strong sense of vocation gave her a powerful incentive to stay single. Yet this latest decision to give up teaching and devote herself to literature cannot have pleased her father. It was one thing to write poetry on the side as her mother had done. But to expect to make a living writing was something else again. Abby's salary as a teacher, though admittedly meager, had at least promised a small security. But now she had rashly decided to throw all that over in order to publish books. For Daniel Hemenway, who had earned his living through hard manual labor, this decision must have seemed foolhardy at best.

If Abby Hemenway experienced pressures from both inside and outside the family to follow a more traditional womanly path, she resisted them. If she was aware of social strictures against independent self-supporting women, she ignored them. An omnivorous reader, Hemenway knew that a good number of American women were making money publishing books. Novelists such as Harriet Beecher Stowe, E.D.E.N. Southworth, Susan Warner, and others had all enjoyed commercial success in the middle decades of the nineteenth century. Because little in Hemenway's own upbringing and education had discouraged her from achieving financial independence, why couldn't she attempt to follow in their footsteps?

Sometime after Hemenway's return from the West she began gathering the materials for an anthology of Vermont poetry. Exactly where the inspiration for this project came from Hemenway does not say. Yet there seems little question that her years in Michigan, that "land of realities" so inhospitable to the muses, had inspired a profound nostalgia for Vermont. When Harriet Beecher Stowe's family moved from Litchfield, Connecticut, to Cincinnati, Ohio, in 1832, the future novelist had exclaimed in a letter back home, "You don't know how coming from New England has sentimentalized us all! Never was there such an abundance of meditation on our native land, on the joys of friendship, the pains of separation." For a budding young novelist such as Stowe, living in the West not only heightened her appreciation for the New England culture she had left behind, but prompted her to preserve it in many of her writings.[8]

Hemenway returned from Michigan with a similar appreciation of Vermont's culture, and like E. L. Godkin, she, too, must have been appalled by the way the West not only lacked any history and tradition, but even gloried in its absence. Like other writers in the Green Mountain State, she felt driven by a need to preserve Vermont's vanishing past, for here, too, manners were changing, customs were disappearing, the old values were passing away. Moreover, she also believed that a knowledge of the past would act, as Emma Willard had written some forty years earlier, as a school of "republican manners and republican virtues"—qualities then endangered not only by the rise of the boisterous West but also by the looming sectional conflicts of the day. Whether or not Hemenway remembered that Vermont, too, had once been pioneer country with a "get rich quick" flavor of its own, she probably preferred not to dwell on this aspect of her state's past.

Thus Hemenway, who had discovered how poorly the Michigan muses sang, shared the sentiments of novelist Alice Carey recalling her own girlhood in a rural Ohio town. "In the far west where pioneers are still busy felling the opposing trees," Carey wrote in 1852, "it is not yet time for the reed's music; but in the interior of my native state which was a wilderness when my father first went to it, and is now crowded with a dense and prosperous population, there is surely much in simple manners, and the little histories every day revealed, to interest us in humanity."[9]

Unlike Harriet Beecher Stowe and Alice Cary, who chose to celebrate their native culture through fiction, Hemenway planned to celebrate hers by publishing Vermont verse both past and present. Anthologies of poetry had been popular items in the antebellum literary marketplace since the early 1840s. One native Vermonter who had already made a considerable national reputation for himself as a collector and publisher of verse was Rufus Wilmot Griswold. His *Poets and Poetry of America* came out in 1842 and was followed in 1849 by *Female Poets of America*. On a more modest scale, another Green

Mountain native named Anne Lynch Botta—herself a poet of some note—had compiled a collection of local prose and verse for Rhode Island. *The Rhode Island Book* was published in 1842 and may have prompted Hemenway to do something similar for Vermont.

Yet Hemenway envisioned a different sort of poetry anthology from those published in other states. As she wrote in the preface to *Poets and Poetry of Vermont,* instead of featuring the region's "*leading* native poets," her collection would represent the "general poetic literature" of Vermont "from its earliest settlement to the present period," and include poets from all over the state, many of whom were unknown even in their local communities. A love of history prompted Hemenway's effort rather than a desire to uncover literary genius. She shared the concern of many Vermont writers that the state's past was in danger of vanishing. These authors, as the Ferrisburgh novelist Rowland E. Robinson later observed, "wrote with less purpose of telling any story than of recording the manners, customs, and speech in vogue fifty or sixty years ago." Daniel Pierce Thompson, one of Vermont's most popular nineteenth-century writers, was a case in point. He had relied almost solely on local legends, tales of revolutionary bravery and rugged frontier life, as the subject matter for his many stories.[10]

Hemenway, too, wished to record the local and familiar in her collection of verse. She chose poetry to give voice to "those who claim no poetic name," those for "whom poetry has been but a casual interest."[11]

Today we think of poetry as high art, practiced mainly by professional writers. But a hundred years ago it was a much more homely form of expression. Abby herself had grown up reciting poetry and hearing it recited. On long winter evenings hill country families such as the Hemenways had gathered around the light and warmth of the fire and listened as one relative or another declaimed verse after verse of poetry. This

From the Gazetteer

✶ ✶ ✶

St. Albans

"June training in Vermont; A Serio-Comic History by L. L. Dutcher" includes an "old Vermont song" of Green Mountain Boy vintage.

[By way of introduction, Dutcher writes, "There are many things which influence a state in its progress and contribute to shape its destinies, which, isolated by themselves, appear to be of little importance. Of this character are the manners, habits, customs—and songs, sports and pastimes—of a people, which, whatever we may think of them, are nevertheless legitimate and indispensible subjects of historic record."]

Ho! all to the borders, Vermonters come down,
With your breeches of deer-skin and jackets of brown,
With your red woolen caps and your moccasins, come
To the gathering summons of trumpet and drum.
Come down with your rifles, let gray wolf and fox
Howl on in the shade of their primitive rocks,
Let the bear feed securely from pig-pen and stall,
Here's a two-legged game for your powder and ball.
Leave the harvest to rot on the field where it grows,
And the reaping of wheat to the reaping of foes,
Our vow is recorded, our banner unfurled,
In the name of Vermont, we defy all the world.

[Volume II, page 351]

recitation of verse was more than simply entertainment for Abby and her fellow Vermonters. Like family stories, it was also the traditional method of passing down the values and folkways of northern New England culture. Important events, such as the celebration of the Fourth of July, the dedication of a new cemetery, or the death of a local dignitary, would customarily be marked by the recitation of verses composed especially for the occasion.[12]

Already by midcentury much of the poetry traditionally recited by Vermonters at their firesides or at public gatherings seemed destined for oblivion. The proliferation of books and periodicals that accompanied the advent of cheap paper meant that reading poetry would soon replace reciting it from memory. At the same time, as Abby's mother had discovered, women as well as men were finding it easy to publish short verse in their local newspaper's poetry column, and farm wives had already begun the tradition of cutting out their favorite poems and pasting them in scrapbooks.[13] But newspapers and scrapbooks are ephemeral. If the invaluable oral tradition contained in such verse was to be saved for posterity, it must be put between the covers of a book. This was precisely Abby Hemenway's plan. She would preserve the ephemeral by publishing it in a permanent form.

Once Hemenway returned from the West she accepted no more teaching positions, but lived with her parents in Ludlow and devoted all of her time to collecting, compiling, and editing her projected volume of Vermont poetry. Some Vermont poets had already published their verse in books or periodicals. Others Hemenway solicited personally through relatives and friends. But to ensure that she would have as wide and representative a sample as possible, she sent out notices to the various county newspapers announcing that "Abby M. Hemenway, of Ludlow, is engaged in getting out a book of poetry to consist of selections from the published and unpublished productions of Vermont poets." Not every newspaper printed Abby's notice, but the word spread. In the end a "flood of manuscript," or three thousand pages of verse, were submitted from every corner of the state.[14]

Abby left no record of how she planned to pay for this

ambitious literary project. Nor do we know how she talked George A. Tuttle, the Rutland publisher, into printing her anthology. Yet her scheme for choosing which poets and poems to include was masterful. Well aware that an unknown schoolteacher from Ludlow would not be taken seriously as the sole judge of poetic talent in Vermont, Abby put together an "examining committee" to help her make the selections.

The committee members, whose identities were kept secret until long after the book was published, included four men and two women. All were contributors to *Poets and Poetry*, and Hemenway counted one, the Reverend Henry A. Saunderson, as an old literary friend from her Black River Academy days.[15] The other men were Anson A. Nicholson, a lawyer practicing in Brandon; the Reverend William Ford, editor of the *Northern Visitor*, a religious and literary periodical in Brandon; and Albertus B. Foote, editor of the *Rutland Herald*. The two women were Mrs. A. H. Bingham, whose husband was principal of the Brandon Seminary, and Julia Caroline Ripley Dorr, of Rutland, the most distinguished poet of the five. Dorr's reputation extended well beyond the borders of Vermont and she could count Emerson, Longfellow, and Oliver Wendell Holmes among her friends. Her presence on the examining committee brought a critical acumen to the process of selection, which neither Hemenway nor the other members possessed.[16]

From the hundreds of poets who submitted manuscripts, the committee chose the works of 110 for inclusion in *Poets and Poetry*. While today most of the contributors to an anthology of verse would consider themselves professional writers or teachers of literature, Hemenway's collection, like others of that time, brought together men and women from all walks of life. Here we find lawyers and doctors, farmers and housewives, clergymen and newspaper editors. Of the 47 women in the collection, 4 had already published volumes of their poetry, but only Julia Dorr and Anne Lynch Botta had national reputations as literary figures. Botta's fame rested less on what has been described as a "modest literary output" than on her New York salon, where famous and not-so-famous writers could meet on an equal footing in an atmosphere "free of petty gossip and backbiting."[17]

The men in *Poets and Poetry* who were known outside Vermont's borders include the nature poet, Carlos Wilcox; Charles G. Eastman, dubbed by English critics "the Burns of New England"; John Godfrey Saxe, whose verses were once as popular as those of Oliver Wendell Holmes; and the renowned eighteenth-century playwright, Royall Tyler.[18]

The introductory poem, "Vermont," was commissioned for the volume. Written by William Brown, a retired minister and newspaperman, whom Hemenway describes elsewhere as "a ripe scholar and devoted Christian," it sets the tone and introduces many of the themes to be found in this collection.[19]

> Land of the mountain and the rock,
>   Of lofty hill and lowly glen,
> Live thunder-bolts thy mountains mock;
> Well dost thou nurse by tempest's shock
> Thy race of iron men!
>
> Far from the city's crowded mart,
>   From Mammon's shrine and Fashion's show,
> With beaming brow and loving heart,
> In cottage homes they dwell apart,
> Free as the winds that blow.
> . . . .
> On Champlain's waves so clear and blue,
>   That circled by the mountain lies,
> Where glided once the light canoe,

With shining oar, the waters through,
The mighty steamboat plies.

And now among those hills sublime,
 The car doth thunder swift along,
Annihilating space and time,
And linking theirs with stranger clime
In union fair and strong.

The Southland boasts of vines and flowers,
 Of cloudless skies and silver waves,
Of spicy groves and orange bowers,
Lovely as dreams in youth's sweet hours—
But 'tis a land of slaves!

. . . .

And if, through Southern pow'r and pride,
 This broad, green land, in future time,
Shall hear the slave-roll by the side
Of Bunker's shaft, that marks where died
Her sons in strife sublime;—

Lo, as the bugle-echo thrills,
 New England's sons shall rally then,
And build their homes by mountain rills,
High up among our wild, green hills,
And sing free songs again!

The hills were made for freedom; they
 Break at a breath the tyrant's rod;
Chains clank in valleys; there the prey
Bleeds 'neath Oppression's heel alway—
HILLS BOW TO NONE BUT GOD![20]

Vermonters, these verses proudly maintain, are a race of patriotic, freedom-loving, hardy folk uncontaminated by urban vice or the evils of slavery. Yet progress has not passed them by. The steamboat plies Vermont's lakes and the railroad "thunders" around its hills.

Brown's poem is but one of more than two dozen in the collection that extol the Green Mountain State. Many of these verses are sentimental evocations of Vermont as a region where independent, thrifty farmers happily toil in their fields; their virtuous, loving wives cheerfully mind the home fires; and their carefree children play tirelessly among the ever-blooming summer flowers. Sentimental and nostalgic, these poems look back at an earlier time with a sense of something lost—innocence, love, beauty—for those who left their childhood Vermont homes to live elsewhere. Other poems, however, contradict this nostalgic image of an untroubled past, where verse after verse evokes the sorrows and hardships of life, and the prevalence of death. For every poem recalling happy, carefree childhoods there are others lamenting the premature deaths of beloved sons or daughters.

Religion, a source of consolation for these and many other nineteenth-century poets, is a pervasive theme in this collection. Here are poems about God's presence in nature, poems urging readers to place their trust in God rather than in human institutions. Put up with life's sorrows and trials, counsels one, "For yonder lies the better land!"[21] An image employed by several of the poets portrays the colorful Vermont autumn as a harbinger of death and decay:

> Yet sweet to die 'mid Autumn hours
> When mourning forests sadly wave;
> Better are withered leaves than flowers,
> To strew upon my early grave.[22]

Perhaps the best nature poet in the anthology is Carlos Wilcox, a clergyman who died of consumption in 1827 when he was in his early thirties. Hemenway calls Wilcox a man of exalted character haunted by "shades of sadness and mystery." She published three of his poems, including one called "Midnight," which concludes with the following melancholy lines:

> I seem alone 'mid universal death,
> Lone as a single sail upon the sea,
> Lone as a wounded swan, that leaves the flock
> To heal in secret or to bleed and die.[23]

Various members of the Barton family are also included among the poets in this collection. Uncle Asa is represented by a single poem written to comfort his daughter Lucia after the death of her mother in 1851. Near the end of the volume are four bittersweet samples of Abigail Dana Hemenway's poetic writings. Finally, the very last poem, "Vermont," is by Lucia Barton. This paean to "My native State, so *free*, so dear," serves as a concluding sentimental tribute to the beauty of Vermont's "rugged scenes" and the virtues of its citizens in their "cottage homes."[24]

During the months just prior to the publication of *Poets and Poetry of Vermont* Hemenway made at least one trip to Rutland to see her publisher, Charles Tuttle, and conduct other business connected with the volume. The second week of September 1858 found her living with the family of Albertus Foote, one of the members of her examining committee, and arranging for photographs to be taken of a selected number of her poets. Eleven of these portraits would be included in the dozen or so "presentation," or deluxe, copies of the anthology.

A letter Hemenway wrote on September 11 to her old poet

friends, the Reverend Henry Saunderson and his wife, Elizabeth, is typical of many she would compose during her ensuing editorial career. It began in a chatty, comfortable vein:

> *My Dear Mr. and Mrs. Saunderson,*
> Hoping you are now at home, nicely seated after and much refreshed by your journey. Allow me to drop abruptly in and talk to you a moment of my gettings along (gettings, there is such a word in the dictionary isn't there Mr. S.; well if there's not, there ought to be hadn't there Mrs. S.) But, Our Book—Oh they [the printers] are getting along *a little*. Do you believe it they have really arrived to page *160* this 2nd week in September. I have an excellent opportunity to practice "Let patience have her perfect work."
>
> Mr. Tuttle, however has promised to put another hand on to it next week, and *says* he will try to get it through this month.[25]

Having made the Saundersons feel comfortable and given them a progress report on her book, Hemenway then proceeded to the real business of the letter, which was to talk both husband and wife into having their photographs taken for inclusion in *Poets and Poetry*. She began by assuring them that other prominent contributors to the collection had already agreed to sit for a professional photographer. "Mowry & Russell are getting us up some fine pictures," she told them, "they have got us up an excellent head of Eastman and Naramore. They are getting us up the head of Saxe now." As a further inducement she noted that "private copies" of each plate were also available from the photographer at reduced rates. She hoped that the Saundersons will "come up the first of next week and set for your pictures (today is Saturday). If you call at Mr. Foote's you will find me quite probably there."

Hemenway's persuasive skills, which she would use to such

Abby Maria Hemenway, 1858.
(Frontispiece in *Poets and Poetry.*)

good effect as editor of the *Vermont Historical Gazetteer,* were already in evidence here. She understood exactly how to make her authors feel both proud of their worth as poets and necessary to the success of her publication. By pointing out that others were complying with her request for portraits she was shaming the Saundersons into doing her bidding, all the while appealing to their Yankee thriftiness.

In the end the portrait of only one Saunderson, Elizabeth, found its way into the deluxe edition of *Poets and Poetry,* along with those of ten other poets in the collection. Hemenway must have made a visit to Mowry and Russell's studio herself, for the fronticepiece shows her seated, hands in lap, attired in a striped dress with full sleeves. A loose shawl covers her shoulders, and her hair is rolled fashionably over her ears. The editor of *Poets and Poetry* looks very much the demure literary lady.

Abby Hemenway's anthology received considerable advance notice both in Vermont and elsewhere. According to one report, even before it was sent to press the work was being heralded in various newspapers as one that would "fill a vacancy hitherto unsupplied." As Tuttle had promised Hemenway, the book was in print by October 1858. It ran to more than four hundred pages, cost $1.00 a copy, and could be purchased with a plain green, blue, or red cover. Elegant, illustrated editions with embossed covers were also available at a higher price. The most elaborate of these was bound in white silk and sprinkled with minute gilt roses.[26]

Although we don't know how many copies of *Poets and Poetry* were printed, we do know that it was successful enough from the start to send Abby back to work almost immediately on a second edition. Meanwhile, the first was greeted with generally favorable reviews. The *Middlebury Register* called it "a treasury of bright thoughts" in which the "peculiar genius and spirit of our people" is exemplified. Yet another notice in the same paper drew attention to the female sensibility evoked in the volume, "the gentle melancholy . . . which elevates life by shadowing it and pleases by saddening it." Equally complimentary reviews came in from as far away as Independence, Missouri. A New York newspaper doubted whether "any State in the Union has furnished more poetry in proportion to its population, worthy of preservation, than Vermont."[27]

Closer to home, however, a critic who signed himself "Ascutney" published a lengthy and stinging denunciation of *Poets and Poetry* in the *Bellows Falls Times*. Dismissing the collection as "pretentious" and filled with editorial and typographical errors, "Ascutney" was particularly vicious about the poems themselves, one-half of which he declared should have been omitted altogether, while the other half needed pruning and editing. Far from being a representative collection of the poetic literature of Vermont, the verses were, in his view, "a motley mixture of the very good, the tolerable, and the intolerable." He further questioned whether the "aimless, senseless, and measureless doggerel" contained in the book could be "properly defined by the phrase 'poetic literature.'" In all fairness, "Ascutney" did point out what he considered to be the "real poetry" in the collection, including the works of Anne Botta, Julia Dorr, and John Godfrey Saxe. He seems to have had an overheated scorn for the more sentimental poems glorifying Vermont and its people. For example, he decried the "undue prominence given to 'Old Ethan [Allen]'" when only one poem in the whole collection is devoted to this Revolutionary hero.[28]

"Ascutney's" review of *Poets and Poetry* induced a storm of protest from the readers of the *Bellows Falls Times*. One letter deplored the "spirit of virulence and acrimony" with which such a "laudable effort" had been greeted. Another spoke of the months of arduous labor that had been destroyed with one touch of a pen and took issue with "Ascutney's" dismissal of such poems as Royall Tyler's "Fourth of July Ode."

> Ask the men of sixty years ago who still linger among us if the "Fourth of July Ode" is not a life-like picture of Independence day in their boyhood? . . . It is from such records as that very ode that our children's children will gain the clearest and most correct idea of

the manners and customs of their fathers in the primitive days of the republic.[29]

Hemenway could not have defended her collection better herself. Meanwhile, excitement over the "Ascutney" review quickly spread throughout Vermont. Contributors to the collection denounced by this critic quite naturally took his attacks personally. Many years later, Hemenway remarked that it was "the only war of poetry ever blowed up in the State."[30]

All this attention, of course, only added to the volume's popularity. As Hemenway herself put it, the book's success was "a speculation verily burst in air."[31] According to a *Times* correspondent, some of the poets who had been included there had already "strung their harps anew" and were writing more verse. All the while questions mounted as to "Ascutney's" real identity. There were hints that he was a poet who had been rejected by Hemenway's committee for inclusion in the volume. One reader of the *Times* went so far to to identify this critic as the one-time editor of a Vermont newspaper who was now a proofreader in the offices of the *New York Sun*. These assertions were never proved, however, and the identity of "Ascutney" remains a mystery.[32]

If Hemenway was upset by "Ascutney's" criticisms, she must also have delighted in all the fuss that provided such wonderful publicity for her book. According to one report, *Poets and Poetry* could be found throughout the state in the parlors of Vermont's best families.

Still, when Hemenway brought out the second and revised edition in 1860, she did make some changes. The new collection contained one hundred more pages than the first. While ninety-one of the original poets were included here nineteen others were dropped. Twenty new authors—thirteen men and seven women, including Abby Hemenway herself—were added. Verses appear by John Hopkins, the Episcopal Bishop of

Burlington, and his more poetically gifted son, also named John (the author of "We Three Kings of Orient Are"). In addition there are also two poems by the distinguished naturalist George Perkins Marsh.

The selections from her own poetry that Hemenway chose to include were taken from *The Mystical Rose*. Four extracts, including "A Bethlehem Legend," "The Magi Visit," "The Baptism," and "The Crucifixion" fill six pages of the volume. The fact that these verses have little to do with Vermont and its people may explain why Hemenway left them out of the first edition. The revised edition, however, contained a number of new poems with biblical themes.

Hemenway's verses are essentially a retelling of the life of Jesus as found in the Gospels. Embellished by her own imaginary rendering of a lush and exotic Holy Land, they describe a world very foreign to the one she had known and reveal a passionate yearning for richer fare than could be found in the hill country of northern New England. These lines describing the visit of the Magi to the Holy Family in Bethlehem are typical:

Gazing on that Blessed Maiden,
On whose velvet bosom lay
Loveliest born of human clay;—
Down they bowed in adoration,
Laid with words of warm devotion
Judah's princely Babe to greet
Costly offerings at His feet:
Treasures rich from Orient lands,
God's dust bright from Afric's sands,
Radiant gems whose rainbow-blaze
Kindled 'neath a tropic's rays,
Odorous myrrh and spices sweet,
Laid with rapture at his feet.[33]

The best known of the newcomers in the second edition of

Poets and Poetry of Vermont was someone who should have been included in the first, Thomas Rowley. Called the "father of Vermont verse," Rowley was a pioneer patriot, widely regarded as "the official minstrel of the Green Mountain Boys," and renowned for his remarkable gifts for poetic improvisation. Why this once-popular poet was left out of the original edition is unclear. The fact that only a few of his verses survived in print may have been one reason. More likely, Hemenway and her committee considered Rowley's rollicking verses too politically radical and crude. The one she printed in 1860 was an invitation to tenant farmers in eighteenth-century New York State to settle in what would become Vermont:

> Come all ye laboring hands
> That toil below,
> Amid the rocks and sands
> That plow and sow,
> Come quit your hired land,
> Let out by cruel hand,
> 'Twil free you from your bands—
> To Rutland Go.
> . . . .
> For who would be a slave,
> That may be free?
> Here you good land may have,
> But come and see.
> The soil is deep and good,
> Here in this pleasant wood,   .
> Where you may raise your food
> And happy be. . . .[34]

As if in answer to "Ascutney's" critique of the first volume of *Poets and Poetry,* Hemenway's introduction to the second edition makes a point of defending the often unsophisticated attempts at verse contained therein. "The boast of the Green Mountain State," she wrote,

> has been that hers was "the land of the free," rather than being the home of the arts or the garden of poesy. Indeed, with a political existence as yet of hardly eighty years, and a rough land of rock, and stone, and tree, where incessant war must be waged on ice and granite, on snow and gravel-stones . . . it would be surprising rather than otherwise, if many stars of the first magnitude had found a place in the literary firmament.[35]

Reviews of this new edition of *Poets and Poetry* justified the additions and deletions. The *Boston Times* noted the "great deal of excellent poetry in the five hundred and more pages," and predicted that the "book will be a popular one in Vermont, of course, and deserves to be so everywhere else." The *Portsmouth Journal* in neighboring New Hampshire said that "the degree of talent presented shows that the cold regions of the North are nurseries of poetry."[36]

Hemenway's *Poets and Poetry* was the first major collection of Vermont verse. In 1872 A. J. Sanborn updated the work with a smaller collection entitled *Green Mountain Poets.* The next significant compilation, *Vermont Verse: An Anthology,* was published in 1931 as one of a series of volumes sponsored by the Vermont Commission on Country Life. The strong regional and historical impulse that had inspired Hemenway's collection is present as well in this later work. As Arthur Wallace Peach wrote in his foreword:

It is the hope of the editors that the four books in the Series may serve as interesting byways from Vermont's past into Vermont's present and also may tend to throw some definite light . . . on the attitudes of mind and heart, faiths, beliefs, and loyalties that woven together through the years have formed those traditional characteristics so generally associated with the state and its people.[37]

Of the 116 authors represented in this twentieth-century collection, 29 were also in the Hemenway volume, including Anne Lynch Botta, Julia Dorr, Royall Tyler, and Carlos Wilcox. Yet this new anthology covered a century and a half of Vermont poetry, more than twice the number of years spanned by *Poets and Poetry*. Abby Hemenway's collection had stood the test of time remarkably well.[38]

In the light of Hemenway's own literary career, *Poets and Poetry of Vermont* served as a prototype, a kind of trial run, for what would become her life's great work: editing and publishing the *Vermont Historical Gazetteer*.

"Not a Suitable Work for a Woman"

---◆◆◇◆◇◆◇◆◆---

Making history is building bridges
over the old stream of time.

Abby Hemenway[1]

Gathering the materials for *Poets and Poetry* had taken Hemenway all over the state, introducing her to many of Vermont's prominent men and women. Once the book was published, like a peddler hawking his wares, she spent a good part of the fall and winter of 1858–59 traveling around Vermont selling copies, which she carried along with her. Indifferent to polite society's strictures against women promoting themselves, or even traveling alone, she derived great pleasure as well as profit from these tours. For one thing they gave her an entrée into Vermont's political and cultural elite, among whom she formed many lifelong friendships. For another, they carried her to parts of Vermont she had never seen before, heightening her interest in the region's rich culture and history.

These tours cemented old friendships and fostered new ones. Hemenway had a collector's instinct for people that was of the same magnitude as her passion for historical facts and documents. She remembered everyone she met and kept up with as many of these as she could, including many of her poets, whose verses she later published in the pages of her *Gazetteer*.

Those who spent time with Abby Hemenway invariably found this small, energetic woman, with her straight brown hair and bright, penetrating blue eyes, good company. Her fund of anecdotes—tales of the adventures she'd enjoyed, the people she'd met—all conveyed in a beautiful speaking voice, delighted her fellow Vermonters. Nor could they fail to be impressed by her wide knowledge of many subjects, from history and literature to birds and flowers.[2]

The first of Hemenway's promotional tours occurred in October 1858 when she was invited to accompany Charles Linsley and his wife to Montpelier. The biannual meeting of the General Assembly was in session, and Linsley, a friend and contributor to her book, was a member of the Vermont House. While in Montpelier, Hemenway was well entertained. She and the Linsleys visited Eliakim Walton's printing office by the courthouse; they also called on two of her poets, Charles Eastman, the "Burns of New England," and G. N. Brigham. Brigham, a homeopathic physician, returned the compliment by entertaining his editor at the Pavilion Hotel.[3]

No sooner did Hemenway return home to Ludlow than she received another invitation, this time to visit her friends the Rockwells in Middlebury. Sylvester Rockwell, a successful sheep breeder from nearby Cornwall, had been a tireless salesman for her book. He only recently had moved into Middlebury, where he had bought an old brick farmhouse and transformed it into an imposing Victorian mansion with a wide veranda running around three sides. A handsome iron fence enclosed the property, and Hemenway remembered it all as very "picturesque."

During her stay at Springside, as the house was called, Hemenway met a number of prominent Middlebury citizens, including Phillip Battell, also a contributor to her book and secretary of the town's historical society. She described him as an "old school gentleman, of artistic, delicate mould." Here she also met two women, Miss Allen and Miss Warner, both recently returned from abroad "fragrant with France and Geneva." Another of her poets, Egbert Phelps, the youngest son of a retired U.S. senator, was full of praise for *Poets and Poetry*. He encouraged its editor to embark next on a collection of Vermont prose. As Hemenway noted many years later, this was the first seed planted in her mind for a historical and literary project that would eventually blossom into the *Vermont Historical Gazetteer*.[4]

Sometime later when Hemenway was in Rutland, presumably on business with George Tuttle, her publisher, she also saw Albertus Foote. Perhaps she even stayed with him. In any case Foote told her of a recent argument he'd had with a friend who insisted that *Poets and Poetry* would have been a better book if it had contained more poems from fewer poets. Foote, as a member of the volume's examining committee, did not share his friend's views and took pains to assure Hemenway that the breadth of representation was part of the book's charm. He went further and suggested that her next publication should include samplings of prose and poetry from every town in the state. A second seed had been planted.[5]

A third seed was sown later that winter when Hemenway came across an article by the Reverend Pliny H. White, urging the people of St. Johnsbury and other towns in the state to collect and preserve their own history. White, a one-time lawyer and businessman, had only recently accepted the call to become a Congregational minister in Coventry. A prolific writer and respected local historian, he was also a leading member of the

Pliny H. White, Vermont historian
and frequent contributor to the *Gazetteer*.
(From the collections of the Vermont Historical Society.)

Vermont Historical Society, founded in 1838. Biography was White's forte. No one else in the state could rival his detailed knowledge of the many influential men peopling Vermont's past. In his article, White warned that if each community did not begin to record and preserve its own history, much information of great historical value would be lost. As Hemenway later recalled, the notion expressed by White that "our past has been too rich and, in many points too unique and romantic to lose, impressed us, and that permanently."[6]

Pliny White's urgency to recapture a vanishing past was shared by other American historians and antiquarians (to most people at the time the terms were interchangeable). These individuals saw themselves as intervening at a crucial moment in history to preserve neglected records from oblivion.

The writing of local history had a long tradition in New England stretching back to the seventeenth century. From the beginning, according to David Jaffee, "history was critical to New England self-definition." The region "was as much an ideal created in stories told about its past as it was a place mapped out on the ground by settlers."[7]

A new resurgence in writing local history occurred in the 1820s. In New England's older communities the chief impulse driving this effort had been, according to David Hall, "the struggle to re-imagine a lost world." Antiquarians in these towns mourned the widening gulf between themselves and their Puritan ancestors. Paradoxically, however, they also felt a kinship with the past, viewing it as a harbinger of the present, and they sought to breach that gulf in their writings.[8]

In more newly settled regions such as Vermont, where history was rooted not in distant colonial days but in a closer revolutionary past, other factors prompted the writing of local history. The accelerating pace of economic and social change in the first decades of the nineteenth century led many Vermonters to glance back wistfully to an earlier and better time, a time before emigration westward and cityward had carried away their towns' most promising youths, a time when the old customs and traditions had been cherished, when the old virtues had been practiced. The impulse to write local history was, as one practitioner put it, to "encourage a love of home by its attraction," to draw back "the wanderer to his birth—and quiet in a measure that restless spirit of change."[9]

Elsewhere in New England the writers of local history were lone individuals concerned chiefly with recording the history of their own family and community. In Vermont, however, the impulse to produce local history was from the start more of a group effort and grew out of attempts to publish gazetteers. In 1814 Josiah Dunham sought cooperation from "gentlemen of science and information" to gather material from the various communities in the state on such matters as topography, town incorporation, schools, churches, statistics, and biographical sketches of eminent local citizens. Dunham even sought the help of the legislature to promote the work and secure subscribers.[10] Dunham never published his gazetteer, but the proposal was revived nine years later when Zadock Thompson began collecting information "relating to the settlement and history of our townships" for his proposed *Gazetteer of the State of Vermont*, which was published in 1824.[11]

County efforts were also underway in the Green Mountain State to stimulate the writing of local history. As early as 1847 Middlebury had formed its historical society with the express purpose of securing such works for every town in Addison County. Samuel Swift, a highly respected lawyer in Middlebury, was finishing up his history of that community. Appearing in 1859, it was the first such publication in the state. John M. Weeks's *History of Salisbury* followed soon after in 1860. The prime impulse behind this effort is spelled out by Swift in the opening pages of his *History of the Town of Middlebury:* "Already nearly all the men who had shared in the occurrences and toils of the first settlement had passed away; and their immediate descendants, who are the next best witnesses will soon follow."[12]

Despite these worthy objectives, the Middlebury Historical Society was finding it hard to persuade other towns in the county to follow suit. An article published in the *Middlebury Register* on April 27, 1859, spoke of the difficulty these communities were having raising the funds for such projects "on account of the limited sale which must attend them." This reluctance of towns to publish their histories may have prompted the Vermont legislature to take the initiative. In 1858 the General Assembly, probably at the urging of both the state and the Middlebury historical societies, passed a law authorizing towns to provide financial assistance to any persons prepared to write their community's history.[13] Because the law contained no provisions for helping out the towns financially with these works, it is unlikely that the measure had much effect.

Pliny White's warning that the past was becoming "more and more indistinct and irrevocable" with the passing of each day struck a responsive chord in Abby Hemenway. In his call to preserve a vanishing past at the local level he articulated what she had been groping for herself. Egbert Phelps's idea of collecting the best prose in the state meant as little to her as had the idea of publishing only the best poets. Such an anthology would have given voice only to the educated elite. By contrast, the mountain of verse submitted for inclusion in *Poets and Poetry of Vermont* had revealed a rich regional culture.

In one of the book's most popular poems, Charles Eastman's "My Uncle Jerry," the hero personifies a historical source that had all but disappeared by the late 1850s. Uncle Jerry, an early settler from Connecticut, is a little "odd . . . and ancient in his manners." He won't talk much about politics anymore, Eastman says,

But if you care to hear about
  When he was in his glory,
The early days of old Vermont
  That shine for us in story,

. . . .

Or anything of matters when
  Our freedom we were winning,
He'll talk from dark to twelve o'clock,
  And just have made beginning.

. . . .

There's much, he says, about Vermont
  For history and song,
Much to be written yet, and more
  That has been written wrong.[14]

To record for posterity stories like the many Uncle Jerry had to tell was a task that met Abby Hemenway's tastes exactly. As she later described it, even before she finished reading Pliny White's article, "the third seed had fallen,—a plump seed, that we did not hesitate one moment to plant."[15]

While compiling *Poets and Poetry* Hemenway had not only read verses that lamented the loss of the first generation of Vermonters, but she also would have remembered stories told by the older members of her own family around the fire on long winter evenings. As a child she'd done her own part to keep the past alive, gaining a reputation as the Hemenway family raconteur, and she would have agreed with Dorothy Canfield Fisher that in Vermont, as in other settled communities, "family history often and vividly recounted becomes as real to every generation as personal experience."[16] She would have understood, too, that those who knew the history of the early days, men such as Charles Eastman's Uncle Jerry, were also the keepers of local lore and tradition; their stories must be saved.

Without question the inspiration for compiling the *Vermont Historical Gazetteer* came as much from Hemenway's experience collecting the verse for *Poets and Poetry* as from anything Pliny White or anyone else may have said. As is so often the case with inspiration, he articulated something she was already groping for. Yet she wanted to go beyond merely collecting the writings of the educated and well-to-do politicians, lawyers, ministers, and other professional men. She wanted to save the stories of women as well as men, of ordinary folk as well as extraordinary ones.

With characteristic determination, and without so much as a backward glance, Hemenway decided to take up Pliny White's charge and begin single-handedly the work of collecting and publishing the history of every town and village in the state. The task was daunting, but that doubtless made it all the more appealing to this energetic, ambitious, and successful editor.

Vermont may have been small, but Hemenway's resolve to publish the local history of her entire state was matched by no other person or institution in the country. If she was to some degree inspired by early antiquarianism in Vermont, which saw the collecting of town history as a statewide effort, her own plan was far more ambitious than anything previously attempted. Zadock Thompson had included individual town histories in his *Gazetteer* published in 1824, but these sketches were considered too brief by younger Vermont historians such as Pliny White and the members of the Middlebury Historical Society.[17]

Hemenway's conviction that she could manage such a vast and complex historical enterprise as a single woman on her own is astonishing. Less remarkable is the choice of history itself as the subject of this new literary venture. In the nineteenth century, before the field of history was professionalized, it was considered a branch of literature.

Ever since the early days of the republic women had been seen as particularly suited to the study of history. Even the writing of history was becoming accepted as a womanly occupation. In the decades between the Revolution and the Civil War, more than a hundred American women wrote and published history books. Although they were not historians in the modern sense of the word, combing archives for original material to be analyzed and dissected, these women did gather, arrange, write, and publish accounts of the past. Some, such as Emma Willard, produced textbooks to be used in female seminaries. Others, including Frances Caulkins, a native of New London, Connecticut, wrote the histories of their hometowns, while still others published historical compendia, intended for the home libraries of ordinary people.[18]

These women historians saw their calling as primarily didactic. Frances Caulkins justified the educational value of her own work when she wrote in the preface to her 1860 history of New London: "It is the ardent desire of the writer to engage the present generation in this ennobling study of their past history, and to awaken a sentiment of deeper and more affectionate sympathy with our ancestors." For Caulkins the writing of local history had a religious as well as a patriotic purpose. "The hand of God is seen in the history of towns as well as in that of nations."[19]

At work for their town, their state, their nation, and for God, nineteenth-century American women who wrote history shared a profound sense of mission, and Abby Hemenway was no exception. She later remembered her single-minded zeal as she confided to her closest friends about this new literary project. She recalled talking of it "as one must of an engrossing thought that is to develop into a lifework" and how her "unquestioning faith" had kindled in some of these friends "a correspondent faith." Looking back on her first years as editor of the *Gazetteer* Hemenway perhaps forgot that the project was initially designed to take a few years, and not a lifetime. But there is little need to doubt her "unquestioning faith," her belief that she was embarked on what she later referred to as a "holy cause." From the start Hemenway's commitment to the work of history had all the marks of a deeply held religious vocation, and the strength of this commitment would sustain her through many difficult times.[20]

Those whom Hemenway told of her plan to publish the local histories of every county in Vermont suggested that she start with her own county, Windsor, or neighboring Rutland. But because, as Hemenway put it, "this new and larger work was to come, rather from others than ourself," she quite sensibly thought it wiser to begin where some town history was already being collected. Addison County fit this criterion and had the further advantage of being the alphabetically logical place to begin.

Sometime during the spring or summer of 1859 Hemenway traveled from Ludlow to Middlebury, where she stayed again with her friends the Rockwells. Her plan, as she described it to the whole family gathered in Springside's "pleasant sitting-room," was to issue a quarterly magazine of the history and literature of Vermont. "History must be its back-bone, cranium, limb, nerve and sinew," Hemenway told her friends. By her account, Sylvester Rockwell "heartily endorsed the plan" and suggested they speak first to Philip Battell. If the secretary of the Middlebury Historical Society approved—and Rockwell was certain he would—so would the other members of the Society.[21]

They called on Mr. Battell, a town leader and benefactor, who was not as enthusiastic as they had hoped. He liked the idea well enough. "He looked a little grave, smiled while looking grave," Hemenway remembered, but he also implied that it was going to be much harder work than perhaps Miss Hemenway realized. Battell gave her a long list of names of people in the county who had been appointed to write their town's history and suggested that she discuss the matter with them and see what they thought of it. Hemenway later learned that this was a rather underhanded attempt to discourage her. But Philip Battell did not know the woman he was dealing with.[22]

Undaunted, Hemenway made a date with the Rockwells to revisit Middlebury and returned to Ludlow, where she immediately began to prepare for Battell's suggested tour of Addison County. She spent the next few months composing letters to each prospective town historian. She also ordered one thousand printed circulars describing her proposed undertaking, enclosing a hundred of them with the letters she mailed off.

Where Hemenway came up with the money simply for the postage, much less the cost of printing the circulars, is pretty much guesswork. All we know about her plans to finance the *Gazetteer* is that she expected to pay her travel expenses from sales of *Poets and Poetry*, and the cost of publication through obtaining advance subscriptions, a common practice for the editors of nineteenth-century periodicals.[23]

By mid-September Hemenway was ready to start. Her book trunk and newly purchased carpetbag were packed with circulars together with copies of *Poets and Poetry* to sell along the way. She was anxious about what lay ahead and dreaded meeting so many strangers. But she was also eager to get started, feeling, as she described it, a "propellative power" urging her along her "chosen path." Then, half an hour before the train was to leave for Rutland, the mail brought her a letter from Sylvester Rockwell. She later remembered thinking that the envelope's appearance had not been promising, and when she opened it she quickly discovered why.[24]

The enclosed sheet was signed by several Middlebury College professors, all apparently members of the Middlebury Historical Society. These "unbelievers at the College," as

Hemenway dubbed them, made it very clear that they re-garded her whole plan as "an impracticality . . . not a suitable work for a woman. How could one woman," they demanded incredulously, "expect to do what forty men had been trying for sixteen years and could not?" Indeed, they suggested, she would break down before she had toured half the county. Of course, they didn't want to discourage her completely. Write another book by all means, they told her, but leave out the history. Instead, they suggested that she "make a volume of prose selec-tions, for which the best writers of Middlebury [presumably including themselves] would contribute."[25]

"Middlebury had shut her door," Hemenway noted in her recollection of this devastating rebuff. The first real setback in her new career, it was surely rendered all the more painful by Sylvester Rockwell's apparent betrayal. Somehow this friend, until recently one of her staunchest supporters, had fallen under the influence of the professors at the college, men who were clearly uncomfortable that a woman might succeed at a task they had struggled with for so long with only limited success.

Whether Hemenway knew it or not, forty-five years earlier Emma Willard had been similarly rebuffed by the authorities at Middlebury. To prepare herself to teach advanced courses in science and the classics at the Female Seminary she opened in her home adjacent to the campus in 1814, Willard had requested permission to attend classes and examinations at the college, only to have her request summarily denied.[26]

Much as Emma Willard's resolve to give women the equiv-alent of a college education was strengthened, not broken, by Middlebury's denial of her request, Hemenway's own determi-nation to move ahead with her plans never faltered. It was a blow, certainly, to be treated with such condescension, and she did not leave Ludlow for Middlebury that afternoon as planned. She even toyed with the thought of beginning with some other county. Remembering, however, that the letters and circulars had already gone out announcing her tour of Addison, she determined to proceed with her plans but with one minor change. Instead of starting with Middlebury she would go first to Orwell, where she had an open invitation from Julia Barber, another poet friend, to visit whenever she chose to come. The very next day, without even waiting to find out if Barber would be at home, Hemenway took the train to Brandon, changing there to the stagecoach that carried her through Sudbury to Orwell.

"The memory of that ride is lovely, even today" Hemenway wrote near the close of her long career. After the pain of the previous day, "rolling along leisurely in the open stage . . . gliding in the quietude over the delightful landscape" proved a benign start to her tour of Addison County. At "exactly 6 p.m." the stage driver "reined his horses up to the little post-office at Orwell village." Julia Barber, it turned out, was away from home. But she had left a message, informing Hemenway that she had been invited to stay with the Reverend Rufus Spaulding Cushman, the one person in town whose support was essential if she was to get any cooperation from Orwell for her *Gazetteer*.[27]

The Rev. Mr. Cushman and his wife, Sarah, had waited tea for their guest in the sitting room of their "little white cottage." Hemenway was instantly charmed by her hostess. "A lily on a tall stalk" was the way she remembered Sarah Cushman. By contrast her husband, the pastor of the Congregational Church, was large and "very manly in personage . . . a staunch Orthodox Divine." After tea Hemenway opened her book trunk and copies of *Poets and Poetry* in their assorted bindings were displayed and admired. Then she read some selections aloud, including "My Uncle Jerry," and her hosts expressed their delight and approbation.

But when she brought up the subject of the new gazetteer

and history, Rufus Cushman's expression darkened. As Hemenway tells it, "He remarked that he had heard something about it when out to Middlebury a few days before," and "said it impressed him then and it did still as a subject more suitable for a man than for a woman." The clergyman even suggested that Hemenway's efforts were connected somehow with the woman's rights movement. Hemenway later remembered her horror at the very suggestion "that there was anything ultra in our work." Yet, while it is true that she never expressed any sympathy for what was then regarded as a dangerously radical crusade, she must also have known that she was hardly conforming to the domestic and submissive model of true womanhood sanctioned by her contemporaries. By editing and publishing books, and by traveling about the countryside to promote them, Hemenway was defying the doctrine of separate spheres for men and women. From the outset of her editorial career she had all but openly declared that she was a public woman who could do work that traditionally belonged to men.

That night Hemenway went to bed torn by whether she should obey her inclination "to fly from the field of the doubter," or stay on the chance that he might change his mind. But Sarah Cushman's "few gentle words" as she said good night to her visitor were a welcome comfort. "We clasped them to our bosom," Hemenway remembered, "and slept sweetly."

Waking the next morning to what she described as a severe equinoctial storm, Hemenway was forced to remain at the Cushmans for the better part of a week. After breakfast the first day the sight of an abolitionist newspaper lying on the minister's desk reminded Hemenway that her Uncle Asa Barton had asked her to convey his admiration for an article that Cushman had written for the same paper. No sooner had she given him the message than the clergyman's whole manner changed. He told her that there was no other contributor to the paper whose work he liked as much as Barton's and proceeded to read Hemenway several articles he, Cushman, had written. Over the course of the next four or five days the wary minister conversed with Hemenway on a good many subjects simply to test her. He found she had "common sense views on them all," and by the time the storm ended Cushman expressed a willingness to give her proposed gazetteer his full support. He also introduced Hemenway to his cousin, Dr. Earl Cushman, who became the magazine's first subscriber.

On the last day of Hemenway's visit, Cushman took her to call on Judge Bottom, the man selected by the Middlebury Historical Society to write the history of Orwell. According to Hemenway's later account the meeting proceeded smoothly. "It was arranged and agreed, the Judge should write the general history and Rev. Mr. Cushman the history of the church, and find us a lady-assistant to obtain subscribers to the Gazetteer and sell copies of the 'Poets and Poetry.'" The work of soliciting contributions for the first issue of Abby Hemenway's *Quarterly Gazetteer* had begun, and it proceeded in similar fashion in every town she visited.[28]

In all but a few communities Hemenway found men willing to aid her efforts or arrange for a suitable person to do so. Her staunchest supporters were often ministers. But women, too, rallied to her cause by volunteering to raise subscriptions for the Addison County number. One or sometimes two of these "lady assistants," as Hemenway called them, were appointed for each town. By the end of December 1859 she had engaged twenty-six Addison County women for this work in the twenty-four towns to be represented in the first number of the *Gazetteer*. In some cases these "lady assistants" were relatives of the historians of their towns, or of the clergymen and others who provided hospitality to Hemenway during her tour of the county.[29]

Over the course of the next twenty years Hemenway would make countless trips in all kinds of weather to towns all over

the state on behalf of the *Gazetteer.* One such trip was the journey from Orwell to Shoreham following her visit to the
Cushmans. The distance of some eight miles was covered in a
wagon driven by a stout man and drawn by two stout horses
over a muddy lakeshore road rendered nearly impassable by the
recent storm. As Hemenway clambered aboard the wagon with
her book trunk and carpetbag, she noted the only other passenger: a woman weighing somewhere between two and three
hundred pounds who was accompanied by two large trunks.
"A pretty good load for clay mud," Hemenway remarked to
herself.

While the wagon crept slowly northward, Hemenway's
traveling companion introduced herself as a Vermont native
recently returned from California. She inquired after her fellow traveler's destination and business. When Hemenway told
her, the woman declared herself pleased "to find one independent woman in Vermont," adding that she "did not want
the help of any man living." Taking issue with this pronouncement Hemenway expressed her belief that no one was
independent, and that she for one wanted the help of a good
many men.

The "independent woman" reached her destination first.
The driver, wearing a glum expression but giving no other sign
that he had overheard anything, helped her out with her luggage. Climbing back into the wagon, he brusquely proclaimed
himself glad to get rid of her, but said nothing more during the
few minutes it took to reach the Congregational Church
parsonage in Shoreham where Hemenway was to stay. Once
there the driver tore his coat on one of the metal straps of
Hemenway's trunk while trying to lift it off the wagon.
Hemenway, "a little afraid of his burliness," offered to pay for
the repairs. But he refused to take a penny, telling her that she
was a "woman who can help yourself or be helped; if it had
been the other woman's trunk, she should have paid for it."[30]

The portly wagon driver had unwittingly picked up on one

of the secrets of his passenger's skill as a promoter of the cause of local history in Vermont. This was Hemenway's willingness to let her independence and competence speak for themselves, while at the same time making those who might be of use to her, such as the Reverend Mr. Cushman, feel important and necessary to the success of her enterprise. In a similar way she managed to convey the impression that, while she might be engaged in what many considered unwomanly work, she entertained no radical views on woman's proper place.

Hemenway's description of her visit to Rowland T. Robinson of Ferrisburgh later that same fall underscores her ability to win over the leading citizens of one town after another. Robinson, an elderly Quaker and town leader, was also a prominent abolitionist whose home was known throughout the northeast as a stop on the Underground Railroad. When Hemenway arrived at Robinson's house the old gentleman at first showed little interest in her project. "Discernibly reluctant with the privileged testiness of old age," Hemenway described his manner of greeting her. But she sparked his interest by telling him that Starksboro, a one-time Quaker community like Ferrisburgh, was supporting her *Gazetteer*. When he asked if she had engaged William Worth to write the history of Starksboro, she was able to tell him yes. She topped this by adding that she had also engaged Henry Miles to write the history of the Quakers, once numerous in that part of the county. After she listed some of the others who had agreed to write the histories of their towns, Friend Robinson was forced to admit that she had won him over to her project and assured her that she could count on Ferrisburgh. By her own account he then credited her with devising "a most cunning plan. It appeals to all the pride in human nature," he acknowledged, adding that "No man will be willing to see all the towns in the county represented and his own left out . . . and when a county is finished, it will waken a county pride and when a few counties, a state pride." He concluded by telling her how pleased he would be to see her succeed, assuring her that the Quakers believed in woman's rights. When Hemenway disclaimed entertaining any such radical sympathies, he replied simply that "thee knows too much to admit it; but thee does what is better than to say it, thee acts it." By the end of their conversation Rowland Robinson had made it clear that he knew what Abby Hemenway was about perhaps better than she did herself.[31]

By late October 1859, Hemenway considered herself sufficiently successful at garnering countywide support for her project to return to Middlebury and make one more attempt to convert the "doubters" in the town and college who believed history was unsuitable work for a woman. With characteristic pluck she went directly to Springside to speak with her erstwhile supporter, Sylvester Rockwell. She knew very well by now that this man who seemed to be such a good friend might also "be a hard enemy," but her resolve was strengthened by the conviction that "our cause was too good." Success would sustain her, she knew, once she began speaking.

And so it did. At first Rockwell seemed mystified that Hemenway should have come at all. Had she perhaps not received his letter urging her to abandon her proposed history of the county? She assured him that she had received it and had come now to give her answer in person. "As soon as I read that letter I knew, you had been overborne to write it," she informed the still-puzzled Rockwell. Without waiting for a response to this presumptuous declaration, Hemenway plunged into an account of her travels about the county, taking care to assure Rockwell that to date over half the towns had promised to provide their histories and support the *Gazetteer* with subscriptions.

When Hemenway finished, Rockwell admitted that he had indeed been talked into writing the letter for the professors at the college. He nonetheless urged her to abandon the project and consider instead Philip Battell's suggestion that she edit a volume of representative Vermont prose writers. He promised that if she did undertake this work she would have all the help she needed from her friends in Middlebury. Hemenway acknowledged that such help was essential, particularly "when a woman undertakes a good work," adding ingenuously that she could not "go out as a man and battle for her cause." But she dismissed the idea of a prose collection as outdated. "Let anyone do it who has faith in it; let one of the professors at Middlebury do it," she told Rockwell.

Sylvester Rockwell, seeing that nothing would dissuade his friend Miss Hemenway from her chosen path, finally relented and with good grace agreed once more to help her. Philip Battell was also brought round to supporting the project and promised to write an essay about the town cemetery. To Hemenway's relief, Middlebury had finally opened its door.[32]

Although Hemenway was astonishingly adept at recruiting men—by catering to their personal as well as their local pride—to help generate historical material and support for her *Gazetteer,* she was a good deal less successful in raising the needed funds for her publication. When she launched the project in the summer of 1859 her only known assets were her earnings from the sales of *Poets and Poetry.* From the beginning Hemenway had a blind faith that the project would pay for itself. Like others who become deeply engrossed in what they are certain is a worthy undertaking, she had little doubt that subscriptions to her history magazine would come pouring in by the thousands.[33]

Her original plan had been to sell enough copies of *Poets and Poetry* to pay her traveling expenses while she toured the county. Fortunately, she was able to enjoy a free spirit of hospitality wherever she went. And, as Frances Babb observed, "the list of those who opened their homes to her reads like an ecclesiastical dictionary of that section of the state."[34] But the cost of publication was another matter entirely. Hemenway had thought this expense could be met easily by raising

From the Gazetteer

∗ ∗ ∗

Randolph

by C. Blodgett

"Reminiscence of the Rev. Tilton Eastman"

[This story employs a rustic theme, to mock the contentious political spirit that accompanied the 1840 presidential campaign, when incumbent President Martin Van Buren was (according to the author) "charged with all the sins that the sons of Adam, our first parents, are heir to," and ultimately defeated by William Henry Harrison.]

[About] May 3d, the Probate court had business at the house of widow Benjamin Griswold, in the Centre Village of Randolph, and towards evening of that day, Parson Eastman, knowing we were there, called in as he was passing towards his own home; and after our official business seemed about closed, remarked, that he had just come from Loren Griswold's, and as the day was rainy, several farmers gathered in, and among other matters talked about was the best time to plant potatoes: each having a theory of his own, and all argued his side with more or less zeal. Some contended that early planting insured the best crop, while others were sure they had been far more successful with late planting. Still others contended that potatoes should invariably be planted during the new of the moon, while the fourth class were confident that when planted in the first half, or new of the moon, the potatoes were apt to be more in numbers, but smaller, and far more likely to be watery, than when planted in the latter part, or old, of the moon. [Eastman] said that during all this description, he sat and listened, until, by and by, they asked *his* opinion—when *he* considered the most favorable time: and I told them "I intended to plant *my* potatoes just when I got ready; and if I didn't have a good crop, I should lay it to 'Van Buren.'"

[Volume II, pages 1004–5]

subscriptions to the magazine. Other historians, including Zadock Thompson, had used this method. But perhaps the success of her first book had made Hemenway overly sanguine about the financial prospects of this new publication.

The first hint that this plan might not work as well as she had hoped came on this same fall tour when she visited New Haven. Lewis Meacham, a town officer, was her principal contact there, and, as was so often the case, it had taken some persuasion to convince him of the validity of her plan. Having won Meacham over, Hemenway then told him of her scheme for supporting the publication through advance subscriptions. Surely, she reasoned, the people of Addison County would not refuse to pay twenty-five cents to see the history of their town in print. While Meacham agreed that no one should begrudge her such a small sum, he also warned that he knew of families in New Haven and other towns who would not give two cents for her history.[35]

Popular resistance to the 1858 law requiring towns to underwrite the publication of their histories was making life difficult for other Vermont historians. As Hemenway soon learned, in Whiting, a small farming community south of Middlebury, the Reverend Whitfield Walker had petitioned town meeting for several years for funds to print a history he had written. But Whiting voters consistently refused to spend a penny for this purpose. When Hemenway asked Walker to contribute his history to her *Gazetteer* he was understandably delighted.[36]

Vergennes was another community where a surprisingly stubborn opposition to the underwriting of its town history arose. Hemenway blamed this lack of cooperation on a political quarrel among the town fathers. The historian designated by the Middlebury Historical Society was widely known as a "warm Democrat," and the Whigs, who dominated Vergennes politics, were not happy with this choice. According to Hemenway they had "flamed up" at the very mention of history. In a referendum on the issue the Whigs carried the vote, and Vergennes became one of the few communities in Addison County that failed to produce a chapter for the *Gazetteer*.[37]

In the end Hemenway wrote the annals of Vergennes herself from what published sources were available. She included a description of her own visit there. Standing on the bridge spanning Otter Creek she noted how business had declined in the "Little City," despite the coming of the railroad. Still, the busy "hum of machinery, modulated by the water-chorus" from the falls, blended pleasantly in her ears. She stopped for a moment to listen and found herself moved by the pull of two forces. While "the white, ever-boiling waves, rolling and tossing like a brave spirit" urged her to "tarry and worship at the shrine of Nature," a stronger voice, which she calls Labor, tuned in with quickening energy, proferring a more compelling message. "What thy hand findeth to do, do with all thy might," it said. Strengthened by this momentary reverie, Hemenway walked off the bridge with a new firmness to her step.[38]

6

"The Morning of Local History in Vermont"

—•◦◊◦•—

He came to the state when the town was new
When the lordly pine and hemlock grew
   In the place where the court house stands.
When the stunted ash and the alder black
The slender fir and the tamarack
   Stood thick on the meadow lands.

Anonymous[1]

Sometime early in the winter of 1859, before the snow flew, Abby Hemenway, then thirty-one years old, returned with her book trunk and carpetbag to her family's house in Ludlow, where she began the hard work of editing and collating the materials for the first number of her *Vermont Quarterly Gazetteer*. For the next seven months she labored upstairs in her "solitary little library," the room that would serve as her editorial office for the ensuing four years. In addition to working on the manuscripts that were sent to her, she conducted an extensive correspondence with her historians, "lady assistants," and other helpers.[2]

Hemenway doubtless also spent time that winter reading or rereading the works of her predecessors in the field of Vermont history. The chapters in the *Gazetteer* that she wrote herself—a number of which are scattered throughout the five volumes of the completed work—indicate her heavy reliance on such historians as Zadock Thompson, Samuel Williams, and Hiland Hall. In the Vergennes history, for example—one of the four she wrote in the Addison County number—she credits Thompson, Hall, and Samuel Swift, Middlebury's historian, for the facts included in her chapter. All of these early Vermont historians had in turn been strongly influenced by the writings of Ethan and Ira Allen. Their version of the past had solidified the myth of Ethan as a selfless war hero. It had also perpetuated the Allen brothers' carefully orchestrated propaganda campaign that equated the fight waged by the early settlers against their foes in New York State with the battles fought by freedom-loving Vermonters in the American Revolution.[3]

Thompson, Williams, and Hall, by surrounding the early history of Vermont with patriotic propaganda, were simply echoing the writings of other American historians in the early decades of the nineteenth century. Even George Bancroft, the nation's first major historian, preferred to immortalize the old myths rather than apply scholarly scrutiny to traditional accounts of the young republic's rise from the shackles of its colonial past—this, despite his training in Germany under Leopold von Ranke in the most up-to-date scientific research methods. Bancroft's three-volume *History of the United States*, published in the 1830s, chose to perpetuate the notion of America's greatness by insisting on her citizens' commitment to democratic virtue. He showed how manifestations of this democratic spirit were visible all through the nation's history, from the Revolution and the making of the Constitution to the expansion westward. By treating this patriotic myth as if it were serious history, Bancroft succeeded in discouraging other historians from employing scientific scrutiny to their own writings on the nation's origins. Not until after the Civil War would historians infuse a new critical spirit into their writings on the nation-building events of the Revolution and Constitution.[4]

In her new role as editor of the *Gazetteer* Abby Hemenway had little reason to question the story she was handed of Vermont's revolutionary past. It was the story she had grown up with, and, while she might dispute the accuracy of certain details in individual accounts, she had little reason to doubt the overall picture provided by her predecessors. Where Hemenway did differ from early historians of Vermont is in the kind of history she valued. Thompson, Williams, and Hall focused on rescuing the revolutionary generation from oblivion. They emphasized political and military history. Hemenway, while ready to include the revolutionary and political story, was more interested in preserving the fast-perishing records of the early days in Vermont, particularly the fledgling state's social and cultural history.

Abby Hemenway did not dictate to her town historians a particular slant to be employed in their essays. Her requirements, at least for the first few numbers of the *Quarterly*, were minimal. Each town would be responsible for furnishing its own history, providing a "reliable record of facts" and "interesting events," as well as "biographical sketches of the first settlers and most noted citizens." She also asked that "specimens of the fairest articles of prose and poetry" accompany these histories, "to bring forth as our farmers do in their agricultural fairs our best literary productions."[5] As in previous Vermont histories, the *Gazetteer* would provide geological information, supplied by the state's leading geologists. The size and style of the quarterly were to be modeled on *Harper's Magazine*, each issue would measure six-and-a-half by ten inches and number 150 two-columned pages.

As late as December 1859, Hemenway was promising subscribers that the first *Vermont Quarterly Gazetteer* would be published the following February with subsequent numbers appearing at regular three-month intervals. She envisioned the whole project needing less than four years for completion. But from the start the plan was too ambitious. It was impossible to meet the printers' deadlines, because, as Frances Babb has noted, local historians could "neither be threatened nor cajoled" into getting their chapters in on time. Hemenway had trouble, too, with her printers, including delays and losses, as well as haggles over finances. Last but not least, the Civil War broke out.[6]

Undaunted, Hemenway threw herself into the project with her characteristic energy. Years later, she recalled the many long letters she wrote that winter, remembering "the enthusiasm that kindled as we wrote swiftly on, and as the responses came back." She worked, as she told it, "on no ten hour system," but labored at filling "the great gap in the history of Vermont" with little thought of the time she put in. Fourteen hours a day, six days a week, she toiled at her papers in her upstairs room. Only on Sunday did she rest.[7]

Little remains of Hemenway's extensive correspondence that winter and spring, so there is much we don't know about how she put together this first number of the *Gazetteer*. The issue of finances is especially murky. For example, while she used her earnings from *Poets and Poetry of Vermont* to meet the expenses of her autumn tour of Addison County, there is no way to know if they also helped pay for her paper and postage that winter.

The biggest expense, of course, was printing. Hemenway, like many other local historians of the time, was her own publisher, and thus had to engage the printer herself. In theory, the decision to print was usually put off until sufficient advance subscriptions were paid for. But historians, like other writers then and now, were sometimes overly optimistic in estimating potential sales and proceeded with publishing their books despite a shortfall in their subscription lists.[8] Ignoring warnings that Vermonters might not be as willing as she had hoped to pay for her *Gazetteer,* Hemenway persisted in her optimism, and sometime that winter she secured the services of Rand & Avery, a printing establishment in Boston. She blithely informed them that she was planning a run of 6,000 for the first issue. Because Addison County's population was only 24,000, she was clearly anticipating a statewide readership.

Rand & Avery quoted Hemenway a price of more than $5.00 per page for the 6,000 copies. This meant that for a proposed issue of 150 pages she would have to come up with more than $750. What Rand & Avery failed to tell their new client was that paper of the size she wanted would have to be specially cut to order, which of course added considerably to the cost. But she wasn't informed of this extra expense until the third number of the *Gazetteer* was going to press. Was Rand & Avery taking advantage of her because she was a woman? Hemenway doesn't say, but she later admitted, "It would have been a great help to us at this time to have had an experienced printer friend whom we could have consulted about paper and type." Hemenway's uncle Asa Barton was the obvious person to advise her, except that he had been a newspaper editor back in the 1840s when conditions were very different. It also would have helped if Hemenway had listened to warnings not to be overoptimistic about advance subscription sales.[9]

To cover her costs Hemenway proposed charging twenty-five cents for individual issues of the *Quarterly.* A year's subscription could be had for $1.00 and a subscriber could obtain fourteen issues, or the total number she expected to print, for $5.00. As she told one of her Addison County historians, she needed to sell 3,000 to "draw the work," but by late May 1860

Subscription form for the *Vermont Quarterly Gazetteer*, used by
Hemenway's "Lady assistants."

she had the payment for only 1,800. In the end she was forced
to secure various small loans from family and friends.[10]

A series of letters concerning the history of Panton, an
Addison County town on the shores of Lake Champlain, opens
a window onto Hemenway's first season of editorial work for
the magazine. Early in January 1860 she wrote the Panton historian, John D. Smith of Vergennes, urging him to send in his
chapter as soon as possible. "I heard several weeks since that
you were progressing finely," she told him. "I hope now, to see
it [the Panton history] in a few days." She asked Smith to
include with his chapter "the best possible specimen of poetry
you can for Panton." Hemenway had sealed the letter and was
about to send it off, when the day's mail brought Smith's manuscript. She sat down immediately to read it, then unsealed her
own letter and added a postscript.

After thanking Smith for his "well prepared history," his
editor then faulted him for failing to include the story of Peter
Ferris, an early settler of Panton, who sheltered Benedict
Arnold and his troops during the naval engagements with the
British on Lake Champlain in the fall of 1776. "Copy or
rewrite it just as you please," she urged Smith, "but *please* furnish it for me—We desire not only to make our magazine the

From the Gazetteer

* * *

Chelsea

by C. W. Clarke

[The following excerpt is a "record of the doings" of the Gloucester County court, which at that time had jurisdiction over "all that part of Vt. lying north of White River and east of the Gr. Mtns." It shows how the early settlers often had to make do with unusual locations in which to conduct government affairs.]

Feby. 25th 1771. Set out from Moretown [now Bradford] for Kingsland [the designated county seat] traveled until Knight there Being No Road and the snow very Deep we traveled on snow shoes or Raccatts on the 26th we traveled some ways and Held a council when it was concluded it was best to open the Court as we saw No Line it was not [known] whether in Kingsland or Not But we concluded we were farr in the woods we did not expect to see any House unless we marched three miles within Kingsland and No one lived there when the Court was ordered to be opened on the spot.

> Present John Taplin Judge
> John Peters of the Quor'm
> John Taplin, jun, Sheriff.

All causes continued and adjourned to the next term. The court, if one, adjourned over to the next Tuesday in may next.

[Volume II, page 871]

---

most reliable record of *facts* ever published—but a little treasury of the most interesting events ever *recorded* or *unrecorded* that have ever transpired in Vermont." Hemenway would seem to be saying here that she wanted her writers to include accounts of local heroes who might not figure in the history books, but who had nonetheless made their mark on important historical events and deserved to be recognized. In this case, a short sketch of Ferris was added to Smith's history of Panton.[11]

Hemenway's next letter to John Smith accompanied the printer's proofs of his history, which she mailed to him at the end of May. In this letter she admitted to trimming his paragraphs a little but assured him that she had been careful to leave the substance intact. She hoped there would be "no feeling" on his part "save regret at the necessity which compelled me to cut down at all your excellent chapter for Panton—when you see how high the number of the pages run—and when I frankly tell you that the cost of every page of the Addison No to me is, simply for the stereotype and printing bill—over $5.00 per page."[12]

If Hemenway thought there would be "no feeling" on Smith's part about her cutting his manuscript, she was wrong. On June 5 she received a curt letter from the Panton historian expressing his annoyance on several points. First, he accused her of spending too much time in her letter talking about the cost of printing the *Gazetteer.* "It seems late in the day," Smith wrote, to "plea[d] the expense of printing as a reas[on] why I should [be] subject to the mor[tification] of seeing such a garbled ungrammatical & erroneous chapter published under my name." Had Hemenway informed him earlier that his manuscript was too long, instead of taking it upon herself to leave out the facts that cost him "much labor to collect & are of the most importance in this locality," Smith would have made the necessary cuts himself. He concluded by telling her that he would not "attempt corrections but would be glad to have my manuscript returned & the whole chapter suppressed— You can then save further expense for Panton & save me the trouble of explanation to the local and state papers after publication."[13]

Hemenway, of course, was neither the first nor last editor to call down the wrath of a writer who believes his work has been butchered. Still, if she was upset by Smith's threats she showed no sign of it in her reply. While conceding that she may have misread some of the statements in his manuscript, she urged him to correct any egregious errors. But she was also very firm with him about cuts, reminding him that

> in regard to condensation I supposed you were aware that I had the privilege of abridgment wherever the article overran the allotted space, of whatever might not be of *general interest.* Had you have said "I am aware that my article doubles the allotted space, if you have not room for it as it is, I choose to have you return it to me that I may condense it," I would cheerfully so have done. As you made no such reserve or request, upon consideration I think you will correct all grammatical errors, & mend up all that is wrong therein in as few words as possible—If there are any strictly indispensable paragraphs omitted reinstate them—but not unless they are so, and return the proofs *soon*, for the whole work has now been kept back several days waiting for the return of your proofs.

Hemenway concluded her letter by assuring Smith that he would get credit for what he had done for Panton whether he gave permission to let his chapter stand or insisted upon its withdrawal. She then pleaded with him not to withdraw hastily: "consider well that whatever I have condensed, it was not from any *local* feeling—or preference for parties—but for the general interest—and from the necessity that compels where manuscripts overrun." Finally, she was careful once again to thank him for the historical work that he had "so well performed" and reminded him to return the proofs in two days. She signed herself "kindly and respectfully, Abby M. Hemenway."[14]

This letter demonstrates how tough as well as persuasive

Hemenway could be with her historians. The skills she had learned in the classroom, to brook no nonsense while at the same time encouraging her pupils to do their best work, applied equally to her role as editor. We do not know whether Smith ever made her suggested corrections and returned the proofs promptly, as Hemenway had urged him to do; but his history of Panton did appear in the *Gazetteer* under his name. When she told him that he would receive credit for his work whether he wished it or not, she was as good as her word.

Not all of Hemenway's time that winter and spring was spent editing the Addison County number of the *Gazetteer*. When she first returned home, before any of the towns had sent in their histories, she went to work on her second county, Bennington. For Addison County, the Middlebury Historical Society had provided her with a list of potential historians. In the case of Bennington she had to begin by finding the writers herself.

While Abby was working away in her "solitary little library" upstairs in the Hemenway house, downstairs the rooms buzzed with activity. At least one of her younger siblings was still living at home. In addition, her mother was by this date a partial invalid and was confined to the house. Since Abigail Dana Hemenway could no longer visit her many friends in Ludlow, they came to see her. While such callers were frequent, they rarely expected more than a friendly greeting from Abby as she passed them on her way to and from her own room. "It would have irked me to have tried to entertain them," she later remarked, conceding that her "mother did better."[15]

Occasionally, there would be a quiet evening when no visitors came and the younger members of the household were out. By eight o'clock Daniel Hemenway had retired to bed, but his wife liked to stay up until ten. Her chores finished, Abigail Hemenway would seat herself at her worktable and call up to her daughter, "I am all alone. Gather up your papers and come down." Ready for the summons, Abby quickly complied and, pulling a chair to the table, would finish the day's quota of letters while her mother sewed. The two women rarely spoke, but even when Abby's head was bent to the paper in front of her she could feel her mother's pleasure in her work. Once a letter was finished Abby would read it aloud. If all the day's letters had been written and sealed and there was still time before Daniel Hemenway called out, "It's ten o'clock, Mother!" Abby would read from one of her town histories. Sometimes, to prolong the pleasure of these evenings alone with her daughter, Abigail Dana Hemenway would surreptitiously delay her husband's bedtime call by moving the big hand of the clock back, thus postponing the ringing of the chimes. Abby later spoke of these as happy times to look back upon.[16]

The individual town histories found in the first number of the *Quarterly Gazetteer* were arranged much as the advance publicity had led readers to expect. Each opens with an historical essay describing the early settlement of the town and its physical appearance, with short sketches of noted citizens. This essay is usually followed by a series of brief histories of the town's churches written by local clergymen. The chapter concludes with an example or two of local prose and poetry. Although Hemenway had promised to include geological information for the whole county in a separate chapter, the failure of the state legislature to publish recently conducted geological surveys of Vermont prevented its inclusion.[17]

While the overall pattern of the individual town histories in this first number of the *Quarterly Gazetteer* is similar, there are many variations both in content and quality. Some of Hemenway's historians were careful to place their communities in the larger context of state and national history. A good example of this treatment is John Strong's essay on Addison, the site of Vermont's earliest white settlement. After a brief physical description of the town, Strong begins his narrative with the July 4, 1609, entry of Samuel de Champlain onto the lake that would soon carry his name. Recounting how the naming itself took place at Chimney Point, Strong goes on to describe Champlain's battle with the Iroquois and with a Vermonter's pride points out that it was fought two months before Henry Hudson found the river bearing his name, four years before the Dutch settlement of New York, and eleven years before the landing at Plymouth.[18]

John Smith, in a different vein, opens his chapter on Panton with an eloquent justification for preserving Vermont's heritage. Hemenway could not have expressed it better herself. "To the casual observer," Smith writes,

> it may seem idle to expect, that in our quiet farming towns in Vermont, with so many evidences of peaceful, happy prosperity presenting themselves on every hand, events and incidents of former days can be gathered, worthy of a place in our common history. But a little reflection must convince anyone that the change of our former dense forests, and almost impassable swamps, into the present productive farms, could not be effected without great trials and severe sufferings; and when we consider the turbulent state of the times, our sympathy is increased for the first settlers in their trials, our conviction strengthened that they must have witnessed scenes of thrilling interest, and our desire quickened to rescue the names and deeds of those brave and earnest men from the oblivion that is fast covering them.[19]

Rescuing the "deeds of brave and earnest men" from oblivion in these turbulent times spoke to a sense of urgency that many New England historians shared as they watched dissension over the spread of slavery threaten to split the nation in two. While Hemenway sat quietly at her desk in Ludlow and

From the Gazetteer

*　*　*

Randolph

From a biography of General Martin Flint
by his children

[This story illustrates the strength of opposition in some Vermont towns to the antislavery movement. It is taken from the biography of Martin Flint, a successful and influential Randolph farmer. The occasion was a proposed antislavery lecture in the Randolph Congregational Church by the prominent abolitionist Orson S. Murray.]

There was a strong feeling of opposition to this meeting, and boys and men, moved by a seditious spirit, came with eggs and other missiles, and succeeded in driving Mr. Murray from the place of meeting. Martin Flint, though no friend of oppression in any form, was not, at the time avowedly an antislavery man; absent from home, the story of this outrage upon the rights of free speech, and the mob-spirit manifested upon this occasion, reached him. Mortified and aroused, he determined that Mr. Murray should be heard, and made public declaration to that effect. Procuring the return of Mr. Murray, notice was given and preparations to prevent a recurrence of similar outrages. A temporary police was organized, and the most powerful men, physically, stationed in various parts of the house; and thus the meeting passed off quietly.

[Volume II, page 1060]

Smith at his in Panton, fighting had already broken out in Kansas over the issue of free soil, and John Brown's raid on Harper's Ferry—an abortive attempt to free Virginia's slaves— had raised the pitch of anger high on both sides. Fearful that the very freedoms they had fought for in the Revolution might disappear in whatever maelstrom lay ahead, these chroniclers of Vermont's past felt a pressing need to preserve for posterity the deeds performed by their ancestors in the name of liberty. Hemenway echoes this sentiment in the verses she chose—from an unknown poet—for the cover of the first issue of her *Quarterly*.

> She stands fair Freedom's chosen Home,
> Our own beloved Green Mountain State.
> Where breathes no castled lord or cabined slave;
> Where thoughts, and hands, and tongues are free.[20]

In his history of Panton, John Smith not only invokes the timely theme of freedom so much in the minds of Vermonters that winter of 1859–60, but he is also careful to assure his readers that he has confined himself to "local facts and incidents of the town of Panton . . . of which I have good evidence."[21]

Hemenway would have applauded such dedication to historical accuracy. In common with other local historians of her day she had a passion for data and for a straightforward presentation of events as they happened. When she suspected that one of her historians had not got his facts straight she didn't hesitate to say so. For example, she disputed a point in Samuel Swift's account of Middlebury concerning the identity of the first child born of a white settler in that town. In other instances, as in the case of Panton, when what she considered important information had been left out of a particular history, she was careful to inform her readers where that information could be obtained.[22]

Hemenway's attention to historical accuracy is evident also in the four Addison County town histories she wrote herself. In the case of Bridport, for instance, she is careful to cite the sources she used in her account, and, if there are several versions of a particular incident, to provide them.[23]

One story Hemenway tells describes Ethan Allen's successful escape in 1772 from seizure by the Yorkers—those who upheld rival claims to Vermont's lands. Allen and his companion were staying at the Bridport home of a Mrs. Richards when soldiers from Crown Point arrived to apprehend them. The two Green Mountain Boys, however, managed to slip out of the house undetected. In Zadock Thompson's version, Allen's companion is Eli Roberts of Vergennes; in Josiah Goodhue's version he is Seth Warner. The accounts of their escape differ also. While both depict six armed Yorkers arriving at the Richards' house to arrest the two Green Mountain Boys, Thompson's account simply says that Allen and his friend slipped out an open window at bedtime. Goodhue, however, gives a larger role to Mrs. Richards, who placed Allen and Warner's guns under their hats near the open window.

> While the lady was busy about the house, and the company engaged in conversation, Allen stepped out without hat or gun, and in a short time Warner followed without attracting attention. When missed the Yorkers remarked, "They havn't their hats, they havn't their guns," and fell to talking again; but as they [Allen and Warner] did not return, they examined into the matter, and found both hats and guns were gone.

Waiting outside for the conversation to resume after their absence was noted, the two Green Mountain Boys had slipped up to the window undetected, grabbed their hats and guns, and fled to the house of a neighbor named Moore, whose family also happened to be the source for Goodhue's version of the story.[24]

Hemenway's inclusion of Goodhue's account highlights aspects of her approach as a historian that are worth noting. First, when she had two versions of a story and didn't know which was more accurate, she included both. Second, this account shows her recognition of oral tradition as a vital source for local history. Goodhue's version, unlike Thompson's, is fuller and can be traced back to persons who were actual parties to Allen and Warner's escape. Furthermore, the Moores learned of the account from the men's own lips at the time the incident occurred. Goodhue's version also relates the part played by women in the incident, which Thompson's does not.[25]

Finally, the inclusion of Goodhue's version underscores Hemenway's love of the "homely stories," as she called them, "of our forefathers, [and] foremothers," accounts of the lives of ordinary men and women, and the parts they played in Vermont's history. On her tour of Addison County in the fall of 1859 nothing had given Hemenway greater pleasure than to sit in a village kitchen or parlor and listen to the older members of the household talk of the early days. When she passed through Ferrisburgh, she had spent the night with a family named Rogers, and she inserted a description of this visit in that town's chapter in the *Gazetteer*:

> In the evening we went back and lived over the early days of the settlement, the trials and expedients of those hardy, honest pioneers; listened to the story of one good church-going man, who, the first winter of his residence in town, having no sleigh or sled, fitted runners to the trundle-bed in which he took his wife and children to meeting every Sabbath day; when the mountain squall threatened, covering over the heads of the happy load with an old quilt or coverlet, so that at the door where the meeting was held the plump little troop were turned out from the bunk where they nightly snuggled down to sleep, warm and rosy as if fresh from their slumber. There was to us godliness and beauty in the homely story.[26]

Such sentimental musings on the "godliness and beauty" of pioneer days in Vermont are interspersed here and there

𝔉𝔯𝔬𝔪 𝔱𝔥𝔢 𝔊𝔞𝔷𝔢𝔱𝔱𝔢𝔢𝔯

⋆   ⋆   ⋆

North Hero

by Marie S. Ladd

Section on "Character and Habits of the First Settlers"

[The town histories in the *Gazetteer* contain many stories of encounters with wild animals, especially bears. Such tales, passed down from one generation to the next, provided entertainment — something in pretty short supply in early Vermont. Bears and other predators also stood for all the threats that the wilderness posed to the early settlers, which included harsh weather, rocky soil, and the many difficulties of making a living and raising a family in such inhospitable surroundings.]

A woman whose husband had been at work for several days, some distance from home, finding her small stock of provision entirely gone, fastened her children in the house to protect them from the bears, ignited a stump in order to have fire when she returned, and set out with a large club, with which to defend herself from the prowlers of the woods. She reached the fort safely, and procured food; on her return, she encountered a bear which she managed to frighten by a great flourish of her stick, accompanied with other athletics which kept time to a species of vocal music, fitting to the occasion, and which, I believe, the first settlers denominated "hooting"; all of which proved so efficacious, that she was enabled to return to her little family uninjured.

[Volume II, page 564]

throughout this first number of the *Gazetteer*. For example, in an account of her stay at the Strong Mansion in Addison, Hemenway meditates on the superior character of small-town Vermont:

We looked upon Addison, and remembered she was once a country town, with reasonable expectations of becoming one of the first business towns in the State; . . . and, must confess we like Addison better as she is. To us, this town, where the first Vermont settlement was made, is sacred ground. It is a pleasant truth, that, secluded from the taint of a large and changing population, shut out from the evil that destroys, rich in beauty, rich in soil, rich in flocks and herds, she retains what is most praiseworthy of all, much of her primitive simplicity of manners, unaffected courtesy, and whole-hearted hospitality.[27]

Was Addison in 1860 the way Hemenway wished all Vermont towns could be? Or, as seems more likely, did she recognize that not all communities could be kept from changing, and hoped instead that some at least might be saved to function as sacred places canonizing particular versions of the past, as Bunker Hill and Plymouth Rock did in Massachusetts?

When finally published on July 4, 1860, the first number of the *Vermont Quarterly Gazetteer* contained 120 pages of double-columned text. At the back are 8 pages of tables listing the names of the men and women who had felt "a sufficient interest in gathering up and preserving the fast perishing records, and traditions of our forefathers, to patronize a Magazine devoted to that purpose." Years later Hemenway remembered thinking it "a patriotic work; dated for a patriotic day . . . It was the morning of local history in Vermont."[28]

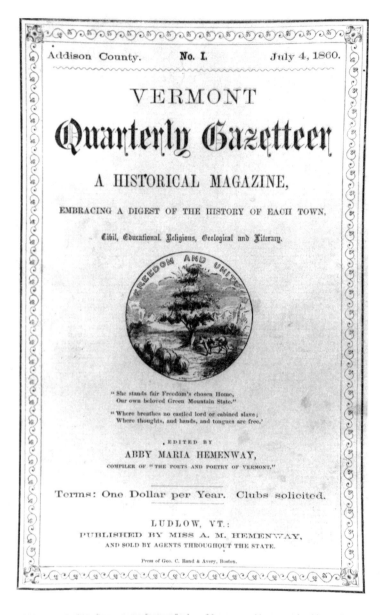

Cover of the first number of the *Vermont Quarterly Gazetteer*
issued July 4, 1860.

Touring Bennington County

———•◦✿◦•———

Our patriot sires are gone,
  The conqueror, Death, lays low
Those veterans, one by one,
  Who braved each other foe;
Though on them rests death's sable pall,
  Yet o'er their deeds no shade shall fall.

No, ye of deathless fame!
  Ye shall not sleep unsung
While freedom hath a name,
  Or gratitude a tongue;—
Yet shall your names and deeds sublime
  Shine brighter through the mists of time.

Anne Lynch Botta [1]

As early as December 1859, while Hemenway was waiting for her Addison County historians to send in their manuscripts, she had begun recruiting men and women to help her both with the work of writing and collecting the various

Bennington County town histories and with obtaining subscriptions. In Addison County, she had established a system of
town agents and "lady assistants." Their principal job was to
sell subscriptions, for which they were paid a small commission.
No one was ever asked to obtain such orders without pay, she
later wrote, adding that in Bennington, "some ladies gave their
subscribers the commission, and two sent in the whole amount
saying we had more need of the money."[2]

Hemenway made similar arrangements in all the other
counties, and, beginning with Bennington, she assumed the
added burden of finding the town historians herself. To obtain
the needed help in this southern and historically rich Vermont
county, she began by mailing out circulars to potential contributors, workers, and subscribers, informing them about the proposed Bennington issue of the *Quarterly*.[3]

William G. Brown, author of the introductory poem in
Poets and Poetry of Vermont, was a recipient of one of these circulars. A one-time resident of Whitingham and editor of a
Baptist newspaper, the *Vermont Observer*, Brown had since
moved his family to Chicopee, Massachusetts. There he had
been in search of "some congenial literary labor" when
Hemenway's notice about the Bennington County number
arrived in the mail. Brown wrote Hemenway offering to help.
The two agreed that he would begin by acting as the general
agent for four counties. His immediate charge was to engage
the services of historians for each town in Bennington, but his
prime duty was to sell the magazine. Once Brown had collected
a thousand subscriptions Hemenway promised that she would
make him a full partner in the enterprise. Precisely what this
meant she did not say.[4]

Sometime in the early winter of 1859, Brown visited
Hemenway in Ludlow where he signed a contract guaranteeing
him a partnership once he had secured the requisite number of
subscribers. Hemenway gave him a small advance and sent him

off with as many copies of *Poets and Poetry* as he could carry to sell along the way. As she later observed, Brown was more successful in selling published poems than unpublished history. But thrifty Vermonters, like most people, were more likely to buy a book in hand than a magazine they had never seen. To Brown's credit it must be said that he did succeed in engaging thirteen of the sixteen historians for the Bennington number. He also made his tour of that county during the winter and had to fight his way through snow drifts and over mountains from one town to the next. By the time he finished the journey, his original enthusiasm had evaporated. Brown returned to Chicopee never again to work for the *Gazetteer.*[5]

Hiland Hall picked up where Brown left off. A resident of Bennington, one-time congressman, and most recently governor of Vermont, Hall had been a member of the 1856 convention that met in Philadelphia to nominate the new Republican Party's first presidential candidate. After retiring from public service in 1860, he became president of the Vermont Historical Society and would devote much of the remainder of his life to chronicling the early history of the Green Mountain State. At the end of her own career Hemenway claimed that for twenty-five years Hiland Hall "was the most extensive contributor" to the *Gazetteer* "of any man in the State."[6]

Hemenway and Hiland Hall first met in Montpelier in the fall of 1859 while the latter was serving his term as governor. Anxious to secure his help, Hemenway called on Hall at the State House. As she entered his office the governor rose, and, giving Hemenway his hand, said that he recognized her name as belonging to "the lady from the south part of the State who is engaged in historical enterprises." He went on to say that he had heard of her work in Addison County, and was himself interested in history, and he urged her, when she had finished Addison, to come and visit him in Bennington. As the county with "the finest history in the state," Hall assured her, it "will

Hiland Hall, onetime governor of Vermont and president
of the Vermont Historical Society.
(From the collections of the Vermont Historical Society.)

not be willing to fall behind Addison." He then promised to be her right-hand man there. "I will do anything you may ask for Bennington," he assured her.[7]

Hemenway did not forget the governor's promise, nor his invitation to visit him in Bennington. Sometime after July 4, 1860, with the first number of the *Quarterly Gazetteer* in print, she filled her carpetbag with edited manuscripts for the second number of the *Quarterly* and boarded the train for Rutland, changing there to another train that carried her to Bennington. She was met at the station by Hall, who drove her to his "simple, comfortable old farm-house," pointing out buildings and sites of historic interest along the way.[8]

Dolly Tuttle Hall, the governor's wife, was at the house when they arrived. Hemenway described her hostess as a "true lady of the olden school" whose "queenly appearance" marked a strong mind and character. Later that day, when Hemenway poured the papers from her capacious carpetbag onto a table in the Halls' sitting room, she noted her hosts' expressions of pleased surprise. The governor remarked that "he had not supposed so much manuscript could be gathered in the County. He did not need to have said a word," Hemenway later remembered, "it shone in his face." All the "anxiety that he had felt about Bennington County had melted in that moment." Hall then left the room, returning in a few moments with another pile of manuscripts, which he laid on the table with the rest. Hemenway watched him as he stood there "looking upon the heap of records for his dear, old Bennington county as a mother stands at times and looks at her family group."

Work began promptly the next morning with the arrival at ten o'clock of the Halls' son, Nathaniel, a lawyer who was to assist them in going over the edited manuscripts. Each town history was read and discussed. They started with Bennington (a historian for Arlington had yet to be found) and continued in alphabetical order, taking turns reading each paper aloud.

Hemenway spent a week in Bennington and later remembered only one substantive disagreement between her and Hiland Hall. The governor, who owned a copy of *Poets and Poetry* but had not read it, announced that he wanted all verse left out of the next number of the *Gazetteer*, telling its editor that he "did not think Bennington County had ever done herself much honor in poetry." At these words Hemenway noted the "soft cloud" that came over Dolly Hall's face as she spoke of her sorrow at seeing the verse of her favorite, Anne Lynch Botta, left out. Hemenway then explained to the governor why poetry was essential to the enterprise. Without it, she told him, she could not obtain enough subscriptions to pay the printer. This was especially the case "among the general class of people in our farming districts and small villages, who mostly preferred something lighter than history." Then, almost as an aside, she informed Hall that his friend George Houghton had given her some poetry by the Reverend Theodore Fay to be included in the Bennington number. The governor turned to her with a look of disbelief: "Did Houghton give you that?" he asked, adding that he had never heard anyone "say so much against poetry in your work as Mr. Houghton." At this Hemenway felt a smile creeping round her lips. Then Dolly Hall spoke up, insisting that if Houghton wished his friend Mr. Fay represented, she wanted Mrs. Botta.

Under such pressure the governor had little choice but to give in. He still believed, however, as he told Hemenway, that a good local history might go a long way to instill a love for history itself. Hemenway assured him that she had no intention of suppressing "any fact of interest" in her *Gazetteer* "for any sketch of prose or poetry." She then told Hall how her own passion for history dated back to her youth, told him of her interest in Napoleon and his battles, and her enjoyment of the writings of the great English explorer William Parry, particularly his accounts of his voyages in the Arctic. Hall, duly impressed, remarked that she was the only person he had encountered who admitted to liking Parry's *Voyages*, a lengthy ponderous work, and said it showed that she "could bear with patient invest-igation—have the spirit of it." He went on to say that he and his wife had been wondering how Hemenway had come "to choose so hard a field." Now they understood that she had "a natural love of fact and research. I will help you," he added, "wherever I can on history, but spare me the poetry!"

When work on the manuscripts was completed Hiland Hall, his son Nathaniel, and Hemenway discussed what to do about the towns that had yet to send in their histories, or, as in the case of Arlington, how to find someone willing to write one in the first place. Hall told Hemenway that the townspeople of Arlington were so ashamed of their Tory sympathies during the Revolution that no one would willingly take on the job. Even after she informed him that the Reverend Frederick A. Wadleigh, pastor of the Episcopal Church in Arlington, had "given us his word" that he would write the history, Hall insisted that it was of no use. In the end the three agreed that Hemenway would call on Wadleigh herself and see if Hall's pessimism was warranted.

The day before Hemenway left the Bennington farmhouse Dolly Hall sealed their friendship by pressing into her guest's hands the last rose from her garden and urging her to make them "a little visit every year."

After leaving the Halls, Hemenway's plan was to visit sev-eral towns which, like Arlington, had been delinquent in send-ing in their histories. She went first to Manchester where she made arrangements with Henry Miner to write the history of the town of Winhall. From Manchester she headed north to Dorset. There her town historian, L. B. Armstrong, blamed his delay on the refusal of the descendants of William Jackson, the first Congregational minister in town, to give him needed infor-mation. Hemenway soon solved that problem. The evening promised to be warm, so she hired an open buggy and, enjoying a view of the "beautiful Dorset hills," was driven to call on Jackson's eldest daughter, a Mrs. Baldwin. After "talking the subject up with her," an agreement was soon reached: The minister's daughter would send the historical materials on her family to Ludlow for Hemenway to collate. In her recollection of the incident, she noted, "Thus we wrote our first biography for the work, 'The Jackson Family of Dorset.'"[9]

To hear Hemenway tell it, she endured a lot more than a pleasant buggy ride and a "talking up" when she went the next day to call on the Reverend Frederick Wadleigh, the designated historian for Arlington. She had written ahead informing the minister she was coming, but when she arrived at his house, a woman—presumably Wadleigh's housekeeper—met her at the door only to announce that he was not at home. When Hemenway asked if she was expected, the woman admitted she was, but said the minister had been called away to a funeral on the other side of town and did not know when he would return. "He left word," she told Hemenway, "if you came today for you not to be detained, he has decided not to write Arlington." Hemenway, unwilling to be put off so easily, told the woman she would wait three days if necessary, and entered the house to watch for Wadleigh's return.[10]

He came within the hour. Hemenway later could not recall the initial words that passed between them, so worried was she by the prospect of losing Arlington. "We had never felt so anxious for any town before, never for any town since," she remembered. Locked in her memory, however, was the image of Wadleigh standing with his back toward her as he ran his hands over the contents of the bookcase in front of him. She had been pelting him with reasons for writing the history; he seemed not to hear her and excused himself: He was "very busy" and must look for a paper. But then she knew he had heard her for he began explaining that certain of the principal families in town, as well as members of his own church, objected to having the history written. It would hurt his reputation as pastor if he wrote it. Hemenway, close to despair, told him that she might have saved herself the trouble of coming, because Governor Hall had already warned her that she wouldn't get Arlington.

The figure standing at the bookcase flinched. "He did, did he?"

Without hesitation, Hemenway replied, "He did!"

At this Wadleigh turned and gave her a glance that demanded a direct answer. "What did Governor Hall say was the reason?"

"Because you at Arlington are ashamed of your Toryism."

Wadleigh's whole manner altered abruptly. "You may tell Governor Hall, we think we can manage that!" he exclaimed. Wittingly or unwittingly, Hemenway had given the minister a lever to use with the Arlington townspeople. As she later put it, "he saw at a glance what the Governor said, others would say, it would be said through the state." Facing his visitor squarely Wadleigh now assured her that "he would save Arlington from that reproach."

Back home in Ludlow, Hemenway wrote Hiland Hall to thank him for his hospitality and report on her success in obtaining Wadleigh as the Arlington historian. Hall in his response commended her persuasive powers. Employing a rustic metaphor of the sort Hemenway herself appreciated, he told her that while she was visiting them at Bennington he had observed that she "could throw grass and apples." But he was glad to see that she "could throw stones, too," for he thought she would often need them before she finished her work.[11] Like Rowland Robinson before him, Hiland Hall recognized and applauded Hemenway's talent for shaming her historians into doing her bidding, her skill at playing on their overweening masculine pride and love of competition.

When Hemenway returned from her Bennington visit she likely found a pile of press notices for the Addison County number of the *Gazetteer*. Before leaving on her tour she had sent copies of the magazine to every newspaper in the state. She mailed others to those Boston and New York periodicals that had reviewed her *Poets and Poetry*.[12] One national paper that brought the *Quarterly* to public attention was the *Historical Magazine*. Published in New York under the editorship of John Gilmary Shea, this monthly, founded in 1857, claimed for its audience a group of younger historians and antiquarians working to bring a critical spirit to the study of American history. Its founder, Charles B. Richardson, a Boston publisher, had seen the need for a scholarly journal that would provide a medium of communication for the numerous organizations throughout the country devoted to the study of history. The *Historical Magazine*—at least in its early years—reported diligently on the work of these local historical societies. Pliny White was a frequent contributor, and in the June 1860 issue Shea praised the "very commendable activity in historical pursuits . . . now manifesting itself in Vermont." In his notice of the *Quarterly Gazetteer* in the same issue, Shea remarked that "the title scarcely conveys the idea of this work. It is really a history of the counties and towns of the State of Vermont." He also noted a novel feature of the *Quarterly*, that of including "specimens of the literary productions of natives of each town and county." Shea gave this first issue of the *Gazetteer* his approval and ended by remarking that "no higher names of sanction can be found than those gracing Miss Hemenway's prospectus."[13]

At home in Vermont, notices of the Addison County number of the *Quarterly* appeared in such newspapers as the Burlington *Free Press*, the *Burlington Times*, and the *Middlebury Register*. The *Times* spoke admiringly of the "exhaustive dissection of each town in Addison County . . . in a form not so condensed as to be dry and dull, nor so much in detail as to be frivolous." The *Register* had nothing but kind words for Hemenway's editorship, attributing the magazine's success to "her energy and discretion."[14]

But a letter to the editor of the *Register*, written by Benjamin Larrabee, a native Vermonter then living in Columbus, Missouri, was more qualified in its appraisal. Larrabee readily conceded that the plan of the *Gazetteer* was "quite unique and has very decided merits." He himself had remarked on a recent trip to Vermont "how thickly the dust of years had settled upon the olden time," how "the stories that gray-haired men were accustomed to tell of Allen, Putnam, Warner . . . and the other heroes of the cradle-days of Green Mountain Independence were too dim to be recalled." He therefore spoke of his pleasure upon being handed a copy of the *Gazetteer*, which brought him "face to face with the period and the people that were about to be lost altogether from my mind." After "a momentary glance at its contents," he had subscribed.

Upon closer reading, however, Larrabee noted certain deficiencies in the format, found it "wanting in the dignity and fullness, the unity, the chronological order, the connection of the parts, the systematic development and completeness of a full-fledged history." He also took the editor and publisher to task for the number of spelling errors in the work, particularly in the history of Shoreham where he had found no less than seventeen misspelled names. "In a town like Shoreham," Larrabee remarked facetiously, "which according to this same history, is 'noted for superior horses,' it could not take a friend of the publisher many horses to get all the needed information."[15]

Larrabee was not the only reader of the *Gazetteer* to notice the errors in the town histories. Samuel Swift sent Hemenway a long list of misspellings and other mistakes that had shown up in her editing of his history of Middlebury. He even suggested rewriting whole paragraphs. Was Swift, who had, after all, published the first town history in the state, displaying his resentment at being edited and critiqued by a woman? Or, like many other authors, did he simply dislike being edited at all?[16]

If Hemenway smarted at this volley of criticism or considered it unfair, she made no public show of her feelings. Instead she indicated her willingness to accept advice from the learned men of the state by printing all of Swift's suggestions at the end of the Bennington County issue of the *Quarterly*. Larrabee's critique of the Shoreham history is there as well. To this she appended an editor's footnote explaining the many spelling errors in the essay as printed and revealing some of the difficulties she faced in her role as editor.

Such humility and willingness to admit error stood in sharp contrast to the attitude most self-respecting male authors of the time would adopt. It also contradicted her tough schoolmarm manner with troublesome town historians such as John Smith of Panton. Did Hemenway feel that, as a woman doing a man's job, such self-deprecation was appropriate? Or, as seems more likely, was she simply being naively candid and assuring her readers that she was doing her best under difficult circumstances?

As Hemenway tells it, back in the autumn of 1859 when she had visited Shoreham on her Addison County tour, she had engaged the Reverend Edward Chamberlain, pastor of the Shoreham Congregational Church, to digest a lengthy history of the town left behind by his predecessor, the Reverend Josiah Goodhue. But as the date of publication for the Addison County number of the *Gazetteer* neared and no Shoreham history had been received, Hemenway was forced to return to the village, collect Goodhue's manuscript, and digest it herself. The day she traveled to Shoreham was stormy and bitter cold. She had gone first by train to Middlebury and there had picked up the twice-weekly stagecoach that carried her the twelve miles to Shoreham. Upon arriving at her destination she sat down immediately with Goodhue's manuscript. It was not only long but illegible in places, "a valuable and interesting accumulation of facts, but not a work ready for the press." Still, short of time and money, she managed to rewrite Goodhue's history in the few days before the next scheduled stagecoach to Middlebury, "and believed we gave a fair summary of every item of interest. Many of the proper names were not legible," she tells us, "but in cases of doubt we referred to [the] Shoreham authority present, and presume we got them mostly correct." Rand & Avery, Hemenway's publisher, added to her difficulties by failing to send her a copy of the final proofs of the chapter. Thus, many typographical errors were left uncorrected. This was not the only time the editor of the *Gazetteer* would be frustrated in her attempt to produce an error-free town history.[17]

Mistakes—factual, spelling, grammatical, and typographical—occur throughout the five volumes of the *Gazetteer*. Taking into account the hundreds of different authors of varying literary and historical proficiency who contributed to the work, many of these errors were unavoidable. Furthermore, revising and editing the essays for publication was a monumental task, which for the most part Hemenway performed single-handedly. No one person could check the multitude of facts, much less the spelling of the thousands of names that appear in the *Gazetteer*. Nor could Hemenway afford to pay for help with editing and proofreading. Volunteers such as Hiland Hall, who assisted in making the Bennington number substantially error-free, would be few.

As Hemenway worked on editing each successive number of the *Quarterly Gazetteer*, financial problems continued to plague her. On the inside front cover of the third issue of the magazine, which came out in April 1862, she spells out these troubles. "The income of this publication," she tells her readers, "has been barely enough to pay its printing expenses. The editorial labor and expense bestowed upon it has never been even partially remunerated." To help alleviate this problem she urged every current subscriber to add another name to the subscription list and warned that publication of the next number would not occur until enough of these had been received to cancel the printing bill.[18]

Despite these efforts, keeping the subscription list high enough to pay the printing costs remained an uphill battle. When Joel Munsell, a historical publisher in Albany, New York, wrote Hemenway commending her for a "work bravely begun and nobly executed," he also declared that her policy of charging twenty-five cents per copy of the magazine was ruinous. "You are throwing pearls before swine," he told her, warning that at such a price "with all of Vermont on your subscription book you will come out of the campaign impoverished." Munsell's words had their effect. Hemenway not only raised the price of the next issue to fifty cents, but she also hired Munsell as her printer, beginning with the fourth number of the *Quarterly*. Unfortunately, neither of these changes had much impact on revenue.[19]

Meanwhile, Hemenway did everything she could to provide inducements to those willing to sell subscriptions. With the publication of the Bennington number she instituted "Club terms." If four individuals in a given town joined a club and bought a subscription, she would send them the fourth number of the *Quarterly* free. If four in a club agreed to take out yearly subscriptions, their club had a choice of bonuses: a copy of *Poets and Poetry* (the revised edition of which came out in 1860) or six photographs of leading Vermont poets. If eight yearly subscriptions were taken by a single club the members could choose from an "elegantly gilt copy of the Poets," or twelve photos.[20]

Had all gone according to plan the second number of the *Gazetteer* would have appeared in October 1860, but delays put off scheduled publication for a full year. "I have been obliged to wait beyond all expectations for our slow printer on the Bennington number," Hemenway would write in late July 1861. The initial cause of this setback is not known. Most likely Hemenway had been delinquent in keeping up her payments to Rand & Avery. But the onset of the Civil War also contributed to the delay. By the time the printer got down to work on this second issue in the spring of 1861, all his help had enlisted in the Union army. Not until October of that year was the second number of the *Vermont Quarterly Gazetteer* finally published.[21]

8

$\mathfrak{Songs}$ of the $\mathfrak{War}$

——•❦✿❦•——

We sing Our Country's song to-night
With saddened voice and eye;
Her banner droops in clouded light
Beneath a wintry sky.

Oliver Wendell Holmes[1]

On October 8, 1861, a notice of Abby Hemenway's *Gazetteer* in the Burlington *Free Press* credited "the disturbed state of the public mind about the [Civil] War" with "a retarding influence" on the timely publication of the magazine.[2] Loyalty to the Union cause was strong in the Green Mountain State. Following President Lincoln's call for troops on April 15, 1861, Vermonters, who had given him 80 percent of their vote the previous November, responded immediately and with enthusiasm. The president asked Vermont to send one regiment, and Governor Erastus Fairbanks wasted no time in ordering its formation. When the General Assembly met in special session on April 23, that normally parsimonious body voted to contribute one million dollars to the war effort and to raise not one regiment but seven. As George Perkins Marsh, the eminent Vermont scholar and statesman, observed at the time, "Our people, slow to move, are now roused and swayed by a spirit mightier than any that has stirred them since Bunker Hill."[3]

From the outset, the citizens of the Green Mountain State expressed their vigorous determination to fight for the preservation of the Union and destroy those who were tearing it apart. Most Vermonters, including Abby Hemenway, her mother, and her uncle Asa Barton, also believed that slavery was a great wrong and should be eliminated. But it was the open rebellion in the South that roused their war fever at the start. As Governor Fairbanks declared in his speech to the legislature on April 23, "We shall discredit our past history should we, in this crisis, suffer Vermont to be behind her sister states in her patriotic sacrifices for the preservation of the Union and the Constitution."[4]

In the ensuing weeks and months Union fervor ran high. On village greens flags flew and companies drilled. Citizens gathered in town halls, and in homes all over the state women set about making gray uniforms with emerald trim for the newly enlisted soldiers. In Ludlow, at a town meeting on June 30, 1861, two thousand dollars was appropriated to purchase clothing for the volunteers and furnish each one with ten dollars in cash. Less than a month later the bloody reality of war was brought home to Vermonters as news reached them in late July of the heavy Union losses at Bull Run. Vermont was a long way from the battlefields of Virginia, but the terror felt on the home front was palpable, particularly for those sending sons and brothers into the conflict. Hemenway's youngest brother, Daniel, then twenty-one years old, enlisted on October 4, 1861, and on the 7th she wrote of "getting up a box to send to our soldier."[5]

In an effort perhaps to distract herself from the horrors of the burgeoning conflict, Hemenway took no reprieve from her labors for the *Gazetteer*. Single-mindedly devoted to her work, she pressed on, determined that no obstacle, not even a civil war, should get in the way of her "cause."[6] She spent most of the summer after the opening of hostilities at home in Ludlow, working on the town histories for the next issue of the *Quarterly*. This third number, which did not appear until the spring of 1862, would complete Bennington County and begin Caledonia. Already, Hemenway's initial scheme to have each issue cover the town histories of one county was expanding.

Information on the canvassing and the work of editing and collating the histories of Caledonia and subsequent counties appearing in the *Gazetteer* is unfortunately sparse. In the last years of her life Hemenway would publish a memoir in periodical form entitled *Notes By the Path of the Gazetteer*. This idiosyncratic publication included descriptions of her first year as editor of the magazine, ending with an account of her tour of Bennington County in the summer of 1860. For the remaining counties, a few scattered letters and occasional references to her travels and editing in the *Gazetteer* are all that remain.

Only one of Hemenway's letters survives from the summer of 1861. She wrote it to the man she called her "antiquarian father," Henry Stevens. Founder and first president of the Vermont Historical Society, Stevens, a native of Barnet, was an eclectic man of business with a passion for collecting. People valued his vast store of historical knowledge, and Stevens corresponded widely with historians and antiquarians from all parts of the country.[7] In her letter to him Hemenway described the difficulties she was having with "our slow printer on the

Bennington number," but, more importantly, she wrote of the worrisome tendency of her town histories to take up more and more space in the columns of the *Gazetteer*. The Reverend Thomas Goodwillie's essays on Caledonia County and the town of Barnet alone filled "40 solid pages," she told Stevens. She begged him not to tell anyone about this, "for fear they will think it [the *Gazetteer*] will never get done." Despite this concern, she couldn't resist boasting that "Caledonia has beat Addison on their town histories out and out," and she lauded Thomas Goodwillie as the answer to an editor's prayers. Not only had he written two excellent historical essays, but he had also taken care to read his own proofs. Secretly Hemenway was pleased that her town historians were producing richer and more detailed histories.[8]

A second letter to Stevens, on October 7, showed her still in Ludlow, sending out copies of the second *Quarterly* to impatient subscribers. Stevens and his wife had apparently invited her to pay them a visit in Burlington, but she warned that it would be a week or so before she could get away. There were still 1,500 copies of the *Quarterly* to be mailed, and she confessed that some towns that hadn't yet received theirs were "getting wrathful." After thanking Stevens for his "kind words of encouragement," she asked him to provide her with some "dry old statistics" for her chapters on Chittenden County.[9]

Hemenway's friendship with Henry Stevens was a great boon to her work as editor of the *Gazetteer*. He allowed her to comb through his vast collection of historical materials, consisting of 3,485 books, about 6,500 pamphlets, another 400 volumes of newspapers, and some 20,000 letters. And, as the above letter to Stevens suggests, he also supplied her and her historians with both original sources and invaluable historical data that found their way into the *Gazetteer*. She later credited Stevens with having contributed more than anyone else to the "statistical and antiquarian resources" of her magazine.[10]

Abby Maria Hemenway c. 1870.
(Volume V of the *Vermont Historical Gazetteer.*)

Following her visit to Stevens, Hemenway spent a good part of the fall of 1861 touring Essex County in northeastern Vermont. These periodic excursions to one or another part of the state served as a vital restorative for the overtaxed editor. For one thing, they took her away from her desk and papers and helped her put aside for a time the financial and other editorial worries that hounded her. For another, these tours familiarized her with the history and character of every corner of Vermont, introduced her to new people and new towns, and added immeasurably to her rich fund of stories, facts, and anecdotes, many of which found their way into the pages of the *Gazetteer*.

Fifty years after Hemenway's death Katherine Waterman recalled the many visits the editor of the *Gazetteer* had made to Fayston to see her mother, Sarah Brigham Mansfield. Waterman described Hemenway's face as "always pale," her "dark hair plainly combed." At the same time she was full of life, had great enthusiasm for her work, and invariably laughed at those who criticized it. Waterman especially enjoyed hearing Hemenway read aloud. Her "quaint style and expression . . . was to me most wonderful."[11]

Hemenway's visit to Maidstone, a tiny hamlet of less than three hundred people bordering the upper Connecticut River, was an idyllic interlude on that fall tour. So moved was she by the experience that she devoted two columns of the town's history to recording it, thereby providing for her readers a rare and richly detailed description of one of many such visits around the state.

Hemenway arrived in Maidstone on a deliciously mild autumn day, making her way first to the farm owned by the town's designated historian, Moody Rich. The son of a German immigrant who had bought land in Maidstone back in 1784, Rich, now in his eighties, was the only living person who remembered the town when it was first organized. His farm, situated high on the banks overlooking the Connecticut River, boasted a magnificent prospect across rich bottomlands to the majestic White Mountains on the eastern horizon, a view that Hemenway, with characteristic hyperbole, called "unsurpassed in all Switzerland-like New England."[12]

After spending a night or two with Rich, Hemenway passed several days with the family of Dr. John Dewey, a once-eminent physician, who in 1841 had retired with his wife to a 200-acre farm. Known for their old-fashioned hospitality, the Deweys opened their rustic homestead to friend and stranger alike. Hemenway pronounced the doctor "the finest spirit we met in all that tour," portraying him as a venerable, learned gentleman above whose long, bushy, snow-white beard beamed a face of marked serenity. Even his voice, though he might be discussing such dark subjects as the Civil War, was, by Hemenway's account, both "genial and inspiring."

The "patriarchal simplicity" of the Deweys' house and its magnificent setting entranced her. Hemenway tells her readers that had she been born there she might have been a poet "and the story of Maidstone yet have remained unwritten," so inspired was she by the house, the people, and the view. "We would stay forever! such was the feeling—impression, effect—such attraction—earth, air, river, meadows in the sun, mountains over beyond, those famous white giants of New Hampshire . . ." But, she admits, "it wants the pen of a Harriet Beecher Stowe" to describe such a scene.

Yet when Hemenway turned her back on the view and took her readers into the Deweys' rustic, low-roofed farmhouse she came close to rivaling the author of *Uncle Tom's Cabin* in her description of its snug interior.

> The cozy, open fireplace was so inviting, the turkey roasted so deliciously, the cranberries so fresh, and the low chamber-room where you slept had such little soft carpeted stairs winding soon and quietly up thereto, and so bright paperings therein, wall and curtains, such cheerful red quilts and rugs and cushions . . . You found the house so like a bird's nest—brown without but feather-lined within; you visited so good below, and slept so good above, you concluded these people in Essex about the happiest people in the world.

Cheered, or "imparadized" as she put it, by the "little comforts and, aye, luxuries," of this deceptively simple-looking
farmhouse nestled so unobtrusively in its grand setting,
Hemenway wished she could remain in Maidstone forever. But
she had other towns to visit and moved on after a few days. By
the first of December 1861 she was back home at her desk in
Ludlow, reading and editing manuscripts as they came in and
keeping up as best she could with her historians, agents, and
other assistants. On New Year's Day, in a letter to one of her
many correspondents, she wrote of being greatly pressed by the
complexities of her business "with more than a hundred neglected towns or subscription lists therein to look after." Not surprisingly, in the chaos of papers surrounding her, an occasional
letter or manuscript did get lost.[13]

Hemenway also traveled that winter, but only to places easily reached by train. The end of January found her in Winooski
Falls, where a huge snowstorm kept her for the weekend at the
home of Judge David Reed, author of the history of
Chittenden County, the essay that would open the fourth number of her *Quarterly*. On Monday morning, January 29, before
leaving for St. Albans to supervise work on her Franklin
County chapters, she took advantage of a free hour to write a
rambling, rather incoherent letter to John Bulkley Perry, her
historian for Swanton, a Canadian-border town. Perry was the
pastor of the Swanton Congregational Church and a respected
geologist and antiquarian. In her letter, she thanked Perry
especially for his recent offer to act as an agent for her magazine. "Suffice to say your proferred aid comes like a benediction
after prayer," she told him, particularly because funds obtained
from subscriptions and other sources had been "barely enough
to pay the printing expenses." She admitted to Perry that her
own costs had yet to be covered, nor had she received any remu-
neration for her editorial labors.[14]

The generosity of Vermonters to the war effort was making it harder than ever for Hemenway to raise subscriptions for the *Gazetteer*. Persuading the citizens of the Green Mountain State to spend money on nonessentials had never been easy, but as the war dragged on this task grew increasingly difficult. By the time the third number of the *Quarterly* appeared in April 1862 the optimism of the early months of the conflict had faded. Vermont troops had spent a long, cold, unhealthy winter encamped in Virginia. With the coming of spring, concern for their welfare and for that of the Union army as a whole deepened. On April 16 a bloody battle was fought at Lee's Mills, resulting in the first heavy casualties for the state's troops. Thus, just as the new number of the *Gazetteer* appeared, the attentions of Vermont's citizens were directed elsewhere. Who cared to read about the exploits of long-dead Green Mountain Boys when a new generation of soldiers was being tested on the battlefields of Virginia and the West?

In early July 1862 Hemenway received a letter that moved her deeply enough to publish it in the *Gazetteer*. Written by John Ufford, her historian for Fairfax in Franklin County, the letter told of the difficulties he was having writing his essay. Ufford described his spirits as so clouded "by the overwhelming fear that our armies before Richmond had been cut to pieces," that he did not feel much like work or play.

Echoing the anguish suffered by other Vermonters on the home front, Ufford told Hemenway that his two brothers in the Union army had both "seen hard service and yet they are willing to endure and suffer for the perpetuity of our glorious government, more free than the world has ever before seen." Ufford spoke movingly, too, of the pride he felt in his native state: "When nearly every heart is wrung by the fear of the loss of near or dear friends, she still sends forth her sons to the battle-field. Mothers and sisters hide their anguish and bid sons and brothers go forth,—the maiden kisses her lover and tells him, his country first,—fathers cheer up their sons by telling them of the immortal deeds of those who first fought for independence."

Ufford conceded that "amid such scenes as this" he found it hard both to focus his mind and to set aside time for his town history. As he phrased it, "the harvest of men taken out of the State has weakened the force left at home, and those here must work harder to make up the deficiency." For this reason, too, he had little success finding agents to canvass the towns for subscribers to the *Gazetteer.* "The men are all too busy in these busy times," he explained, telling Hemenway nothing she did not already know. He did, however, give her the names of some women who might be willing to help sell subscriptions.[15]

The sketch of John Ufford accompanying his letter in the *Gazetteer* tells how this man, one of the youngest of Hemenway's historians, had attempted to enlist in the 11th Vermont Regiment, only to be turned down because of a minor physical defect. In the end Ufford completed his history of Fairfax, but shortly thereafter he contracted typhoid fever. He died in June 1863, at the age of twenty-eight.[16]

The passing months of the war would show Hemenway and others in Ludlow the true horror of this "Southern Rebellion," as so many in the North called it. Beginning in the summer of 1862, the newspapers reported little else but accounts of bloody battles: Antietam, Fredricksburg, Chancellorsville. Lists of soldiers dead or wounded were printed alongside these accounts as they came in. All around her she would have seen families lose husbands, sons, and brothers. Some died on the battlefield, others in hospitals and prison camps or on the way home. The Ludlow town historian, Joseph Harris, noted that "of those who were spared to return home, nearly all came back wounded, and many maimed for life."[17]

As for Hemenway's own feelings about the war, the dozen or so letters that survive from this period, all written to one or another of her historians, barely mention the conflict and then only in connection with the *Gazetteer*. Did patriotic fervor lead her, like so many of her Vermont sisters, to join a Ladies' Aid Society, wartime organizations that made, gathered, and shipped supplies to the soldiers in the war zone? As a child she had never been particularly handy at needlework, but the Union army's desperate need for woolen socks may have shamed her into making the effort. One Brattleboro woman later remembered that it was considered a disgrace for a woman "to attend a concert or a lecture without taking a soldier's sock for knitting work." Hemenway herself took pains to tell the readers of the *Gazetteer* about an elderly Burlington woman she knew who, though too infirm to join those "who from week to week met to labor for the health and comfort of the soldiers in the field," nonetheless kept her fingers busy at home on behalf of the war effort. "Many were the gallant fellows," Hemenway wrote, "whose feet were protected by the stockings which she had knit."[18]

Apart from the care Hemenway took to ensure that information on individual Union army volunteers for each town was included in the *Gazetteer*, her only other known contribution to the war effort was a book of patriotic verse, *Songs of the War*. This small paperbound volume published in 1863 contained, as its editor describes them, seventy-three of the most popular war songs. Here are regimental marches from each of the New England states, many of them written to already existing tunes. Other verses urge farmers to turn their plowshares into swords and enlist; still others discourage deserters. Sentimental lyrics abound here as well, from poems mourning the untimely deaths of youthful recruits to others praising the heroism of women on the home front. One of Hemenway's favorites was "Send Them Home Tenderly." These verses, composed by a woman signing herself simply "Stella," were inspired by Bay

State Governor John Andrew's order that "the bodies of the Massachusetts soldiers dead in Baltimore be immediately laid out and tenderly sent forward by express to me." Another of Hemenway's favorites was the battle hymn, "To Canaan," which she likened to a Cromwellian war song.[19]

Despite the patriotic fervor exhibited in this collection, little of it can rightly be called poetry. "Rhymed propaganda ground out for the home front," is how one critic describes most Civil War verse, and the depiction fits here as well.[20] True, a number of nationally known poets are represented, including Henry Wadsworth Longfellow, Oliver Wendell Holmes, and Thomas Bailey Aldrich. But with the possible exception of Longfellow's rousing verses on the ramming of "The Cumberland" by a Confederate ironclad, none of the poems in *Songs of the War* would make their way into modern collections of verse. Nor do we find any of the rousing Civil War songs that are remembered today, such as "The Battle Hymn of the Republic," written in the fall of 1861.

Songs of the War appeared at a time when Union prospects for victory seemed dim and the most notable verse to come out of the conflict had yet to be written. Yet for all its deficiencies as poetry, the collection does convey the spirit of the times: the initial excitement and optimism as Northern regiments marched out of their village greens and off to war; Vermont's single-minded devotion to saving the Union; and, finally, the mood of discouragement that swept over the North in 1862 as victory seemed to elude the Union troops. Significantly, only one poem, "On the Shores of Tennessee," mentions slavery, a subject close to Hemenway's heart but of indifference to most Northerners at the outset of the war.

Why exactly did she publish *Songs of the War*? The book is small enough to slip easily into a pocket. Did she hope that Vermonters would send copies to their soldiers at the front and

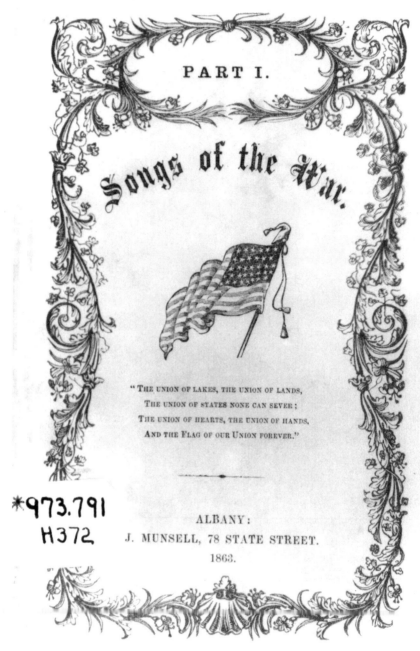

Front cover of *Songs of the War*. Note that it is called Part I, indicating that Hemenway hoped to publish one or more sequels. She never did.

thus encourage patriotic singing around the campfire and on long marches through the Virginia countryside? Or was publication of *Songs* simply a desperate attempt to raise money for her own patriotic "cause," the *Gazetteer*? Whatever her reasons, Hemenway's unqualified support of the Northern war effort is suggested by the picture of the Union flag and the verse on the cover of this little book:

The Union of lakes, the Union of lands,
  The Union of states none can sever:
The Union of hearts, the Union of hands,
  And the Flag of our Union forever.[21]

The first mention of the Civil War in the *Gazetteer* came at the end of the second number, where a list, compiled by Hiland Hall, gave the names of Bennington County volunteers who enlisted in the Second and Fourth Vermont Regiments. Hemenway added her own patriotic footnote to the account of the Bennington war effort by including a notice cut from the pages of the *Rutland Daily Herald* telling of a gift to the state from one of Bennington's native sons. After learning of the legislature's generous appropriation of men and money to the Union cause, Trenor W. Park of San Francisco, who also happened to be a son-in-law of Hiland Hall, mailed Governor Fairbanks a check for $1,000 to help defray "the expenses of fitting out her sons for battle," and support "the families of those who may fall in defense of the flag of our Union." Hemenway pays tribute to Park's great generosity by pronouncing him a "true-hearted patriot, and a worthy son of the Green Mountain State."[22]

When the fourth number of the *Quarterly Gazetteer* appeared in October 1862 Hemenway told her readers what material on the Civil War they could expect to find in future issues. A section on military matters was already a regular feature in most town histories, and information on the current war would now be added. As she had stated on numerous occasions, she intended the *Gazetteer* for future generations, not simply the present one. Thus, she persuaded ex-Governor Fairbanks to write for posterity an account of "the organizing, officering, equipping, subsisting and sending into the field the first six Vermont regiments" during his administration. Following Fairbanks's essay is a table listing the officers and volunteers from the whole of Caledonia County, including their company and regiment.[23]

Despite Hemenway's determination to publish her *Gazetteer* in a timely manner, only two numbers appeared in 1862, one in April and another in October. Although preparation of the historical materials destined for future issues progressed remarkably efficiently, lagging subscriptions continued to cause delays. At the close of 1862 Hemenway had more than enough Chittenden County town histories to fill two *Quarterlies*. The first Chittenden County number appeared in January 1863; the second, held up for lack of funds, waited until the following August. Meanwhile, she told her readers, two more issues, completing Chittenden and covering Essex and Grand Isle Counties, neared readiness for publication.[24]

As early as the late winter of 1862 hints of discouragement began appearing in Hemenway's surviving correspondence. On March 11, in a letter to one of her historians, she spoke bitterly of the slow progress she was making. Seemingly unconscious of the war's drain on the state's financial resources, she blamed the people of Vermont for failing to support the *Gazetteer*. "It is considerable to be able to make any headway with so faithless a generation," she told her correspondent.[25]

But Hemenway's frustration and discouragement would only deepen. A year later on June 9, 1863, she wrote John Bulkley Perry that volume six was "about ready for distribution," but admitted to "coming into arrears for funds to meet our largely increased printing bills." This she attributed partly to the increased cost of paper, which had doubled since the start of the war, but also to the failure of many to renew their subscriptions. "I almost feel that I have been a little sluggish of late," she admitted. "I have not intended to be but the work has been *heavy on our hands* and the people *some hard* to reach. I mean their heads, hearts & pockets, on behalf of the enterprise." Still, for all her apparent sluggishness, Hemenway determined to push on with the work, telling Perry that she hoped to bring out three more numbers of the *Quarterly* before the New Year. Such optimism sprang more from desperation than realism, however. The August 1863 issue of the *Quarterly* was the last to appear for the duration of the Civil War.[26]

"Into the One Sovereign Fold"

———•◦✛◦✛◦•———

When I glance at the Protestant world I cannot
find one thing to make their religion beautiful.
They have parted with those pure and lovely
doctrines which the Catholic holds most sacred:
those forms which render the services of our Holy
Religion so sublime, so tenderly beautiful, and
have taken in their stead the cold formalities of
a *protesting* creed.

Debbie Barlow, Claremont, N.H.[1]

By the late winter of 1864, the editor of the *Vermont
Historical Gazetteer* had little choice but to acknowledge
at least the temporary demise of her magazine. In partial com-
pensation for this great vacuum in her life, Hemenway turned
her energies and attention to a new "cause," one that dramatically altered the spiritual tenor of her being.

On Thursday, April 28, 1864, William Henry Hoyt, a former rector of the Episcopal Church in St. Albans, but by then
a convert to Roman Catholicism living in Burlington, made the
following entry in his diary:

Miss Hemenway here today & dined with us & at tea & to pass the night—At 6 o'clock we went up to St. Joseph's school & convent buildings, near the French Church, in the chapel of which Miss Hemenway made a profession of the Catholic Church and the Bishop gave her conditional baptism. Anne [Hoyt's wife] & self standing as sponsors.[2]

Abby Hemenway was then thirty-five years old. The journey carrying her to this day had been a long one, dating back to her girlhood when she had begun writing her poetic life of the Virgin Mary. As Hemenway later recalled in the introduction to *The Mystical Rose*, the reading she did for the poem as well as the writing of it gradually but steadily overpowered her Protestant religious sensibility. "Lost in a labyrinth of beauty, pious allegory, ancient and mystic, luminous legend, lovingly warm with words that burn, shedding odors as incense from a censer, we were overwhelmed."[3]

The first four books of the poem, Hemenway tells us in this introduction, were written before she had read any traditional life of the Virgin. Later, however, when she had access to a wider range of books, she read everything she could lay her hands on, from Middle Eastern history and mythology to poetry and the writings of the early church fathers. Somehow she managed to appropriate "every coveted relic or tradition handed down by historian, Christian or pagan, from the archives of Latin Church, Hebrew or Greek." For most of her young adulthood, even while she worked on her collection of poets and the beginning of the *Gazetteer*, writing *The Mystical Rose* constituted in Hemenway's mind her chief literary labor, and this labor would lead her, as she later expressed it, "into the one Sovereign Fold."[4]

As a child, Hemenway would have had few opportunities to meet any Catholics. None were recorded living in Ludlow until the building of the railroad in the late 1840s. Nearby

Plymouth, however, did contain an Irish settlement, including 122 Catholics clustered near the local iron foundry.[5] The arrival in February 1848 of immigrant Irish workmen, to begin constructing the Ludlow branch of the Central Vermont Railroad, probably marked her first exposure to any significant number of Catholics. She was then a student at Black River Academy and would have noticed the small shantytown that had been built to house the families of the laborers, including a large number of children. Hemenway's student years were marked by a number of fatal accidents suffered by these new immigrants. The most poignant occurred in the fall of 1849 when three young Irish boys were killed playing with gun powder intended for blasting a rock cut for the railroad above the village.[6]

Even if Hemenway was curious about these Irish families, as a committed Baptist she would have been discouraged from befriending them. Nor could she have learned much about their alien faith even if she had wanted to. There was as yet no Catholic church in Ludlow, and mass was said only on the rare occasions when a priest passed through town.

Ludlow was by no means the only town in Vermont to experience an influx of Roman Catholics in those years. Since the 1830s the number of Irish and French Canadians entering the state had risen markedly. At the time of Hemenway's birth a thousand Catholics had settled in Vermont. By 1840 that number had grown to more than three thousand (most of them concentrated in the Champlain Valley), and a decade later to twenty thousand. As early as 1835 Nathaniel Hawthorne, visiting Burlington, was struck by the great number of Irish immigrants he found swarming "in huts and mean dwellings near the lake" and lounging about the wharves.[7]

Protestant Vermonters, like other native-born New Englanders, felt increasingly threatened by the quantity of Irish and French Canadians moving into the state. Because more than half were illiterate and most were desperately poor, many of these newcomers were forced into manual and domestic labor, with little chance of bettering themselves. Looking down on these immigrants, with their strange customs and traditions, Vermonters were particularly suspicious of their loyalty to a foreign church that since colonial days had inspired distrust if not outright hostility. Indeed, for many Americans, Catholicism was *the* unmitigated evil. As the historian Ralph Gabriel has phrased it, "What the capitalist was to Lenin in 1917 and the Jew to Hitler in 1935, the Catholic was to the American democrat in the middle of the nineteenth century."[8]

Vermonters' antagonism toward the growing number of Catholics in their midst had manifested itself in a variety of ways. In 1835 fifty-six men petitioned the state legislature to prohibit the building of monasteries and convents in the Green Mountain State, declaring that such institutions enslaved the mind, restricted freedom, and favored despotism. No bill addressing these demands ever became law, but when St. Mary's Church in Burlington burned on the night of May 8, 1838, many people assumed that an anti-Catholic agitator was responsible even though no one was ever charged. Unfortunately, the zealous rantings of Vermont's first missionary priest, Jeremiah O'Callaghan, who traveled tirelessly around the state administering the sacraments and denouncing the Protestants, did little to calm such hostility.[9]

Yet, in the midst of nationwide fears of a Catholic menace the antebellum years had also seen a wave of native-born American converts. According to one estimate, 350,000 conversions to Catholicism occurred in America in the nineteenth century. Of these some 57,000 took place between 1831 and 1860. Many of these converts, like Abby Hemenway, could trace their ancestry back to the early days of settlement. Many, too, were solidly middle class, coming from families where the women as well as the men had been well educated. These erstwhile

Protestants brought to what was a largely immigrant church an infusion of educated, articulate, native-born Catholics, whose significance was reflected in the number who became priests, nuns, and even bishops. By the end of the nineteenth century, a good many notable New England families, with names such as Ripley, Dana, Hawthorne, and Bancroft, could show at least one Catholic member.[10] Hemenway had much in common with these converts. If her family was not particularly notable, both parents could at least claim a solid phalanx of New England forebears. Moreover, her own education had been superior for a Vermont woman of her day. While at Black River Academy she had studied Latin, Greek, and French, which she later put to use in her research for *The Mystical Rose*.

During the war years, when Hemenway was working on the Chittenden County histories for the *Gazetteer*, she began spending more time in Burlington. There she had access to better libraries and would have been able to undertake the kind of reading that allowed her to finish the poem.

By Hemenway's own account it was in the course of her work as editor of the *Vermont Historical Gazetteer* that other influences in addition to the writing of *The Mystical Rose* began leading her away from the Baptist Church and toward Rome. When the first volume of the *Gazetteer* (comprising the town histories of five Vermont counties) was published in 1867, she inscribed a copy to Vermont's Catholic Bishop, Louis De Goesbriand, telling him that it was "in prosecution of this work" that she "became acquainted with the Catholics and their faith."[11] She did not specify what particular aspect of this work as historian and editor had brought her a greater knowledge of the Catholic faith, but one likely influence was her research on Ethan Allen's daughter, Fanny, an early Vermont convert to Catholicism who later became a nun.

The sketch that appears in the *Gazetteer* is based on an interview Hemenway conducted in the early 1860s with a woman who claimed that her mother had visited Fanny Allen in her French Canadian convent. Although Hemenway does not name her source, the woman was almost certainly Julia Smalley, a prominent Catholic convert whom Hemenway later described as her good friend and "the most gifted lady writer in northern Vermont." Smalley was the author of a popular book entitled *The Young Converts*, which tells the true story of the three Barlow sisters of Claremont, New Hampshire, all of whom became Catholics in the 1850s. It may well have been Smalley who introduced Hemenway to the close circle of Vermont Catholic converts in Burlington, including William Henry Hoyt.[12]

Whether or not Smalley or her book influenced Hemenway's decision to enter the Catholic Church, the life of Fanny Allen was undeniably crucial, providing as it did a heroic model for her to follow. Ethan Allen's daughter had inherited his rebellious spirit. Not only had she defied the wishes of her mother and stepfather by joining the Catholic Church, but she had gone one step further and entered a nursing order, the Religious Hospitalers of St. Joseph. Intrigued by the idea that Ethan Allen's daughter had gone over to Rome and become a nun, Fanny's friends and acquaintances journeyed north to Montreal to visit her; when she took her final vows, there was standing room only in the church. In the few short years before her death in 1808, she is said to have been responsible for encouraging a more sympathetic understanding of Catholicism, not only among her Vermont friends but also among the English-speaking patients at the Hôtel-Dieu, a hospital where she occasionally worked as a nurse.[13]

Hemenway was drawn to Fanny Allen partly because she saw her as a kindred spirit, a woman like herself who had chosen to take the unconventional path, to brave the disapproval of family and society and compose a life for herself on her own terms. But there was a further bond between these two

Vermont women. As children, both had been visited by visionary figures, apparitions that each later claimed had started them on their long journey toward Rome.

Fanny Allen's vision is described in a greatly embellished account Hemenway wrote for children in 1865. Twelve-year-old Fanny had wandered some distance from her family's house and was playing quietly on a beach close to the rushing waters of the Winooski River when she looked up to see "a fierce-looking monster with widely distended jaws breaking the current of the stream and making rapidly toward her." Fanny, frozen with fear at the creature's hideousness, was unable to move or scream. But then, just in the nick of time, a venerable, mild-looking man appeared at her side, drove the monster away, and then lifted Fanny gently in his arms. After carrying her a safe distance from the river he put her down and disappeared as quickly as he had come. For days Fanny searched in vain for this kind man who had rescued her, but she never saw him again. Years later, however, when she was looking for a religious order to join in Montreal, Fanny recognized his face in a picture of St. Joseph that hung over the mantel in the parlor of the Religious Hospitalers' convent. At that moment, Hemenway tells us, Fanny realized that the beast from whom she had been rescued "was only the figure of that more monstrous beast, heresy," and that her fatherly rescuer was none other than St. Joseph, who had led her into the Catholic Church and was now telling her to enter this convent.[14]

Hemenway's source for this story probably lay in an account published in Paris in 1854, which concluded that it made little difference whether Fanny had actually seen the monster and the old man, or whether they were simply her spiritual impressions—the moral was still the same, the monster standing for heresy and unbelief; and her rescuer St. Joseph, standing for the true faith, Roman Catholicism.[15]

The similarity between her own visionary experience and

that of Fanny Allen was not lost on Abby Hemenway. In both cases kindly parental figures had appeared to these women in their girlhood. The motherly apparition who comforted Hemenway in that "enchanted dell" near Jewell Brook and whom she later identified as the Virgin Mary was perhaps not as heroic a figure as the man who rescued Fanny from her monster. But for Hemenway, "Mary Mother," as she came to call her, had acted as an equally powerful force guiding her out of the wilderness of error into what she believed was the true Church.

Some years after her own conversion to Catholicism, Hemenway wrote a play about Fanny Allen that drew on the same French source as well as oral tradition. *Fanny Allen, the First American Nun* was not published until 1878, but a careful reading of this pious drama in five acts opens a window onto Hemenway's own experience as a convert and suggests some of the reasons why she left the Baptist for the Catholic Church.

The play begins with Fanny trying to persuade her mother and stepfather to allow her to attend a convent school in Montreal. She tells them she wants to learn French, but her real reason for going is to find out if Catholics are indeed as bad as the book she has been reading says they are. Her mother and stepfather agree to let her go on one condition: that she be baptized an Episcopalian. When Fanny objects, insisting that she is no Christian, her mother responds, "You do not know yet what you are." Fanny's next words could well have been spoken by Hemenway herself: "True, true," she readily agrees, "Who does know what they are? I do not know a man or a woman whom I think does. I never met a person who appeared to know exactly what they believed. If you find them thinking one way to-day by to-morrow they will have taken another tack."[16]

Hemenway's own impatience with the state of Protestant Christianity in Vermont can be gleaned from an essay she tucked away in the *Gazetteer* chapter on St. Albans, a railroad town in Franklin County. In it she recalls a visit to the cemeteries sited on a hill above the town. Remarking that the names on the gravestones were more familiar and of more interest to her than those on the doorplates of the houses below, she reflects that "the men who dwell in our grave-yards seem not like the present generation." Baptist though she is, she then commends that "noble class of old Congregational fathers of the earlier day in the state: men who did cordially hate the intrusion of the Baptists and Methodists in the towns where they had planted their churches." To her mind this first generation of Congregational ministers "had a more honest belief in their Calvinism than the men of today, and a grand large-heartedness, withal to act out the part of an 'elected' child. . . . They read their own divines, kept the Sabbath-day up to the high Puritan mark—believed implicitly, or almost, the sermons preached from their tall, narrow, box-like pulpits. . . . They stood up grandly and sturdily in their moral worth, and in their patriotism."[17]

Hemenway had seen something of the current condition of the Protestant churches in Vermont on her travels around the state and in her editing of the town histories that crossed her desk in Ludlow. In her own county of Windsor, she had watched membership in the Baptist and other evangelical churches fall and Calvinist beliefs and disciplinary practice erode.[18] She had also spoken to dozens of clergymen throughout the state. No single group of men had proved such staunch supporters of her historical efforts as the clergy. Not only had they readily provided hospitality when she visited their towns, but as the acknowledged men of learning in many Vermont communities they also figured prominently among the ranks of her historians.

Some of these clerical historians shared Hemenway's concern about the current condition of Protestantism. The Reverend J. H. Woodward, for one, went to considerable

William Henry Hoyt, convert to Roman Catholicism
and Abby Hemenway's godfather.
(Frontispiece from Louis de Goesbriand, *Catholic Memoirs
of Vermont and New Hampshire,* 1886.)

lengths to explain why his Congregational church in Westford,
like so many others, was "wasting away." He began by describing the years from 1815 to 1832 as "a season of unusual religious interest" in Vermont, crediting a powerful succession of

revivals with increasing the number and strength of the churches. Then, according to Woodward, in the mid-1830s a reaction, a period of "unhappy excitements," set in. Prominent among these excitements was another wave of revivals that swept across Vermont and New York, employing soul-shaking conversion techniques and stressing the individual's ability to take control of his or her spiritual destiny. A number of other issues were relevant: anti-Masonry, abolitionism, gold fever in the West, and finally the building of the railroads, all of which, Woodward claimed, had focused people's attention on worldly matters, leading to "an absence and dearth of spirit." Writing on the eve of the Civil War, Woodward concluded that "the whole course of events for the last twenty-five years in New England, has been averse to a state of religious prosperity."[19]

Woodward and Hemenway were not alone in their distress over the spiritual decline they saw around them. Plenty of other New Englanders lamented the growing emphasis upon a felt, subjective religious experience, one that relied on private judgment with only the Bible for guidance. In her play about Fanny Allen, Hemenway, speaking through her heroine, articulates rather ungrammatically the dilemma facing those bewildered nineteenth-century Americans in search of a true church: "My father believed in God without a Bible, when a God with a Bible and no additional revelation, is not sufficient to decide among the multitude of sects, who is right?"[20]

Many in New England had welcomed this movement away from dogmatic and theological conformity, declaring that churches and creeds, even the Bible, were obstacles to an intuitive knowledge of God. Whereas orthodox Christians celebrated God's intervention in human history, these liberals wanted to free the individual from history's shackles to achieve, as the Boston Unitarian minister Theodore Parker put it, a "clear conscience unsullied by the past."[21] Hemenway's uncle Asa Barton, for one, was a great admirer of Parker. In a letter to his daughter, Lucia, in 1865 he spoke of his "uncommon interest" in the Unitarian minister's sermons on Theism, which, according to Barton, showed "very clearly the absurdity of popular theology" as practiced in the orthodox churches. "We are not to be condemned for mere belief," he assured his daughter, "but for our conduct in life."[22]

Other New Englanders, however, including Barton's niece Abby, deplored the erosion of orthodoxy and sought instead an alternative that retained traditional Christian theology and continuity with the past. Down in Massachusetts, the Catholic convert Sophia Ripley, a one-time Transcendentalist, longed to escape disputatious Protestant sectarianism for a "heart religion" that recalled the revivalism of Jonathan Edwards, while rejecting its Calvinist roots.[23]

Some dissatisfied Protestants found a satisfactory resting place in the high church branch of Episcopalianism. Influenced by the Oxford Movement in England, whose leaders sought to link the Anglican Church more closely to Catholic tradition, these Episcopalians called for a renewed sense of Christian discipline, worship, and holiness.[24] Other dissatisfied Protestants had moved directly to the Roman Catholic Church, and still others, such as William Henry Hoyt, Hemenway's godfather (who was raised a Congregationalist), had passed through the Episcopal Church on their way to the Roman.

Hoyt came to Vermont in 1836, serving first in Burlington and Middlebury before assuming the rectorship of the Episcopal church in St. Albans. Although the St. Albans parish flourished under Hoyt's ministry, he was never entirely comfortable with Episcopalianism. When he began introducing Catholic liturgical practices and Gregorian chants into his church services, the Episcopal bishop of Burlington, John Henry Hopkins, became genuinely alarmed. He admonished the St. Albans pastor both privately and in print, all to no avail. On July 24, 1846, Hoyt wrote the bishop resigning his rectorship and that evening he boarded a boat to Montreal, where on the following day he made his profession of the Catholic faith. A month later Hoyt's wife, Anne, also joined the church.[25]

The Hoyts continued to live in St. Albans for another ten years. During this time a number of William's former parishioners followed him into the Catholic Church. One June Sunday in 1854 an attendant at mass noted that "the communion rail was filled with Americans who had been converted to the Catholic faith within the last few years."[26] What influence Hoyt had on Hemenway's decision to join the Roman Catholic Church is not known, but her choice of him as her godfather shows that she shared the respect of many other Catholic Vermonters for this man, who is credited with leading a Catholic revival in the state.

The most important New England convert to Catholicism, however, was the native Vermonter Orestes Brownson. Born in poverty on a farm in Stockbridge, a village in the northwest corner of Hemenway's own Windsor County, Brownson had spent the early part of his adult life moving restlessly from one church and creed to another. Then in 1842 he was converted to Catholicism and quickly became one of its leading apologists. Many letters to Brownson from other converts tell of the powerful effect his writings had on their decision to enter the church.[27]

Apart from Hemenway's research for *The Mystical Rose* and her sketch of Fanny Allen in the *Gazetteer* no record survives of other reading that might have influenced her decision to become a Catholic. Yet her later correspondence with Brownson does reveal a long-standing familiarity with his writings.[28] She may well have paid particular attention to this passage from his memoirs written in 1857, which describes so eloquently the enormous gulf that divided Catholics from Protestants.

To pass from one Protestant sect to another is a small affair, and is little more than going from one apartment to another in the same house. We remain still in the same world, in the same general order of thought, and in the midst of the same friends and associates. We do not go from the known to the unknown; we are still within soundings, and may either return, if we choose, to the sect we have left, or press on to another, without serious loss of reputation, or any gross disturbance of our domestic and social relations. But to pass from Protestantism to Catholicity is a very different thing. We break with the whole world in which we have hitherto lived; we enter into what is to us an untried region, and we fear the discoveries we may make there, when it is too late to draw back. To the Protestant mind this old Catholic Church is veiled in mystery . . . We enter it, and leave no bridge over which we may return. It is a committal for life, for eternity.[29]

In a poem written in 1865 that recounts her own conversion Hemenway echoes Brownson's sentiments. "Our First Annunciation Day" pinpoints the moment she made the final break with her past as a Protestant and crossed over into a new and unfamiliar world. In her case, this moment came, appropriately enough, on the feast day commemorating the angel Gabriel's announcement to the Virgin Mary that she was to become the mother of God. The date was March 25, 1864, and the place, quite naturally, was a Catholic church, probably one of the two in Burlington.

The poem depicts Hemenway's struggle in reaching her final decision to become a Catholic, dwelling particularly on the powerful temptation she endured to resist the forces pulling her into the Catholic Church. In what she saw as a battle for her soul between Mary and the devil, she describes her inability to cross the threshold into the church.

> Fain would enter, fain would lose the soul's pollution.
> Could not enter! Could not enter!
> Dare not venture!

Then on the Feast of the Annunciation, "the wiles of sense," as Hemenway calls them, prevail; "the world the flesh and Satan" lose their grip on her. "The Virgin's arm is stronger," she explains, particularly on this her feast day. Mary beats back the devil, much as Fanny Allen's St. Joseph drove away the river monster. Hemenway falls on her knees; the struggle is behind her.[30]

Where poetic imagery leaves off in this recounting of Hemenway's conversion to Catholicism matters little. The real struggle had likely been going on in her mind and heart for some time. For most American converts, the process was both lengthy and private, marked by extensive self-examination and often painful deliberation over certain doctrines. Furthermore, as seems likely in Hemenway's case, the decision to become a Catholic was frequently made without consultation with other church members. Often converts did not even seek out a priest until after they had made the decision to enter the church.[31]

The appeal of Catholicism for a woman like Abby Hemenway is not hard to understand. This authoritative church grounded on a firm doctrinal and theological base, a church whose history she could trace back to Jesus himself, satisfied her longing for moral certitude. As the recent convert Fanny Allen tells her mother in Hemenway's play, there is no room for doubt in Catholicism. "The church's orders are all worthy of obedience . . . it approves of nothing but what is good."[32]

Perhaps, too, she believed that her "rampant individualism needs the counterweight of a rigorous orthodoxy; needs the clear demanding structures to ballast me with connectedness, a protection against the dangerous voyages of the imagination, and to ensure my return to sanity and to home." The words are those of Sara Maitland, a late-twentieth-century British writer and convert to Catholicism, but they might well have been spoken a hundred years earlier by Abby Hemenway.[33]

The Catholic Church also offered Hemenway what one historian has described as "a sanctified deviance" from nineteenth-century American Protestant culture by allowing converts like her to renounce their Protestant heritage and embrace Catholicism, whose churches, cluttered as they were with statues, holy pictures, and stained-glass windows, seemed to them true places of worship. Their liturgies, too, contained an ancient and mysterious richness. The medieval chants, the colorful vestments, the incense, the Latin mass, and, above all, the sense of history and tradition all spoke to Hemenway's ardent and romantic nature.[34] By embracing the Roman Catholic Church Hemenway was publicly declaring her difference from other people. She now had a license to behave in unconventional ways. As the historian Jenny Franchot writes of Sophia Ripley, "Catholicism both created and compensated for her occupational and cultural marginality."[35]

In this newfound religion, with its call for submission to a nurturing mother church, Hemenway had discovered not only an authoritative alternative to the uncertainty and confusion of mid-nineteenth-century Protestantism, but also a replacement for her earthly mother. At the time of her daughter's conversion Abigail Dana Hemenway was in her mid-sixties. She would live for only a few more years (she died in 1866). For her eldest daughter, the church as "Holy Mother" represented this beloved maternal figure in more enduring form.[36]

There was yet another valid explanation for Hemenway's attraction to Catholicism. Well educated and ambitious, she was one of a growing number of American women who had chosen not to marry and to pursue instead "a noble work in a good cause." These single women believed they were following a sanctified path, comparing themselves to celibate nuns in a Catholic convent. Elizabeth Blackwell had spoken of "tak[ing] the veil" when she began her career in medicine. Some Protestants were even heard to speak enviously of the Catholic Church for the support it gave to such women by providing communities and cloisters for them. As Hemenway had learned from Fanny Allen and other converts, Catholicism also offered women a wider range of identities than the domestic feminine ideal lauded from most Protestant pulpits. Female icons existed for Catholics, while they did not for Protestants. Hemenway could model herself after ardent women mystics whose devotion to God came before their devotion to man. She could eschew marriage with impunity, because the Catholic Church regarded celibacy as a higher calling than matrimony and praised virginity as superior to maternity.[37]

That Hemenway herself shared such a reverence for the celibate life can be seen in her religious poetry. For example, in *The Mystical Rose* she compares the chaste love between Mary and Joseph to that which the angels have for one another, "a love more deep than that of the flesh."[38] By taking a vow of celibacy and renouncing sex, Mary has chosen a higher calling. But Hemenway, by embracing the single life so prized by the Catholic Church, had also found a justification for renouncing marriage. Only as a single woman could she hope to forgo the dependency and the denial of personal identity traditionally expected of married women. As Susan B. Anthony once wrote, she would not object to marriage "if it were not that women throw away every plan and purpose of their own life to conform to the plans and purposes of a man's life."[39]

But in these very months when Hemenway was considering joining the Catholic Church her own plans and purposes were in turmoil. Her editing of the *Gazetteer* had slowed to a halt. The last issue of the *Quarterly* had gone to press the previous August. Although she continued to collect material for her Rutland County histories and spoke with frenzied optimism about the imminent appearance of further issues, the magazine's finances told another story. The money needed to resume printing was not obtainable and not likely to be so as long as discouraging news from the front continued. By the end of 1863 Vermont had sent more than 25,000 men to fight with the Union army, and one in ten of these soldiers had died in uniform. Yet victory seemed as elusive as ever. If Hemenway wondered what the future held she was not alone.

Beginning in the late winter of 1864, when publication of the *Gazetteer* halted, and continuing for the next two and a half years, Hemenway's new faith filled the great void left by this disruption to her work. Catholicism occupied her heart and mind, and pious poetry rather than history became the principal focus for her creative energies, releasing the suppressed passions of a lifetime in an outpouring of spiritual ecstasy.

Meanwhile, Hemenway had begun spending more and more time in Burlington. Having gone there originally because of work connected with the *Gazetteer*, she continued going because it was the center of Catholic life in Vermont. In the 1860s the Queen City contained more than three thousand Catholics, most of whom were recent immigrants. It was also the site of two Catholic churches, several Catholic schools, and an orphanage. Burlington, too, is where Hemenway would have met William Henry Hoyt, his wife, Anne, and the small group of converts who had crossed over the great gulf separating Protestantism from the Roman Catholic Church.[40]

If Burlington provided a welcoming circle of like-minded Yankees who supported Hemenway's decision to enter the

Catholic Church, she could count on disapproval from just about everyone else. One St. Albans convert described being "harassed to death by people talking against the church and against me." She claimed the whole town had given her up "as one *blinded* by error" and described the Baptists in particular as harboring a bitter hatred of Catholics and "*very* strange ideas concerning them."[41]

A similar reaction in Ludlow probably greeted the news that Abby Hemenway had defected to the Catholic Church. Hemenway's friends and neighbors were unlikely to have had more than a superficial knowledge of Catholicism and that gleaned mostly from local newspapers. Curiosity at best and hostility at worst were the predictable responses. A deacon of the Baptist church of which Hemenway had been a member for most of her life is said to have told her mother that he would rather have lost his best yoke of oxen than her daughter from the fold, as she was "so full of zeal and helpfulness."[42] When Hemenway's official ties with the Baptist Church were severed on September 2, 1865, the church record book reported that a conversation between Deacon Howe and Deacon Batchelder and "Sister Abby Hemenway" gave "abundant evidence that she has withdrawn from the church by joining the Roman Catholic Church." Hemenway was then "excluded" from the Ludlow congregation, a sentence tantamount to excommunication. Had she defected to another Protestant sect she would simply have been "dismissed."[43]

According to one source, Hemenway shrank from wounding her family by even mentioning her desire to become a Catholic, but finally she had asked for her mother's permission, and Abigail Dana, seeing how deeply sincere she was, reluctantly consented. This account also describes the rest of the family as politely resigned to Abby's defection from Protestantism, claiming that "no rift of any sort occurred." By contrast, another source of family lore speaks of Abby's reputation as a "black sheep," tracing this to her decision to become a Catholic and her failure to marry.[44]

Perhaps each version of the Hemenway family's response contains a piece of the truth. Given Abigail Dana Hemenway's intimacy with her eldest daughter, she was the most likely member of the family to plead for tolerance and acceptance of Abby's newfound religion. However much the other Hemenways and Bartons may have disapproved, especially her father and Uncle Asa Barton, as long as Abby's mother was alive that kindly woman would have done her best to keep the peace. The timing of Abby's decision to enter the Roman Catholic Church may also have played a part in muting the initial reaction of family and friends. In the spring of 1864 most Vermonters were too absorbed by the horrors taking place on distant battlefields and too harassed by the exigencies of life on the home front to have much thought or concern for anything else.[45]

Having obtained her mother's permission to join the Catholic Church, Abby would then have sought out a member of the clergy to instruct her in church doctrine. Whether Bishop De Goesbriand or another priest took on this task is not known, but these instructions almost certainly took place in Burlington.

Then, in late April 1864, scarcely a month after deciding to become a Catholic, Abby Hemenway was baptized, taking the name of Marie Josephine. She received the sacrament in St. Joseph's Chapel, a tiny structure adjacent to St. Joseph's French church on North Prospect Street, one of the two Catholic parishes in the city of Burlington. Measuring only 20 feet by 10 feet, the chapel contained two minuscule altars as well as a profusion of statues and holy pictures. In this same cozy sanctuary, so different from the stark meetinghouses of her childhood, Abby attended her first mass the next morning and received her first Holy Communion. This was followed by a celebratory breakfast at the home of her sponsors, William and Anne Hoyt.[46]

In her play about Fanny Allen, Hemenway describes Allen's joy at the time of her baptism in words that surely echoed her own feelings that April day in 1864. "I cannot tell you," Allen informs her mother, "the consolations of the sacrament, when your poor child . . . knelt down to receive the sacred stream upon her brow, which fell upon her in almost sensible sweetness, and suddenly produced a serenity different in kind from anything she had ever before even had the power of conceiving!"[47]

Abby Hemenway never regretted her decision to enter the Roman Catholic Church. She remained a devout and loyal member until her death in 1890, her piety and devotion strengthening with the years. Only a deep commitment to her literary calling precluded her entering a religious order. But from the day of her baptism onward she wore nunlike attire: an austere dark dress, in the folds of which could be glimpsed a string of rosary beads.[48]

10

𝔖erbing 𝔗wo 𝔐otfers

———•◦✿◦•———

When we once come into the fold of Christ we
find everything so different from what we ever
dreamed of.

Abby Hemenway[1]

While the Hemenway house in Ludlow remained Abby's
home for the next two and a half years, the absence of
a Catholic church in town discouraged her from spending much
time there. Sometime during that last summer of the war she
journeyed north to Quebec on a pilgrimage to the Villa Maria
convent, the site of Fanny Allen's conversion to Catholicism.
Hemenway later described passing several happy days in this
quiet retreat. She particularly recalled the sweet pleasure of
waking each morning to the sound of the "early Mass bells in
distant Montreal."[2]

For the next two years, with the publication of the
Gazetteer at a standstill, Hemenway's future was in limbo. One

of the few certainties she could cling to was her new religion. Yet that, too, produced its own dislocations. Having crossed the great divide from Protestantism to Catholicism, Hemenway was now in effect branded by her new faith. In the eyes of her Ludlow friends and neighbors, many of whom had known her all her life, she was irrevocably altered, and these same friends and neighbors must have looked different to her as well. Her erstwhile parishioners in the First Baptist Church appeared as strangers; she was no longer one of them. If some remained friendly, many others shunned her for her apostasy.[3] And the Baptist meetinghouse, once her spiritual home, was now off-limits. Even if she had been welcomed there, Catholic canon law discouraged her from entering its doors.

In a letter to her uncle Asa Barton, written in 1869, Hemenway wrote of having pardoned her Ludlow subscribers to the *Gazetteer* for their "unprovoked enmity and malice." While she gave no explanation of the cause of this estrangement, a Barton descendant has suggested that the forgiveness Hemenway spoke of referred to the "bitter opposition" she encountered in her hometown following her conversion to Catholicism.[4]

Even in Burlington, despite its large Catholic population, Hemenway would have felt both ostracized and disoriented. In her play *Fanny Allen*, Hemenway invokes the horror Fanny's sisters feel when they learn she has become a Catholic. Caroline decries the "burning disgrace" Fanny has brought on the family. "How can we ever have it known in Burlington?" she asks. "Oh, I shall never want to appear in the street after it has been whispered around that our sister is Catholic." Caroline then asks Fanny how she can "go and kneel down in some Catholic meeting of the poor foreigners here, side by side with some shabby creature." Fanny replies that she would not be ashamed, "for Christ was never ashamed of the poor."[5]

These are brave words, though one wonders whether Hemenway's reference to the immigrant poor comes more from her own time than Fanny Allen's. At the time of Allen's conversion in 1807, Burlington was a small village, and even by 1815 probably no more than a hundred Catholics, mostly French Canadian, lived nearby.[6]

There is little doubt, however, that Hemenway herself noticed the sharp contrast between Baptist and Catholic congregations. Before her conversion, those with whom she had attended church on Sunday, if not personally known to her, had at least shared a similar heritage and culture. By contrast, the men and women who surrounded her in the pews at Catholic mass were, apart from a scattering of converts, mostly foreigners, recent immigrants from Ireland and Canada. Many were illiterate, most were poor, and few knew anything of Yankee ways and traditions.[7] Nor were the clergy much more in tune with American culture. At midcentury the vast majority of priests were foreign-born. They expected new converts to cast off their Protestant ways of thinking like so many old clothes and instantly assume the outlook of an orthodox Catholic.

While Hemenway adjusted herself to these unfamiliar hostilities and challenges, the Civil War raged on with no end in sight. That spring of 1864 the horror of the conflict came home to the Hemenway family when they learned that Daniel had been wounded on May 5 in the Battle of the Wilderness, the costliest day in the whole war for the state of Vermont. Fortunately, unlike many injured soldiers who died before they could be rescued from the thick scrub woods of the Wilderness, Daniel was found, treated, and sent home.

But the military stalemate continued all that long summer, filling Northerners on the home front with intense weariness and a longing for peace. In Vermont this spent mood was briefly shattered on the afternoon of October 19 when a gang of Confederates slipped over the border from Canada to raid the three banks in St. Albans and make off with more than $200,000. In the end fourteen of the raiders were apprehended and a good portion of the money was recovered. But, though the whole affair lasted only half an hour, it caused a statewide uproar. As a Burlington newspaper noted five days after the raid, "rumors of all sorts of coming horrors kept prudent people on the alert and nervous people in a state of chronic perspiration."[8]

Hemenway spent a good part of that summer and early fall putting the finishing touches on *The Mystical Rose*, which by October was ready for the press. In 1865 this life in poetry of the Virgin Mary would be published by Appleton & Co., a respectable New York house that thought enough of the book's prospects to print it on good heavy stock edged in glossy crimson. Measuring four-and-a-half by seven inches and bound in rich purple cloth covers, this handsome volume has today the look and feel of a prayer book.[9]

"Fervent" is the word that best describes *The Mystical Rose*. The enthusiastic piety so characteristic of new converts spills out onto almost every one of its nearly three hundred pages. Prayers and ejaculations abound, such as these lines from the invocation:

O, golden Rose of Paradise encrowned!
O, Mother of the sceptered Prince enthroned!
All beauty-floodings of earth, air, or sea,
Poured o'er my soul, I offer thee,
And lay my song-heart panting at thy feet.[10]

Fortunately, such effusions are offset in part by the grounding of the narrative in a wealth of sources, from ecclesiastical histories and Biblical dictionaries to the American writer Bayard Taylor's account of his travels in Syria and Palestine.

The central character of the work is the Virgin Mary, about whom, after all, little historical information exists. In the New Testament she is mentioned only nineteen times and nothing certain is known of her birth, her death, her parentage, or what she looked like. Thus, most of the traditional material that Hemenway drew on for *The Mystical Rose* is rooted in legend, passed down orally for centuries.[11]

The Virgin Mary in Hemenway's poem is a "glorified being, free from taste of weariness, or taint of pain."[12] The story begins with her birth to the elderly Joachim and Anna. The tender relationship young Mary shares with the latter calls to mind Hemenway's close intimacy with her own mother. The great passions of the poem are largely maternal ones. Even Joseph's feelings for Mary, his wife-to-be, show no trace of sexual longing. Rather, he loves and worships her as a saint. Mary, for her part, loves him "as the angels love / With a love more deep than the love of the flesh."[13]

After learning to his dismay that Mary is pregnant, Joseph is visited in his dreams by an angel who assures him that this is the work of God, not man:

Take her! take her! she is holy
Take, but touch not, take not wholly;
Let no breath of passion faintly,
Soil the lips so rapt and saintly;
Wife in name but pure evangel,
She can love but as thy angel;
She is woman sealed but tender
Let no wanton wish offend her;
High and pure her trust as Heaven,
Let such care in turn be given.[14]

The passion in Mary's heart is poured out not on her husband but on the child Jesus, miraculously born without a labor pang or trace of blood, a rarefied image when one considers the painful births most Vermont women of Hemenway's generation had witnessed if not experienced.

So moved was Hemenway by the image of this "freshly fair

first glimpse of God . . . nor cross, nor shadow yet, only the 'Child,'" that she found it hard at first to depict the sublimity of the birth scene. If she wrote it once, she wrote it three times, she tells her readers, explaining that "where one wants words of heaven, and has but earth's, the picture comes out slow, and holds at best the difference between the glory of a thought unspoken and [one] wrote." The intensity of Hemenway's own emotions reaches a crescendo as she describes how Mary, holding the baby to her breast for the first time, "feels the heart of God beat back to hers, and in her transport kisses him a thousand times," crying out to him, "Kiss me with the kisses of thy mouth, for thy love is sweeter than wine!"[15]

Implicitly erotic as this image appears to the modern reader, for Hemenway, who was attempting to convey the fervor of a mystical experience, such erotic language seemed appropriate. This ardent woman, nurtured in New England's austere Protestant climate and culture, was only too ready to lose herself in the sensual imagery found in so much of the pious literature of the Catholic Church. Perhaps, too, the rendering of this birth scene brought home to Hemenway the implications of her own childlessness. She had taken a different path from most women, and like the Blessed Virgin had eschewed the pains of motherhood, but unlike Mary she had also renounced its joys. She would never share with her own child the intimacy she had known with Abigail Dana Hemenway. Instead she must find solace and comfort in the imagined closeness between the Virgin and her son, the infant Jesus.

Although the birth scene in the *The Mystical Rose* has a biblical foundation, many of the other events in the poem do not. The account of the extraordinary light that appeared the night the Virgin Mary was born is, Hemenway tells us in a footnote, based on the oriental writers' tradition of ushering in the births of distinguished persons to the accompaniment of "supernatural aurora." She admits to having given serious thought to the appropriateness of including "this and kindred traditionary embellishments." But in the end she concluded that such "remote testimonies" and "traditional stories" would only enhance the reception of her book by "the curious, the liberal, and the candid" reader. A similar instinct prompted her to charge her *Gazetteer* historians to enrich their town histories with legendary lore.[16]

In her account of Jesus' public life, death, and resurrection Hemenway stays reasonably true to the Gospels and official Catholic teaching. But other incidents in Mary's life rely wholly on tradition enriched by Hemenway's fervent imagination. The Virgin's death, for example, occurs not at Ephesus nor in Jerusalem, as in most accounts, but on the Greek island of Patmos, in a fisherman's hut belonging to Jesus' disciple John. As John and Mary Magdalene watch by Mary's bedside bathed in "moonbeams pale, cloud-like and still," the Virgin is carried up to heaven where she enjoys a reunion with her parents, Joachim and Anna, and her husband Joseph. But no account is given of Mary's meeting with her son Jesus. As Hemenway explains: "The glories of his PARADISE / No mortal heart may know, or attempt to describe."[17]

While *The Mystical Rose* received little or no attention in Vermont newspapers, it did get favorably noticed in the Catholic press, and would later provide Hemenway with an entrée into Catholic literary circles. Over the course of the next decade she wrote two more books in the same vein. A second volume, *Rosa Immaculata or the Tower of Ivory in the House of Anna and Joachim*, published in 1867, recounts the life of the Virgin Mary from her birth to the incarnation, adding richly imagined vignettes of her saintly parents. The third and last volume, *The House of Gold and the Saint of Nazareth. A Poetical Life of St. Joseph*, came out in 1873 and is essentially more of the same. Neither of these accounts adds much to what

Lydia, Abby, and Carrie Hemenway, c. 1865.
(Permission David Hemenway.)

had already been written. As Frances Babb succinctly notes in her dismissal of both these later poetic works, Hemenway "wrote herself out in her first volume and then continued to write two more books on an already exhausted subject."[18]

Hemenway's transports of religious ecstasy and her absorption in poetic visions of a distant world did not stop her from paying attention to more mundane matters. In September 1864 she sold a piece of land she owned not far from her parents' house in Ludlow. The 1½-acre parcel had been bought in 1862 with a loan of $600 from Abby's brother Charles, who may have looked upon it as an investment in his sister's future. She made a handsome profit selling the piece in 1864 for $970, and, after paying her brother back in full, she pocketed the remainder. Perhaps this $370 helped to pay off old debts incurred while publishing the *Gazetteer* or provided a much-needed financial cushion while she looked around for gainful employment. Her sale of the parcel within six months of her entry into the Catholic Church suggests further that she was already cutting ties to her hometown, if not to her family.[19] On December 24, for example, she was in Burlington enjoying her first "happy Christmas Eve" as a Catholic by attending midnight mass.[20]

A few months later, on April 9, 1865, the bloodiest war in the nation's history came to an end. That very day, even before the news of Lee's surrender at Appomattox Court House had reached Vermont, the Reverend A. Stevens, pastor of the Congregational church in Westminster West, preached a victory sermon, which Hemenway later published in her *Gazetteer*. Although she normally discouraged her historians from including homilies in their town histories, this sermon, preached while the bells celebrating the rebel defeat at Richmond were still ringing, evoked for her with particular clarity "how the people of Vermont had received the end of the war."

"The nation is frantic with joy," Stevens declared in his opening words. "The merchant forgets his sales; the mechanic and farmer their work. . . . Eloquence, poetry, piety, patriotism and humanity are stirred everywhere, and speak the best they can, the unbounded joy of the nation." But, he reminded his congregation, the war, every agonizing moment of it, had been necessary. A government whose cornerstone was "laid in slavery" deserved to be crushed, and "God had to write it out in blood, before we [the North] could see the self-evident truth—slavery is a sin." Only now that the slave power has been crushed, Stevens told his flock, is it appropriate that "joy fill the land at its fall—that demonstrations be loud and far spread, clothed with piety, adorned with poetry, fired with eloquence and made wild with enthusiasm so that every citizen can give utterance to the sentiments of a freeman's heart."[21]

While some people in Vermont shared the strong antislavery sentiments of this sermon, many did not, men and women who simply felt relief that the war was over and that they could now get on with their lives. But Stevens's words spoke directly to Hemenway's personal response to the Union victory; they articulated sentiments that she believed, whether rightly or wrongly, were shared by the entire state.

The coming of peace found Abby Hemenway at age thirty-six still without a settled future, and as yet no prospect of resuming the editorship of the *Gazetteer*. For the past seven years she had lived and worked under her parents' roof, enjoying the privacy of her own room, the comfort of her mother's presence, and no worries about food or shelter. But her new religion had changed all that. Now she needed a Catholic church close by where she could attend mass and receive the sacraments. There was none in Ludlow and this meant she would have to leave home and find a way to support herself.

A woman living alone, apart from her family, was an anomaly in nineteenth-century America. Since few jobs provided single women with suitably respectable, well-paid work, most were obliged to live with their parents or some other family member. Mary A. Dodge, a successful journalist, wrote in 1864 that she needed $600 a year to live comfortably on her own.[22] But how was Abby Hemenway to earn such an income? Her editorship of the *Gazetteer* may have been her vocation, but it had kept her perpetually in debt. Even if she returned to teaching she was unlikely to make enough to live independently.

If Hemenway struggled with her future as a single Catholic woman, she was not alone. According to Patrick Allitt, most women converts who had entered the church out of religious conviction suddenly found themselves in a community "that shared a range of ideas and beliefs on many other issues quite at odds with their own."[23] For example, the Catholic clergy were if anything more uncomfortable than their Protestant counterparts with the self-sufficient single woman. Submissiveness in women, either to their husbands or to monastic rule, was encouraged, and Hemenway is likely to have been pressured by Bishop De Goesbriand and the priests she knew in Burlington either to marry a good Catholic or enter a convent.[24]

But the reality of Hemenway's life, that of an independent literary woman, did not fit very comfortably with these Catholic ideals. As editor of the *Gazetteer* she had grown used to far more autonomy than most nineteenth-century women had dreamed of, much less enjoyed. For seven years she had been her own boss, directing and managing her own publishing enterprise. To throw all this over in favor of marriage or the religious life amounted to denying that her literary calling was God-given. Hemenway's activities during the two and a half years following her entry into the church suggest that she was not about to forsake either her literary career or her independence. Instead, she set about looking for a suitable niche for herself in the world of American Catholic letters, a world that in the middle of the nineteenth century was largely dominated by converts like herself.[25]

The publication of *The Mystical Rose* introduced Hemenway to this new world, and with the coming of peace in the spring of 1865 she left Vermont on what we today would call a job search. Early in May she boarded a train for the start of a four-month tour that carried her, among other places, to

Chicago and Boston, cities boasting large Catholic populations. Her first stop on this tour was South Bend, Indiana, the site of a small Catholic college, Notre Dame, founded in 1844.

Hemenway's timing was propitious, for the very month of her arrival at Notre Dame witnessed the publication of a new Catholic weekly, *Ave Maria*, "devoted to the honor of the Blessed Virgin." The introductory issue even contained a poem of Hemenway's, "Our First Annunciation Day," and identified her as the "authoress of the 'Mystical Rose'" whose "happy sequel" was her entry into the Catholic Church.[26]

While the head of Notre Dame, Father Edward Sorin, took principal credit for the publication of *Ave Maria*, its de facto editor was Mother Angela Gillespie, founder of the Sisters of the Holy Cross, one of the leading teaching orders in the United States. When Hemenway first met Mother Angela this formidable woman had just returned from successfully managing a large military hospital in Mound City, Illinois. She had since resumed her duties as superior of St. Mary's convent and principal of St Mary's Academy, both of which stood on a hillside not far from the men's college campus. Thanks to Mother Angela's insistence on high academic standards, St. Mary's was one of the best Catholic schools for girls to be found anywhere in the country.[27]

Frances Babb has suggested that Father Sorin or Mother Angela put Hemenway in charge of the children's department of *Ave Maria*. While there is no evidence connecting her to the magazine's editorial staff, for the next decade or so her religious poetry did appear now and again on its pages. Also, beginning in September 1865, she contributed a children's column to the weekly. These letters from "Marie Josephine" (Hemenway's baptismal name) to "Dear Children" began by describing their author's summer travels and continued with a lengthy account of Fanny Allen's childhood vision of St. Joseph.[28]

During her stay in South Bend, Hemenway lived at the convent with the Holy Cross sisters, sharing their meals and

UNIVERSITY OF NOTRE DAME, IND.
FOUNDED 1842, CHARTERED 1844.

An engraving of the Notre Dame Campus and
Sacred Heart Church, c. 1866.
(Permission Notre Dame Archives.)

prayers. This lively community of Catholic women seems to have agreed with her, for she lengthened her visit from one month to two. Some years later a fellow boarder at St. Mary's, Flora Stanfield, remembered the long talks she and Hemenway had shared during their weeks there together. Stanfield did not think Miss Hemenway could write poetry but did think her "a most interesting woman" and she wondered if this recent Catholic convert had ever "relapsed into Protestantism."[29] On July 7, Hemenway's last morning at St. Mary's, she awoke early, feeling overcome with sadness at the thought of leaving. After attending mass at 5:30 she spent the next few hours wandering through a grove filled with holy shrines, stopping at each one with her prayers, petitions, and "adieus."[30]

Hemenway's next destination was Chicago, where she spent a month with her brother Horace (a train conductor), who was living there with his wife, Mary, and their small daughter, whom Abby dubbed her "lilybud niece." But Hemenway spent much of her time in this sprawling midwestern city visiting churches and meeting members of the clergy and other Catholics.

She described this visit to Chicago in one of her early columns for *Ave Maria*'s young readers, which she began writing soon after her return home to Vermont that fall. This column points up how her taste in architecture tended toward the ornate. The more cluttered these edifices were with carvings and holy pictures, the better she liked them. Among her favorites of the seven churches she visited were the Church of the Holy Family, the most expensive and presumably the most elaborate, and the Church of Saint Patrick, where "cherub heads thick as stars" peered down into the sanctuary.[31]

A high point of Hemenway's Chicago stay was the visit she paid to a fellow convert and art teacher, Eliza Allen Starr. Close in age, the two women had much in common beyond their shared Catholicism. Both were single and came from old New England families who had encouraged them to lead creative and independent lives. Starr's move to Chicago in 1856 had followed her conversion to Catholicism. When Hemenway met her nine years later, she was earning her living as a successful art teacher and had acquired a distinctive place in that city's cultural life.[32]

In her *Ave Maria* column Hemenway gave her young readers a tour of Eliza Starr's small house, from the studio filled with plaster casts to the parlor with its "Gothic chair" and "cozy sofa," its "what-not" containing "numerous holy mementos," its walls thickly covered with pictures of "the dear, olden, quaint saints." But Hemenway's favorite room was the bedroom. "I never wanted a room so much in my life," she admitted after describing

the little bed with snowy cover—over its head a Saint Joseph by one of the old painters, and a black crucifix; at its foot is the little oratory, or a little stand with the tiniest vase of fresh flowers, where a little spirit-lamp burns before a picture of the Sacred Heart, and a small image of the crucifixion on the wall behind.[33]

Eliza Allen Starr was living exactly the way Hemenway herself wanted to live, and visiting this modest but cozy house with its ample work space, pious furnishings, and virginal white bed was like walking into a dream. Here was a gifted and respected single Catholic woman composing her own life in the young industrial city of Chicago and succeeding at it.

Chicago was not the answer to Hemenway's prayers, however. Her stay there ended sometime in August when once again she boarded a train, this time for the long journey east. But instead of returning directly to Vermont she went first to Boston, where she stayed with friends and spent her days visiting churches and other Catholic institutions, including the offices of the diocesan newspaper, the *Pilot*.

Hemenway also toured Boston College, run by the Jesuits. There, as she told it in her children's column, she was received kindly by "the good Fathers," one of whom took her to visit an orphan asylum run by the Sisters of Charity. The two were "shown over the whole establishment from basement storerooms and kitchen, to the upper dormitories" where the more than two hundred girls slept. She saw the quilts the orphans had made and the bread they had baked and wrote admiringly of their apparent contentment, orderliness, and good behavior. "Here was a lesson for us," she told her young readers, "of Catholic charity" and its superiority to that employed by the Protestants in New England who "usually leave their pauper-children to the fate of a common poor-house. . . . Did we not almost wish at the time, to be one of those dark robed, white hooded Sisters of Charity, feeding, clothing, sheltering, teaching and leading heavenward the destitute little lambs of their fold, or one of those dear little lambs being led?"[34]

After a week or so in Boston, Hemenway took the train back to Vermont, arriving in Ludlow to find a late summer heatwave baking the little town nestled among the green hills. The clocks in the church towers were striking noon as she stepped onto the familiar platform, and leaving her luggage to be delivered, she chose to walk the few short blocks home. Rounding the corner leading from Pleasant Street to Brook Road, she observed how the shutters of her family's brown cottage were closed against the hot sun. The tree-shaded house looked very welcoming, but she had no sooner reached the gate when her niece Alvaretta rushed out with the news that "Grandma is sick." Passing quickly into the house, through the little sitting room, Abby entered her mother's room. At the sight of her eldest daughter, Abigail Dana Hemenway rose up in her bed, threw her arms around Abby, and with evident relief exclaimed, "My dear child, I had like to die, and you not here! Thank God for bringing you back to me!"[35]

With her daughter safely home, Abigail Dana mended quickly from her illness, leaving Abby restless and anxious to return to that "blessed place," Burlington. As long as her mother lived, Hemenway's conscience and her affections continued to pull her in two directions: toward her earthly mother in Ludlow and the Holy Mother Church in Burlington.

Then, on October 2, 1866, a little more than a year after Abby returned from the Midwest, Abigail Dana Hemenway suddenly and unexpectedly died. No record explains the cause of her death, but the sorrow it occasioned was devastating. Daniel Hemenway, for one, never recovered. He lived for three years in deep mourning for his wife, then he, too, died.

For Abby, the loss was also devastating. No single person had been dearer to her than her mother. Yet the misery she suffered must largely be imagined since only two mentions of her mother's death survive. One is an obituary she wrote, presumably for a local newspaper. After admitting that "our heart is too sorrowful to sing the requiem so appropriately her due," she acknowledges that she cannot "leave to another hand" what she knows her mother would have chosen from hers. Following a brief and rather prosaic life history, the obituary concludes with one of Abigail Dana's poems, that "she may sing her own requiem."[36]

"When We're Gone" is a gentle, self-effacing dirge in which Abigail Dana Hemenway minimizes the impact her death will have on the world around her. As she writes in the last verse:

The flowers, the trees, the grand, old hills—
    The years still gliding on—
Will smile back to the guardian stars,
    As bright when we are gone.

In contrast to these modest verses with their pantheistic view of dying as a simple, natural event, is an elegy Hemenway wrote in 1886 on the twentieth anniversary of her mother's death. "My Relic Box" conveys the enduring pain of this loss by describing a small coffer she lovingly treasured for two decades, its contents a thin piece of muslin and some withered flowers. These, the poem tells us, had lain in Abigail Dana's open coffin until her burial. "Oh, I cannot part with it yet," Abby writes of the relic box, "but yet it stabs / My heart always to see."[37]

Following Abigail Dana Hemenway's death, nothing, not even the presence of her grief-stricken father, kept Abby in Ludlow. Only the mothering arms of the church could console this daughter for the loss of her earthly mother. Seeking the solace of the Catholic community in Burlington, she headed north, this time for good. For the next twelve years the bustling little city on the shores of Lake Champlain would be home.

11

New Beginnings

———•◦◊◦•———

Your history of our mountain State
Although commenced some years too late
. . . .
Will furnish facts, tho' some are lost,
That richly pay the trifling cost.

S. H. Tupper[1]

When Abby Hemenway moved to Burlington in 1866 a postwar boom was in full swing. This port city with its commanding view across Lake Champlain to the distant Adirondacks was benefiting from its location on a body of water that since midcentury had become a major artery for interstate commerce. Its convenience as a junction of railroad and water routes gave Burlington an advantage over other lakeside Vermont towns, as did the abundance of cheap immigrant labor that filled its dockside tenements. In these years the booming lumber business chiefly contributed to the Queen City's prosperity. As early as 1860 40 million feet of board annually had passed through Burlington on its way from

Canada to ports as distant as South America and the Pacific Islands. By 1873, the peak year for the city's lumber trade, that number would reach 170 million.[2]

Summer visitors to Burlington took note of the contrast between the urban blight overspreading the densely packed streets near the waterfront and the lush greenness of the tree-shaded hillside above. The young novelist Henry James spent an hour strolling about the town one August day in 1870. He described the shoreline as "savagely raw and shabby," but "as it [the city] ascends the long hill, which it partly covers, it gradually becomes the most truly charming, I fancy, of New England country towns."[3]

At first Hemenway regarded her move to Burlington as temporary. A "situation" had been offered to her in Indiana beginning in May 1867. What this "situation" was she did not say, but she was probably desperate enough at this point to try anything that promised her a living.[4] Meanwhile, the only address we have for her during these last months of 1866 is St. Joseph's Convent on North Prospect Street. Such religious houses, as she had learned from her stay at St. Mary's in South Bend, offered inexpensive and genteel accommodations for single women, while providing the companionship of a Catholic community.[5]

Wherever she lived during this time, Hemenway kept herself occupied by composing her second volume of religious poetry, *Rosa Immaculata, or the Tower of Ivory*, a recounting of the early life of the Virgin Mary. As she admits in the preface, it was written "for the most part during the first months of a sore bereavement, working for the Heavenly Mother to ease our sorrow for the earthly one; and it is born more of the heart than of the head, and we have not perhaps pruned it as we would in a stronger day." But if the intense feeling that Hemenway poured into these pious verses did not produce particularly good poetry, writing them served as a creative outlet for her abundant energies. Completed in December 1866, *Rosa Immaculata* was brought out the following year by P. O'Shea, a Catholic publishing house in Philadelphia.

After mass one Sunday at St. Mary's, Hemenway was introduced to Lydia Clarke Meech, a sprightly eighty-year-old widow who lived in Burlington with her son, DeWitt Clinton Clarke. Lydia Meech's name, if not her face, would have been familiar. Her second husband, Ezra Meech, had been well known throughout the state. This wealthy gentleman farmer from Shelburne had enjoyed a notable political career, beginning in 1805 when he had represented Charlotte in the General Assembly. In the 1820s he served two terms in Congress with one in between as a Chittenden County judge.[6]

The timing of this initial encounter between Abby Hemenway and Lydia Meech was fortuitous for both. The younger woman needed a home, at least for the winter, and the elder needed a companion. DeWitt's wife, Caroline, had died the spring before, leaving his mother on her own much of the time. Thus, as soon as Lydia Meech learned that her new acquaintance had no permanent home in Burlington, she arranged to have Hemenway board with her.

Lydia Clarke Meech had been quite a belle in her youth. In the 1820s, during Ezra Meech's second term in Congress, Daniel Webster is said to have frequently chosen her for his partner at cards and was several times overheard saying that he thought her the most splendid woman in Washington. Although Lydia had spent much of the remainder of her married life with Ezra on his farm in Shelburne, she had never gotten along very well with his children, particularly his eldest son, Ezra Junior. When Ezra Senior died in 1856 and the son learned that Lydia Meech had been left a life interest in the Shelburne house, he not only contested the will but made matters so disagreeable for his stepmother that in 1857 she decided to leave the farm in Shelburne and move to Burlington to live with the son of her first marriage, DeWitt Clinton Clarke, and his wife, Caroline.[7]

Lydia's first husband, Asahel Clarke, a native of Mt. Holly, had carried on a successful law practice in Glens Falls, New York, until his death of typhoid fever. A legal adviser and good friend of the governor of New York, DeWitt Clinton, Asahel named his second son after him. When Hemenway first knew DeWitt Clinton Clarke—who like his mother was a Catholic— he was prominent in Vermont newspaper and political circles, and was serving as executive clerk of the U.S. Senate. A genial, kindly man in his late fifties, DeWitt was reputedly a witty conversationalist who laced his talk with a limitless supply of jokes and stories.[8]

Upon seeing Lydia Meech for the first time that Sunday in St. Mary's Church, Hemenway was struck by the close resemblance the older woman bore to her son DeWitt, how, despite her advanced years, she had the "same carriage and step, ready, springy, self-exultant."[9]

As Hemenway later learned, Lydia Meech's first summer as a Catholic had been a trying one. If DeWitt welcomed his mother's conversion, her other relatives and many of her friends did not. The threat of ostracism by the elite Protestant circles she moved in had long held her back from entering the church, and when a favorite niece, Sophia Freeman, came to keep her company during the summer of 1866, Lydia's deepest fears were realized. No sooner had the younger woman arrived in the house than she set to work to wean Lydia Meech away from the Catholic Church. As Lydia later told Abby, Sophia "made a great deal of unhappiness for me that summer, trying to turn me back herself, and inducing others to come in and try. . . . She railed about the bishops and priests and DeWitt and all Catholics." When Catholic friends came to call, Sophia "contrived in some way to make it so disagreeable for them and for me" that they soon stopped coming.[10]

Sophia remained with Lydia Meech for four months.

Although she made her aunt's life "perfectly wretched," the niece ultimately failed to persuade this elderly but feisty woman to renounce her chosen religion. When Sophia finally declared that she was leaving to stay with her wealthy sister in Buffalo, her aunt was glad enough to be rid of the persecution, but she worried about spending the winter alone. "Providence sent you to me," Lydia later told Abby; "you were the best Christmas gift I ever had."[11]

The Meech house, a large frame dwelling on Pearl Street, just east of Church Street, stood on two acres of land. The ground floor included a sitting room that also served as a dining room. There over the mantel above the stove hung a portrait of Asahel Clarke. Lydia's bedroom opened off this room. In addition, the downstairs contained a bathroom, kitchen, and two parlors. Abby's and DeWitt's rooms were upstairs. Almost as soon as Abby moved in, Lydia began persuading her new boarder to make the Meech house her home, and what started as a temporary expedient was soon accepted as permanent. Hemenway would live with this new friend until 1874, when the elder woman died at the age of eighty-eight.[12]

From the start, Lydia Meech treated her new boarder like her own child. As Hemenway later recalled, "I had buried my own mother but a short time before I came to her. She [Lydia Meech] put her arms around me and took her place." Both women quickly settled into a comfortable routine, which included saying prayers together twice a day. No further mention was made of the position Hemenway had been offered in Indiana.[13]

The deep friendship between these two women owed much to their shared Catholicism, an intimate bond that drew them together even as it divided them from their Protestant origins. For, as Jenny Franchot points out about other American converts, Abby Hemenway and Lydia Meech found themselves looking out on the familiar but erring Protestant world from the redemptive but unfamiliar enclosure of their newly accepted Catholic beliefs. Together with such one-time Protestants as the Hoyts they made up a small and rarefied group, a band of outcasts who comforted and consoled one another.[14]

Hemenway inserted sketches of a number of these outcasts in the pages of her *Gazetteer*, including three young women who died of tuberculosis. Particularly noteworthy in Hemenway's account of these young Catholics is their effort to deliberately distance themselves from worldly affairs and thus from the society of many of their Vermont contemporaries. One sketch tells of two sisters, Frances and Sarah Smith. A few weeks before their death, one of their Protestant friends who was engaged to be married came to show off her trousseau. Frances and Sarah "looked at the rich dress-stuffs, the beautiful lace work, the lovely flowers. They pronounced everything very pretty, very pretty, beautiful! It was sweet," Hemenway tells us, "to see what an artless interest they took in it all." But when they had examined everything, Frances turned to Sarah saying, "we wouldn't exchange with her for the world would we?" "Oh no!" replied Sarah.[15]

Cynthia Smalley was apparently equally disdainful of worldly matters. The daughter of the writer Julia Smalley, Cynthia refused to read *Harper's Magazine*. By Hemenway's account, when Cynthia was asked why she avoided such amusing, harmless, and elegant reading matter, she replied that Jesus had given her "a pearl of great price to keep, it is very bright now, but it is of such delicacy the least breath contrary to it may dim its luster, and I want to keep it to carry to Him." Cynthia Smalley and the two Smith sisters had apparently all made vows of chastity. Hemenway's nunlike attire suggests that she, too, made a similar vow at the time of her baptism, and her undisguised admiration for these angelic invalids reveals her own striving for purity and perfection as a single Catholic woman.

When Abby Hemenway and Lydia Meech embraced Catholicism they joined a church that was experiencing a dramatic influx of new members, mostly poor immigrants who poured into Burlington from Ireland and Canada. In 1867 Roman Catholics made up slightly less than half of Burlington's entire churchgoing population. On a given Sunday, three thousand people could be seen crowding into the pews at both St. Mary's and St. Joseph's.[16] In an effort to ease this congestion, the diocese was building a new St. Mary's, destined to be the first Catholic cathedral erected in New England.

On Sunday, September 29, 1867, the stone Gothic Cathedral of the Immaculate Conception opened for religious services. The previous Thursday, bonfires and a torchlight procession had greeted Bishop De Goesbriand on his return from a trip to Rome. If Hemenway was not among the throng welcoming the bishop, as a devout Catholic she would not have missed the thanksgiving service held that evening in old St. Mary's and the first mass celebrated in the new cathedral the following Sunday. The ornate interior of the latter matched Hemenway's taste for rich decor, with its rows of tall marble columns clouded with a tint of blue, and its groined arches pointing to a ceiling of deeper blue decorated with brightly colored figures of the saints. A particularly striking feature of the new building was its stained-glass windows, especially the large, central one depicting the Last Judgment.[17]

The most impressive liturgy marking the opening of the new cathedral occurred at the consecration two months later, on December 8, the Feast of the Immaculate Conception.[18] The bitter cold early winter day did not prevent more than a thousand people from attending what the Burlington *Free Press* described as "the peculiar and imposing ceremonies of the Catholic Church."[19]

Abby Hemenway's wholehearted participation in Catholic liturgical life is underscored in a letter she wrote to her youngest sister, Carrie, on March 22, 1867. She began by describing the recent St. Patrick's Day procession, how the participants had marched through the streets of Burlington and into St. Mary's Church, waving banners to the accompaniment of rousing patriotic harmonies from the Hinesburg band. "It takes Irishmen [and] St. Patrick's Day, to wave flags to music," Abby assured her sister. Yet more to her taste was the French mass she attended the following morning at St. Joseph's, which celebrated with less fanfare the feast day of its patron saint.

This same letter to Carrie also conveyed the tantalizing news that Abby, who would turn forty years old the following October, had been receiving proposals of marriage from a Methodist minister. "He has shown himself somewhat persevering, considering I have not ever given him the least encouragement," she told her sister. The lovelorn clergyman, whom Abby doesn't bother to name, had sweetened his offer by promising that he would not ask her to go against her conscience "in religious matters," that he would help her with the *Gazetteer*, and "try to make it a splendid success." But neither of these promises had their desired effect. Instead Abby tried to pawn this clerical suitor off on her sister. "I have no doubt about his liking you," she quipped, adding that she thought the minister would make Carrie "a kind and excellent husband—May I mention you?" she asked, and then moved on to a discussion of the delightful weather and the celebration of the Feast of the Annunciation the following Monday. The day would mark the third anniversary of her reception into the Catholic Church, which, she assured Carrie, was the "happiest and best step" she had ever taken.[20]

Carrie's only known husband was not a minister but a military man, Captain Lemuel H. Page of Brandon, whom she married in 1873, so she apparently did not take her sister up on her offer. Nor does Abby make further mention of this clerical admirer or any other suitor. As a Catholic she would have resisted even considering the minister's proposal, because mixed marriages required special dispensations with strict conditions attached. In any case, even without these obstacles, Hemenway was unlikely to have taken these marriage proposals with any seriousness. By the spring of 1867 the various pieces of her life had finally fallen into place. She had a new mother and a new home, and this measure of stability allowed Hemenway to resume her work as editor of the *Gazetteer*.

The exact status of this work during the long hiatus between the appearance of the sixth number of the *Quarterly* in August 1863 and resumption of publication five years later in August 1868 remains unknown. When work was halted in 1863, five additional issues of the magazine, besides the six already published, had been set into type. J. Munsell, Hemenway's printer in Albany, had been sitting on them ever since. All she needed, apparently, was sufficient money to pay off her debts to the firm, and the remaining town histories of Chittenden County, together with those of Essex County, could be published.[21]

While these five issues were finally in print by the late summer of 1867, how the debts to Munsell were paid remains a mystery. Lydia Meech, with only a small annuity from her late husband's estate, had no money to lend her companion.[22] Yet somehow the editor of the *Gazetteer* obtained sufficient funds to satisfy the printer, either from loans or gifts, and numbers seven to eleven of the *Quarterly* were issued that August. At the same time she printed and circulated a flyer announcing the publication of volume I of the *Vermont Historical Gazetteer* containing all the issues published thus far: the town histories of Addison, Bennington, Caledonia, Chittenden, and Essex Counties. This same flyer revealed the editor's renewed optimism by announcing the imminent publication of volumes II and III, slated to contain the town histories of the remaining eight counties. To make up for lost time, Hemenway had plunged into her editorial labors with renewed vigor. The next ten years would prove the most productive of her career.[23]

Miss Hemenway
wrote her
about Aug 12 '76

CONTENTS

OF

VOL. III,

Vermont Historical Gazetteer.

COMPLETE IN FOUR VOLUMES.

Price per vol., Paper, $5.00 ; Cloth, $6.00 ; Half Turkey, 7.00.

Vol. III., Royal 8 vo., 1200 pages, opens with a completion of the Index of vol. II., followed by an extensive County chapter for Orleans Co., by the late Rev. P. H. White, late Hon. B. H. Steele, Hon. E. A. Stewart, Rev. S. R. Hall, L. L. D., followed by the particular histories of each town in Orleans County, the history of Coventry and four other towns written by Rev. P. H. White. It has also a steel *portrait*, (engraved especially for the vol.,) and a biographical sketch of the Rev. P. H. White. The whole county is extensively done. Among the contributors of town history, church history and biography, are Rev. J. P. Stone, Rev. S. R. Hall, Judge Stewart, H. A. Cutting, M. D., State Geologist.

RUTLAND COUNTY.

Commencing with page 403, fills the remainder of the volume, over 800 pages. The Hon. Hiland Hall contributes THE INTRODUCTORY COUNTY CHAPTER of " RUT-LAND COUNTY IN THE NEW YORK CONTROVERSY. The histories of the town being furnished by; BENSON, the late Hon. Loyal C. Kellogg (very complete) BRAN-DON, the late Dr. A. G. Dana with portrait (with sketches of over a hundred of the first settlers—with church histories, by Dea. Davenport, Rev. Mr. Tuxbury, Rev. C. A. Thomas, D. D., the late Rev. B. D. Ames and the late J. E. Higgins, biograph-ical and papers on business, by George Briggs, Esq.; H. M. Mott, Editor, John A. Conant, Esq., Hon. N. T. Sprague; Account of the Brandon Frozen Well, by A. D. Hager, Past State Geologist and other papers, by others; CASTLETON, by the late Rev. Joseph Steele, the Cong. pastor there for 40 years, the Rev. Mr. Higley and others; CHITTENDEN, by H. F. Baird; CLARENDON, (which was called " The Old Tory Green Mountain Boy times) by H. B. Spofford,—Gov. Hall has seen the proofs, and pronounces the history very good. (DANBY, J. C. Williams, Esq., extensive.) Fairhaven. by A. N. Adams, extensive; all in his published book and more; HUBBARDTON. good, by Amos Churchill, who died at the age of 93, pre-pared and arranged by E. H. St. John; IRA, Bradley Fish, Esq.; MENDON, Mrs. Anna Bourn (a remarkably smart old lady historian); MIDDLETOWN, Rev. Barnes Frisbie, all in his published book and more; MT. HOLLY, Dr. John Crowley; Biographical sketch of Eld. Daniel Parker, by his daughter, Mrs. Sarahette P. Bull; MT. TABOR, by Gideon S. Tabor, Esq.; PAWLET, Hiel Hollister, (often called by our readers, the model town history.) PITTSFIELD, W. R. Blossom. PITTSFORD, Dr. A. M. Caverly, con-densed from his published book and by others. POULTNEY, Henry Clark, Esq.; The Papers of Elias Ashley and others. RUTLAND, Centennial Celebration, by Chauncey K. Williams, Esq., the town and County published historical papers of Henry Hall, Esq.; Church histories, by Williams and Revs. E. Wells, B. M. Hall, and Bishop De Goesbriand, with biographical sketches of and from—REV. SYLVANUS Haynes, the old pastor of West Rutland, by L. L. Dutcher, St. Albans, with anec-dotes, by Rev. Pliny White; REV. BENAJAH ROOTS, first pastor of East Rutland, Rev. A. Walker, D. D., REV. SAMUEL WILLIAMS, LL. D., by Hon. E. P Walton, GEN. HOPKINS, by Mrs. Hopkins; HON. ROBERT PIERPONT, from the Family; DR. PORTER, by the late Gen. Hopkins; COL. W. Y. RIPLEY, by Mrs. J. C. R. Dorr, Biograpical Sketches and Poems, from Prof. James Davie Batler, &c., &c.; RUT-LAND MARBLES AND MANUFACTURES, E. W. Redington, Esq.; RUTLAND AND BURLINGTON RAILROAD HISTORY, etc., etc.; SHERBURNE, Hon. D. T. Taylor; SHREWSBURY, C. W. Hemenway, (brother of the histographer, Miss H.) SUDBURY, Pliny Holmes, Esq.; WALLINGFORD, Rev. H. H. Saunderson, (now engaged on an extensive History of Charlestown, N. H.) Mr. Saunderson's Wallingford, particu-larly good; WELLS, A. C. Hopson.

Three portraits have been engaged for this volume—and a large number more are being negotiated for which it is expected will be added immediately.

The volume will positively appear by or before the first of August. The proof *last* has been read of the last town. We are now at work on a closing Military Chap-ter. The Editress was so fortunate as to secure from the antiquarian collections of Henry Stevens, a complete list of all the Revolutionary officers and soldiers from Rutland County, etc—Henry Clark says, this paper alone is worth all the rest of the papers from Rutland County. Chauncey K. Williams has said the same.

Gentlemen of Rutland County, give us what help you can to help meet the issue of the volume.

CLAREMONT MANUFACTURING CO., Publishers.

Broadside announcing the publication of Volume III of the *Vermont Historical Gazetteer.* Note the number of authors who contributed to this volume, published in 1876. Note too Hemenway's occasional asides. (From the collections of the Vermont Historical Society.)

The months following the publication of volume I of the *Vermont Historical Gazetteer*, with its eleven hundred double-column pages of Vermont history, established Abby Hemenway's reputation as its editor. Up until that time the half dozen issues of the *Quarterly* had appeared too sporadically to inspire much confidence in her ability to complete the work.[24] But the publication of so many issues of the *Quarterly* under one cover restored the faith of Hemenway's readers. On August 22, 1868, the Burlington *Free Press* carried a lengthy notice of volume I expressing satisfaction and relief at the *Gazetteer's* renewed publication. "We thought it possible that the enterprise had been abandoned," the paper acknowledged. After describing the *Gazetteer* as "a great repository of historical facts," the notice reminded Vermonters of their "lasting debt of gratitude to the persistent and laborious editor, who has spared neither time nor pains to make the collection reasonably full and accurate." The *Free Press* conceded that not all the articles were of equal value, adding that they would gladly have been spared "some of the 'poetry,' and a few of the *compositions*—we don't know what else to call them; and we wish the proof-reading had been done by a more careful or more competent hand." Despite these criticisms, the *Free Press* commended the work "to all the sons, native or adopted, of the Green Mountain State."[25]

Equally praiseworthy notices came in from other Vermont newspapers. The *St. Johnsbury Caledonian* remarked on Miss Hemenway's enviable success in recruiting talented historians as contributors. The *St. Albans Messenger* predicted that when completed the *Gazetteer* would be by far the most comprehensive history of Vermont, not simply because of its length, but more importantly because so many of the historians were local contributors "possessed of every facility of observation and tradition to bring out objects of interest that might more easily escape the eye of the more general historian."[26]

One letter of support that must have given Hemenway particular satisfaction came from Philip Battell, the member of the Middlebury Historical Society who, in the fall of 1859, had done his best to discourage her. In his letter Battell confessed that at the time he had considered her plan to publish the history of every town in Vermont unachievable. But her successful completion of this first volume, containing as it did the town histories of five counties, had at last convinced him that she had sufficient "competence and energy" to finish the whole "in a manner worthy of its commencement." He went on to assure her that he was not likely to lose interest in the *Gazetteer* "while so much is done in it so well," and while "so much is being accumulated by it of priceless value to the state."[27]

Meanwhile, notices from outside Vermont included a lengthy and very favorable review in the *Historical Magazine* of New York. In 1860 its editor had described the proposed work as "too full of promised usefulness to be appreciated by a thoughtless and superficial generation." Now he praised Abby Hemenway for producing a history that was both novel in its construction and remarkably comprehensive. Echoing the *St. Albans Messenger*, the editor went on to stress the advantages gained by engaging, as Hemenway did, large numbers of writers with access to "a great variety of materials," who were willing to devote "much patient labor" to composing their town histories. He asserted that such a work "must necessarily be more complete and more accurate than it would have been if only one had done it."[28]

A modern reader might question whether the quantity of historians employed on a work of this sort would necessarily guarantee its greater accuracy and comprehensiveness. But Hemenway's system of putting one individual in charge of each town history, and of making that person responsible for combing available sources for information as well as for writing the chapter itself, did produce many remarkably full and detailed histories of even the smallest Vermont towns. Furthermore, the increasing length of the chapters in the *Gazetteer* attests to the mounting vigor with which her historians sought to accumulate facts. In common with other New England antiquarians they shared the belief that nothing was too trivial for inclusion. As early as 1862 the Vermont Historical Society had recognized that by "collecting from sources that will ere long be inaccessible," Hemenway's historians were preserving for posterity "a vast amount of historical material that is now useful, and will soon become invaluable."[29]

While Abby Hemenway's Catholicism in some respects isolated her from the Protestant world of her childhood, it also served to reinforce her vocation as a historian. By joining the Roman Catholic Church she had publicly declared her difference from other people. She had also chosen a system of beliefs that justified (as New England Protestantism did not) the worth of the single, chaste woman. She now had a license to act differently and a justification for believing that in doing the work of history she was doing God's work, that as editor of the *Gazetteer* she was following a religious calling.[30]

With the *Gazetteer*'s reputation firmly established, Hemenway's commitment to the project quite naturally strengthened. In 1859, when she began collecting materials for her *Quarterly*, she thought it would take a few years to complete publication. Then she would move on to something else. But almost a decade later the town histories of only seven counties had been published, while six remained. At the same time, the essays and other materials sent in by her town historians had steadily grown in length, and the effort put into editing them had also increased. By 1868, as the work assumed entrepreneurial proportions, its editor—quite naturally—came to take her role as editor-in-chief with commensurate seriousness.

"A Work Intended for the Whole People"

———◦◦❖◦◦———

Some village Hampden that, with dauntless breast
  The little tyrants of his fields withstood,
Some mute inglorious Milton here may rest,
  Some Cromwell guiltless of his country's blood.

Thomas Gray, "Elegy Written in
a Country Churchyard"

Following the publication of the first volume of the *Vermont Historical Gazetteer*, when Hemenway was at the height of her powers as an editor and historian, her confidence manifested itself in the increasing length and fullness of the town histories that followed. As early as 1867 she was talking about bringing out supplements for Addison and Bennington Counties, an indication that she knew she had hit her stride. She wrote of having on file several papers "of considerable information" for the counties whose histories had already been published, including "Antiquarian Relics" from Henry Stevens and additional biographies.[1]

In October 1872 Hemenway received a formal acknowledgment of her contribution to local history when the Vermont Historical Society elected her an honorary member. She had been attending meetings of that society for several years, and her friendships with its leaders, including Pliny White, Henry Stevens, and Hiland Hall, had been important to her since the *Gazetteer*'s inception. It was, after all, thanks to Pliny White's inspiration that the magazine had been launched in the first place, and, until his premature death in 1869, he was a faithful contributor to its pages. Her "antiquarian father," Henry Stevens, the founder and first president of the society, had shared with Hemenway his vast store of historical knowledge and allowed her to comb his extensive archives. Finally, former Governor Hiland Hall had long been one of her principal supporters in Bennington County. In 1862 he had introduced a resolution at one of the society's meetings supporting her local history efforts.[2]

Evidence of a growing esteem for the *Gazetteer* was also apparent at the local level, particularly in the readiness with which town after town agreed to prepare its history. Early in January 1870 Hemenway wrote the secretary of the Vermont Historical Society that she had forty new writers for volume III alone, and the following year, when volume II, embracing the histories of Franklin, Grand Isle, Lamoille, and Orange Counties, was published, she described having six thousand pages on hand for Rutland, Washington, Windham, and Windsor.[3] Once word went around the state that Miss Hemenway was in earnest about including every county in Vermont in her *Gazetteer*, most towns indicated their willingness to be part of the enterprise. Their cooperation was further ensured when they realized that publication costs were met through subscriptions and would therefore not be a drain on town coffers.

Without the incentive of publication in the *Gazetteer* many Vermont communities might have shown little enthusiasm for printing their histories. John M. Moore, a one-time resident of Rockingham, wrote Hemenway sometime in the late 1860s that he had once prepared a history of that village and would have published it if the townspeople had given him any encouragement to do so. He even had a portion of his essay printed in a local newspaper, but to no avail. The town showed not the slightest interest, and in the end Moore donated his manuscript as pulp for the local papermill.[4]

Hemenway agreed with Moore that few towns in any given county could "make up a solitary history of sufficient interest to captivate their inhabitants." But experience had taught her that, when individual histories were combined in counties, enthusiasm rose. "What one [town] lacks another has, and as members of the great whole, equally sharing the interest and importance of the whole, even their own part and history becomes pleasing and acceptable." Rockingham was no exception. When asked to contribute its history for the *Gazetteer*, the town happily complied.[5]

Poorer communities, too, must have their stories told, wrote Amos Churchill, the historian for Hubbardton, a village in northwest Rutland County that over the years had lost trade and business to more prosperous neighboring communities. As Churchill put it, Hubbardton and other towns like it needed to speak up, to tell something about themselves in order to preserve their place among the thriving towns around them.[6]

The *Gazetteer* "is a work intended for the whole people," Hemenway told her readers in one of the many asides she scattered through its pages. This was true, she maintained, not simply because every Vermont town would be represented in the work, but also because the histories themselves reflected the distinctiveness of each community by allowing it to speak for itself through its chosen historian. As she wrote in the preface to volume II, her *Gazetteer* was "a most emphatically original history from the people," the product of "their own town and county historians and multiple local contributors."[7]

While Hemenway over her years as editor gained a clearer idea of what her *Gazetteer* should contain, the modern reader senses an unresolved conflict in her conception of its ultimate purpose. Put simply, how were her historians meant to appeal to local pride and at the same time refrain from shunning the bad in favor of the good, a question that continues to challenge local historians today? On the one hand Hemenway was seeking to preserve a kind of historical memory, one that served both to educate her readers about the early days of their state and to remind them of those qualities of which they should be proud. This aspect of her work meant glancing back, recovering a past of a particular kind, and seeing it in a favorable light. But she was also employing a more modern approach to historical writing by applying a selectively critical eye to some of the old myths that made up the traditional story of Vermont's past. Seemingly unaware of the tension between these two ways of writing history, she continued to use both approaches, adopting an overtly critical stance only when she was very sure of her ground.

Hemenway's success at invoking local pride had been recognized in 1859 by Rowland Robinson of Ferrisburgh. No self-respecting person, Robinson had assured her, seeing all the other towns in his county represented in the *Gazetteer*, would want his own left out. When a county was finished, it would awaken county pride, and when a few counties were complete, state pride would flourish. The very appearance of the first volume of the *Vermont Historical Gazetteer* demonstrated how well this appeal to local pride had worked. This hefty book containing the histories of more than eighty towns not only underscored Abby Hemenway's commitment to the cause of local history, it also contributed to a growing statewide esteem for Vermont's heritage. Because her town histories were clearly pieces of a larger whole, the *Gazetteer* was recognized as telling the Vermont story and not simply a smattering of local ones.

The *St. Johnsbury Caledonian*'s review of the first volume of the *Gazetteer* echoed Rowland Robinson by observing that Hemenway's reliance "on the several towns in each county to furnish its own history" was "the salvation of the work, also its interest and value. All people have so much pride as to like to have *their* town appear well in history; consequently it has been often the case that the very best men and writers have freely contributed to the *Gazetteer*."[8]

While Hemenway's success in appealing to local pride undoubtedly helped both in the writing of history and in the selling of subscriptions, it had a dangerous side as well. Such pridefulness might easily encourage a local historian to concentrate only on those people and those events that would redound to his community's credit. Arlington, for one, had been too ashamed of its Tory past to want its history written.

But Pliny White in his history of Coventry, an Orleans County town situated just south of Lake Memphremagog, more willingly portrayed the bad as well as the good. While he praises the admirable qualities of Coventry's first inhabitants, especially their hardiness, White is less flattering about their godliness. We are told, for example, how a Mrs. John Farnsworth, who was suffering a very painful death, wished for someone to pray with her, but no man or woman could be found who would do so. White also questions the enduring courage and integrity of some settlers during the War of 1812. "Tales of Indian cruelty were familiar to every ear," he tells us. "The cracking of a limb in the forest, or the midnight hoot of an owl," was sufficient to alarm the more timid men and women. Only as time passed and no foe appeared did the panic subside. Meanwhile, whenever the British soldiers came into town to purchase supplies they had little trouble obtaining them from individuals "whose covetousness was greater than their patriotism."[9]

Hemenway's own writings in the *Gazetteer* show a similar

preference for including the bad along with the good. She disliked, for example, biographies of great men that ignored their peculiarities, even their sins. As she explained to her readers, "When astronomers may write a treatise describing the sun without spots, lest they disparage that great shining luminary, then let men who would be true historians, or true biographists, photograph a giant character without human mold or spot."[10]

Like most local historians of her day Hemenway expected her authors to feature prominent townspeople in their essays, but she also wanted ordinary men and women included. When T. A. Cutler sent in his chapter for Waterford he included no biographies, explaining that he had "neither presidents nor fools to write about." Hemenway urged him to send in what he could anyway.[11] By contrast, she commended the Reverend John A. Hicks, the historian for Sheldon, on his "estimable biography" of the Reverend Joel Clapp, an early Episcopal clergyman in that town. According to Hicks, Clapp

> ran no brilliant career—exhibited no displays of genius—did no acts to strike a thrill of admiration through the public mind, or warm the hearts of thousands with a glow of gratitude. He belonged to that class of plain and solid men of whom Vermont has been so prolific—men sound in judgment and wise in council— of great physical endurance, . . . who reared amid the rude employments of country life, are yet competent to guide their country's councils in times of peace, and uphold its interest and defend its honor in the hostile conflict.[12]

If Hemenway did not specifically charge her historians to include accounts of women in their essays, the *Gazetteer* is nonetheless an unmatched resource for material on this segment of Vermont's eighteenth- and nineteenth-century population. As Faith Pepe pointed out in 1977, Hemenway considered everything from stories about bears to sentimental poetry important enough for inclusion in her town histories. Had Hemenway engaged a man to edit her *Gazetteer*, Pepe suggests that most of the valuable information describing the domestic and social life of early Vermont women would have been edited out.[13]

A handful of town histories in the *Gazetteer* are written by women, and the history of Stowe by Mrs. M. N. Wilkins is unusual in its amount of detail about the actual conditions under which the first white settlers and later inhabitants of this mountain town lived. In her essay Wilkins doesn't simply give the facts, as many others do, but she enlivens them with stories and homely details. Most notably, she discusses subjects that most other historians carefully avoided, including the town's treatment of the poor. In the first half of the nineteenth century the accepted method in Stowe, as in other Vermont communities, was for the overseer of the poor to contract out the care of destitute persons to the lowest bidders. As Wilkins points out, those who sought such contracts were mostly individuals "who had about all they could do to live themselves, and resorted to this method to get a little money." Under such a system, Wilkins observes, the destitute "often had rather poor boarding places, and were liable at the end of each year, or sooner, to be removed to a poorer one." Thus the establishment in 1859 of a poor farm is applauded by Wilkins as "a great improvement." By her description the inhabitants of the one in Stowe were "furnished with all the usual comforts and even luxuries, of families well-to-do in the world." She admits, however, that the success of such a system "depended much on procuring the right kind of a man to superintend the carrying on of the farm, and managing the persons who came there to reside."[14]

While few of Hemenway's historians went so far as Wilkins did in discussing the plight of their town's poorest inhabitants, Hemenway's insistence on including ordinary people as well as

From the Gazetteer

∗ ∗ ∗

Danby

by J. C. Williams

"Productions of Agriculture [1870]"

No. of farms producing to the amount of $500	130
No. of acres of improved land,	15,027
No. of acres of unimproved land,	8,408
Present cash value of farms,	$678,700
Average price per acre,	$28.90
Value of farming implements & machinery	$32,770
Total amt. wages paid during the year, including board	$24,370

Live Stock ending June 1, 1870.

Horses, 268; milch cows, 1,617; working oxen; 52; other cattle, 714; sheep, 924; swine, 236; value of all live stock, $130,385.

[Volume III, page 667]

∗ ∗ ∗

Fairfax

from the history of the First Baptist Church in Fairfax
by the Rev. L. A. Dunn.

Report of salary to be paid to Rev. Amos Tuttle in 1809.

"The committee report that the church pay Elder Tuttle two hundred dollars in the following articles, viz: $20.00 worth of pork, 15.00 worth of beef, 5.00 worth of tallow, 15.00 worth of rye, 10.00 worth of wool, 25.00 worth of wheat, 10.00

worth of flax. The remainder to be paid in articles conven-
ient for the church. E. Safford, Samuel Cressey, committee.
Voted to accept the report."

[Volume II, page 184]

*   *   *

Cabot

by John M. Fisher

"Freighting"

[Provides invaluable information about the transportation of
marketable goods to and from Vermont in the first half of
the nineteenth century.]

Robert Lance, from Chester, N.H., who came here about
1810, and lived where Hial Morse now does, did the first
teaming to Boston. His team was two yoke of oxen; freight,
salt, whisky, pork, and it took from 4 to 6 weeks to make the
round trip. He usually made two trips a year. A little later
Joseph Burbank began to go with a span of horses, and two
loads a year would usually supply the merchants with goods.
Benjamin Sperry used to team. It is said he was known from
here to Boston by the name of Uncle Ben by everybody.
Hugh Wilson did quite a business at teaming. In the winter
quite a number of men would go to Portland, Me., with their
red, double sleighs and two horses, loaded with pork. In
1838, Allen Perry began to run a 6-horse team to Boston,
regular trips, the round trip taking 3 weeks. The freight
tariff was $20 per ton; his expenses about $50 a trip. When
he came in with his big, covered wagon it was quite an event
for the place. He run his team until 1846, when the railroad
got so near he sold his team and went to farming. The P. & O.
railroad is 5 miles to the north of us, and the Montpelier &
Wells River the same distance to the south.

[Volume IV, page 86]

more prominent folk is echoed throughout the pages of the *Gazetteer*. In the chapter for Poultney, she printed a historical address by Henry Clark delivered on the occasion of that town's centennial in 1861. Too often, Clark asserted, historians had supposed their story fully told when they had "chronicled the march of armies—the installation or dissolution of cabinets." Clark insisted that "history, to include all that belongs to it, should describe more faithfully the life of the people in their homes and hamlets."[15] Loyall C. Kellogg, the historian for Benson, made a similar point when he wrote that

> the annals of an agricultural town are largely formed by the "unhistoric deeds of common life." Our honorable past, in its social, educational and religious character, was made by earnest and self-denying men and women—the fathers and mothers who here planted in hope, and bore faithfully the struggles and trials of life, and now "rest from their labors."[16]

Put this way, Hemenway's history sounds almost modern in its emphasis on the ordinary, on the "people without history" as they have been called, in giving the voiceless equal time and equal space with kings, generals, and presidents. And much of the interest in the *Gazetteer* for modern historians derives from this aspect. Yet Hemenway and her writers, even the most notable of them such as Pliny White, were not modern historians. Rather they were chroniclers, or, as some might call them, antiquarians. Modern social historians, particularly academic social scientists, have tended to ignore the individual in favor of the group (there are notable exceptions, of course, such as Laurel Thatcher Ulrich's recent *Midwife's Tale*). Though these modern scholars use essentially the same sources for their studies as did their nineteenth-century predecessors—including town and church records, account books, and inventories—they have different purposes and thus ask different questions.

Viewing their communities as laboratories that can help create understanding of a larger society, they are more apt to pose the sorts of questions raised by an analysis of quantifiable data.[17]

Most of Hemenway's historians, however, were chroniclers. Their common purpose was to tell a story, weaving such topics as settlement, industry, religion, and education into a chronological narrative intended to demonstrate their town's distinctiveness within a shared regional culture. At the center of the their story were people: the early proprietors, the first settlers, the leading professional men and women of the town.

By telling the story of ordinary folk, the men and women who had created their communities large and small out of the wilderness, Hemenway was giving Vermonters a democratic history, one in which individuals such as the Reverend Joel Clapp were valued equally alongside the Allen brothers and other better-known Green Mountain heroes. Furthermore, since one of the purposes of the *Gazetteer* was to gather and preserve "the fast perishing records and traditions of our forefathers," it was precisely the qualities of men like Clapp that made this northern New England state distinctive. Industry, hardiness, and self-reliance were traits admired by all Vermonters, rich and poor, men and women, and the lives of those individuals from the state's past who met these criteria were worth remembering and preserving. Thus the *Gazetteer*, like so much other nineteenth-century history, had a marked moral and instructive purpose. It was a collection of stories around which all Vermonters, young and old, could gather—as their ancestors had gathered around the hearth on cold winter evenings—to learn about the worthy (and, in some cases, not so worthy) deeds of their forebears.

Much as Harriet Beecher Stowe helped to domesticate American literature by dwelling on the lives of small-town folk in novels such as *The Minister's Wooing*, so Abby Hemenway and her local historians were domesticating history. By including stories of ordinary men and women in even the smallest

Vermont towns these amateur local historians were giving their readers a history that was personal and close to home.[18]

For example, Pliny White's chapter on Coventry, like M. N. Wilkins's history of Stowe, provides unusually detailed information on everyday life in a small Vermont town from its first settlement through years of growth and relative prosperity in the 1820s and 1830s and up to the Civil War. Here we learn that it was the younger girls in pioneer families who were sent out at night to find the cows and drive them home, "oftentimes a laborious task requiring them to search the woods for miles around." We are told that door-to-door shoemaking was called "whipping the cat," and how the scarcity of cash in the early years of settlement forced one man to travel more than fifty miles to procure less than a dollar to pay his taxes. White even provides us with occasional glimpses into the working lives of Coventry women. We learn that the town's first schoolteacher, Temperance Vincent, was hired in the summer of 1803 and taught for $1 per week in a corn barn where the only light came through the open doorway and the wide cracks between the boards. The town's first postmaster was also a woman; Mary A. Holton was appointed to that position in 1822.[19]

Pliny White concedes that Coventry's history spanned "only a brief period of time" and recorded events he called "comparatively unimportant." This suggests that it may have been easier to describe the ordinary and everyday in the histories of communities such as Coventry that were settled after the Revolution. Historians who wrote about towns that had played no part in the military and political dramas of the state's early history had little choice but to describe the commonplace. Furthermore, these towns often boasted people still living who actually remembered the early days of settlement and could provide firsthand accounts of pioneer life.[20]

Unfortunately, there are no footnotes in Pliny White's Coventry essay identifying the sources he used. Luckily, however, we do know how Sylvanus Nye, the historian for Berlin, found much of his information. This is because Nye's notes and papers for his chapter have been preserved, providing a rare glimpse of how Hemenway's historians went about their work of collecting, selecting, and arranging the historical materials at their disposal.[21]

The history of Berlin, then a small hamlet lying between Barre and Montpelier in Washington County, takes up just over twenty pages in the fourth volume of the *Gazetteer*, published in 1882. Nye's essay also observes the usual format. It opens with a brief account of the initial settlement in the summer of 1785. This is followed by a lengthy series of sketches of the town's first settlers, forty-five in all. Then comes a section on religion, and another on military history. For lovers of literature there is a biographical essay on Daniel P. Thompson, the author of *The Green Mountain Boys* and a native of Berlin. Thompson's rousing tale of "The Great Wolf Hunt on Irish Hill," recounting how the early settlers overcame the threat of wild animals, concludes the chapter.[22]

Sylvanus Nye drew on a variety of sources for his history of Berlin, including vital statistics, tax records, military records, newspapers, and legal documents. But his principal source was people. Complying with his editor's charge that her historians engage as many writers as possible, men and women "whose direct personal acquaintance with the subject treated best qualified them to the task,"[23] Nye either spoke with or wrote to several dozen individuals asking for their recollections of life in Berlin. The majority of these people provided sketches of fathers or grandfathers who numbered among the town's first settlers. But others gave information on churches, on military matters, on early schools.[24]

Thus, like many of Hemenway's historians, Nye relied heavily not so much on public records and printed documents as on personal and social memory. This strategy resulted partly from a paucity of written materials, because many Vermont towns had not taken the trouble to preserve their records.[25] Like today's oral historians the authors of Hemenway's town histories collected and published the recollections of eyewitnesses and participants in historical events. The difference is that oral history as practiced today is a technique and not simply a research tool. It is also understood now as a record of perceptions rather than a re-creation of actual historical occurrences. In other words, it provides an insight into how people think about certain events and what they perceive their own role to have been in those events.[26]

According to Charles Morrissey, the term "oral history" was coined in Vermont in 1863 when Winslow Watson, in an address before the Vermont Historical Society, complained that much of the local history of the state was being lost as older residents who remembered it died. "I have been amazed" Watson declared, "by observing in my own local researches, the ravages made by a single decade, among the fountains of oral history in a community."[27]

Hemenway's historians shared Watson's concern that the sources of oral history were disappearing with the passing away of earlier generations of Vermonters who remembered their towns' history. Firsthand recollections of the early days of settlement abound in the pages of the *Gazetteer*. However, the nineteenth-century historian credited personal reminiscence with a veracity not shared by the modern scholar who realizes that the subjective nature of memory makes it an often unreliable guide to the past. For Hemenway, who lacked our psychological wariness of memory's accuracy, the recollections of elderly folk spoke a truth about the past that mere documents could not (a view perhaps not so greatly at variance with a certain kind of memoir appearing today!). And this reliance on memory is another way in which the tension between the "old" and "new" aspects of her work can be seen. Particular faith, she felt, should be placed in the memories of older people who were both personally acquainted with their community and respected by their fellow townsfolk for their

From the Gazetteer

✳ ✳ ✳

Westfield

"Chapter for Westfield."

by E. W. Thurber

"Letter from Hiram Sisco the first male child
born in Westfield"

[An example of the kind of letter town historians received
from individuals no longer living in Vermont, describing
their memories of the early days of settlement.]

Bloomingdale, March 27,_____

Mr. Thurber—I received your letter last evening. I will
write in answer to it this morning. I was the first male
child born in the town of Westfield. Lucinda Barber
was the first child born in the town of Westfield. I
think there were but three families in town when I was
born, viz. Mrs. Barber's, Mr. Jos Stoughton's, and my
father's family—Richard Sisco. I was born on
Stoughton's meadow in some shanty near the river.
You will see by my writing, that I was brought up in
the woods, where there was no schools. My father often
told me that I was entitled to a lot of land for being the
first boy born in town.

Hiram Sisco.

[Volume III, page 364]

"probity and intelligence." She told her *Gazetteer* readers she
believed such people were entitled "to unquestioned belief."[28]
She also trusted the recollections of those who had actually witnessed a historical event more than the published accounts of

it, which might have been obtained from a biased source. Here Hemenway's critical, almost revisionist nature is at work. Yet elsewhere memories are invoked not for purposes of historical accuracy so much as to inspire in her readers a pious pride in their heritage.

For his history of Berlin, Sylvanus Nye had to track down numerous people who no longer lived in Vermont. One was Harry Dewey of Pittsburg, Iowa, the son of an early settler. Some years before, Dewey, like so many others, had moved west carrying his memories with him, including the text of a lyceum talk he had given in the 1840s on the early history of his home-town. When Dewey received Nye's letter asking for his reminiscences he hunted all day among his boxes and files for the talk and other Berlin papers he'd brought to Iowa with him, but could not find them anywhere. Fortunately, a few days later Dewey recovered his lost papers, including the missing lyceum talk, and sent them off to Nye in Vermont.[29]

Nye's history clearly benefited from such a source as Dewey's lyceum paper, which had been written when the latter was still living in Berlin and had access to sources not available to him in Iowa. Although the lecture itself is not included in Nye's chapter, he made good use of its contents. In one form or another most of the information Nye received from his various sources found its way into his history. In cases such as Daniel Thompson's gripping story of the wolf hunt or Mrs. Joel Fisher's historical account of "Berlin Pond and Benjamin Falls," the source is given in full. In other instances the information received is simply incorporated into the history, usually with no credit given for the source used. Dewey was not the only one to send Nye an account of Berlin's early settlement. Nye simply took the different versions sent to him, including Dewey's, and wove them into a coherent narrative.

While Nye's notes tell us much about how he worked as a historian, there is no way of ascertaining the precise editorial role Hemenway played in the published version of the Berlin history. Apart from one letter she wrote in 1879, after Nye's chapter had been set into type, no correspondence between them survives. A few copyediting notes on some of Nye's papers are in Hemenway's hand, but that is all. If she altered or cut his history to any significant degree the papers contain no record of it.

Luckily, in the case of Charles Abbott's history of Worcester we have not only the original manuscript but also a letter from Hemenway to Abbott telling him what to include in his chapter. Thus it is possible both to examine the kind of instructions Hemenway gave her historians and to study the kinds of changes she felt free to make as editor.[30]

In the summer of 1871, Abbott, Worcester's town clerk and postmaster, was considering whether or not to take on the task of writing his town's history for the *Gazetteer*. Born in Thetford, Abbott had later moved with his family to Worcester, a village nestled among the high peaks of northern Washington County. Chronic arthritis had rendered him unfit for farming or other manual labor, so Abbott made himself useful by holding a succession of town offices. Familiar with village affairs and respected by the townspeople for his integrity and his "clear, well-disciplined mind," Abbott was an appropriate choice for town historian.[31]

On July 24, 1871, the editor of the *Gazetteer*, having learned of Abbott's candidacy for the position, wrote him a letter detailing in a businesslike manner the "items and matters" to be "embodied" in his chapter and expressing the hope that Abbott would agree to take on the assignment. She promised that if he did she would send him a copy of volume II "so that you may see what your neighboring Co[unty] towns have done."[32]

Among the "items and matters" Hemenway instructed Abbott to include in his chapter, she listed natural history, early settlement, town organization, and, of course, biographical sketches of deceased "prominent citizens." She specifically requested statistical information such as the results of early censuses but also asked for local lore, including Indian history and tradition. Finally, she was very precise about the many "firsts" she wanted mentioned, from the first house and first school, first church and first graveyard, to first teacher, first clergyman, and first members of the town militia.

Although Hemenway's list of subjects emphasized the early years of settlement in Worcester—that period of the town's history most in danger of loss—she also requested more recent "items and matters," such as accounts of the town's various businesses and organizations up to the present day, including "masons or lodges, temperance and other societies, for moral, agricultural or intellectual improvement." To conclude his chapter, she asked Abbott to provide "specimens of prose,—Quaint Epistles, Epitaphs" from "any creditable writer of any publication."[33]

Compared to the town histories in the early numbers of the *Quarterly Gazetteer*, which had rarely filled more than half a dozen pages, Charles Abbott's twenty-nine-page chapter on Worcester was a lengthy one for a small town. In his very full account, Abbott was generally faithful in following his editor's guidelines. He even ticked off the items in Hemenway's letter as he covered them. In summary, he tells us that although Worcester had been organized in 1803, for the first few decades only a handful of families settled there. Between 1812 and 1816 a succession of cold summers had depleted even that tiny population, so that by 1818 only one family was left in town. In the 1820s more settlers began moving in, and by the 1870s, when Abbott was writing his history, Worcester had achieved relative prosperity for an agricultural hill town. With a population of some eight hundred people, it boasted two churches, one store, one hotel, five sawmills, three blacksmith shops, and one gristmill. But, as he makes clear, no earthshaking events had occurred in Worcester, nor had any of its citizens made great names for themselves in the outside world.

Even though Charles Abbott was diligent in following his editor's instructions on matters to be included, a comparison of the published and manuscript versions of the chapter shows that Hemenway had few qualms about reorganizing, rewriting, adding to, and even omitting portions of the material he had sent her. Like most good editors, Hemenway tightened sentences, reworded phrases for greater clarity, even moved whole sections around to make the chapter flow better. But she also took some questionable liberties. Where Abbott's manuscript cited a measure passed in an 1821 town meeting making nine hours the official length of a day's work, Hemenway inserted a quip into the published version suggesting that Worcester at least "was ahead of the ten-hour law." More troubling, however, was her tampering with an autobiographical account of survival in the wilderness by an early woman settler. While Abbott insisted the essay was just as Alma P. Howieson had written it, Hemenway could not resist smoothing out its rough edges: leaving out an occasional word, changing others. For example, she replaces Howieson's use of the phrase "house dog" with the more familiar "lap dog," and turns a simple and direct description—"the sun shone bright and warm for that time of year"—into the more euphonious "the sun shone pleasantly for that time of year." Hemenway obviously did not share the modern historian's reverance for preserving such records verbatim.[34]

Throughout her years as editor of the *Gazetteer* Abby Hemenway exercised a limited but forceful sway, giving her historians the freedom to tell their own stories while at the same time doing her best to hold them to certain standards, and reserving to herself the right of editorial comment. "All walk amiably together in the garden of the Gazetteer," she would write in 1886. Yet, while such Edenic harmony may have been her ideal, it did not always prevail.[35]

Perhaps nowhere is Hemenway's self-confidence and clarity of purpose better exhibited than in a lengthy and sharp public critique of the scholarly minister and geologist, John Bulkley Perry, whom she had chosen to write the history of Swanton, a border town in northern Franklin County. "Work for a woman's book, Sir," Hemenway had warned him "and you work for her."[36]

Discord in the Garden of the Gazetteer

———◦◦○◦○◦◦———

A historian must not know nationality, when he takes up his pen for another party or nation.

Abby Hemenway[1]

Abby Hemenway's critique of John Bulkley Perry, which she published in the fourth volume of her *Historical Gazetteer*, is noteworthy in part for its articulation of her views on history, particularly the right and wrong way to write about the past. But this critique also shows the degree to which her conversion, together with her voluminous reading in Catholic sources, had awakened a heightened sensitivity to Vermont's Catholic and French heritage and given her the courage to question American values and ideals.

John Bulkley Perry had been serving as pastor of Swanton's Congregational Church when Hemenway engaged him to write the town's history in 1862. But Perry was no ordinary clergyman. He was a sedate and studious man in his mid-thirties whose passion for geology matched his religious fervor. During his years in Swanton he could be seen, a hammer protruding from the satchel at his side, traversing meadows, fields, and forests, familiarizing himself with the region's geological formations. Some of Perry's parishioners complained that he spent too much time "cracking rocks" and not enough time on his ministerial duties. Others worried about his unorthodox theology, particularly his questioning of the literal interpretation of Scripture. They might have worried further if they had known about his fascination with evolutionary theory, which predated the publication of Darwin's *Origin of Species*. Undaunted, Perry went his own way. Using the data he collected while exploring the Vermont countryside, he plunged into one of the century's most bitter geological debates, the Taconic controversy. He helped to prove that the Taconic rock system stretching from eastern New York State to Canada was older than the Silesian stratum. This was an unpopular theory among geologists of the time, but one that was later shown to be correct.[2]

Hemenway had known little of Perry in January 1862 when he wrote offering to serve as Swanton's historian. But she soon learned that he came with the highest commendations from both the faculty at the University of Vermont and from her friend and mentor, Henry Stevens. The latter claimed the Swanton minister as a particular favorite and introduced him to Hemenway during one of her visits to Burlington. Meanwhile, Joseph Torrey, a professor of philosophy and president of the University of Vermont, had assured her that with men like Perry on her roster of historians, she need not fear for the success of the *Gazetteer*. In the end Perry agreed to write, not only the history of Swanton, but also a chapter on the geology and natural history of Chittenden, Lamoille, Franklin, and Grand Isle Counties.[3]

Hemenway must have been pleased to secure the services of

such a respected scholar, particularly since his natural history chapter promised to be the first comprehensive discussion of that subject in the pages of the *Gazetteer*. His reputed familiarity with Vermont's Native American heritage more than qualified him to write the early history of Swanton, the site of a once thriving Abenaki village. Perry was a great catch.

At first all was harmonious between editor and historian. During January 1862 letters went back and forth between them in which Perry went out of his way to be considerate and cooperative. He even offered to serve as town agent, sending Hemenway detailed accountings of the subscriptions he had sold. Money problems, which worsened as the Civil War lengthened, made her particularly grateful for such assistance. But when Perry wrote offering general genealogical and historical aid, Hemenway, sensing perhaps that the Swanton historian wished to assume more control over the work than she was willing to give him, made it clear who was in charge. She was careful, too, to let Perry know what particular subjects she wanted covered: "The history of the Indian settlements & of the French Grants . . . & of the part Swanton took in the 'Patriot [sic] War' [the Canadian rebellions of 1837–38], should receive special attention," she told him.[4]

By early November 1863, Hemenway had a draft of the geology portion of Perry's natural history chapter in hand. The final version of this lengthy essay would fill more than sixty pages when it was finally published in the second volume of the *Gazetteer* in 1872.[5] While this treatise on the geology of northwestern Vermont revealed the originality of Perry's work, the long delay in publication meant that no one, Hemenway included, had any idea of the importance of its contents. By the time Perry's findings on the Taconic rock system appeared in the *Gazetteer*—nearly a decade after he'd written them down—they were no longer news.[6]

Meanwhile, Perry was also at work on his Swanton town

From the Gazetteer

* * *

Charlotte

by Miss Julia Pepper, a poess

"Observation To A Whail.
Dug up in Sharlot, Vt., and now on exerbishon
at the stait Hous."

[In a footnote Hemenway admits that "we do not usually
regard this style [of poetry], and this, moreover, we
understand to be a production of Montpelier rather than
Charlotte; however, whoever has seen 'the whale' can, but
rather appreciate the 'Great Blubber' . . . . An appropriate
notice of this fossil skeleton will appear in an after-chapter
upon the geology and natural history of Chittenden
County—by Rev. J. B. Perry."]

Big reptile! Did you expect
To rub out your foot tracks by
The trail of your Ab Domen,
So that Hager couldn't find you?
Ef so, your'e sold—Great Blubber!
He knew your hand ritin, soon's
He see it! Better not jump'd
Outer the ark, quite
So much in a hurry.
P'raps your's ridin on an Ice Burg
And stopt to warm in Brenden
By a Lignite fire,
              Or may be
You considered lake Shamplane
Was the Pacific Oshun! Great
Setashus Mammallia, Aint
You took in? Mounted on

Paddles how'd you expect to travil
I sh'd like to now, on the Clay
Called Plisterseen? Gess you
Felt some like a fish out er water
Throw'd up by Joner on to
Dry Land. Icthyosorrus,
Farwel.

[Volume I, page 751]

history. By Hemenway's account, sometime early in 1863 he read aloud to her an incomplete draft of his manuscript and she was pleased by what she heard. She particularly liked Perry's sympathetic treatment of the Jesuit missions that had been set up in Abenaki villages beginning in the seventeenth century. When Hemenway commended him for the "great and very kind respect" he had shown toward the Jesuit fathers, he had spoken in turn of his "obligation towards several Canadian priests" of that order who had treated him "with special kindness."[7]

What happened next is not certain, except that the Civil War interrupted both the publication of the *Gazetteer* and Perry's pastorship of the Swanton church. Sometime late in the conflict, facing mounting criticism from his Swanton parishioners for his heterodoxy, he left Vermont to serve as chaplain to the Tenth Vermont Regiment, at which point he stopped work on his town history. When he returned to Swanton sometime in the spring of 1865 the old controversy revived and he did not remain there long. In November of that year he resigned his pastorship, citing ill health as the reason. After a brief ministerial stint in Wilmington, Perry left Vermont for good in 1867 and moved to Cambridge, Massachusetts. Here he drew the attention of Louis Agassiz, the renowned Harvard geologist, who procured him a lectureship at that institution in 1868.[8]

Because Agassiz at the time was battling the scientific forces marshaled in support of the new theory of evolution, a Darwinian sympathizer such as Perry seemed an improbable ally. But Perry, unlike most Harvard scientists, including Agassiz, had little taste for either self-promotion or controversy. He also shared Agassiz's dream of a reconciliation between religion and the sciences. As Kevin Dann has suggested, Perry's humility and theological background were probably as important as his geological abilities in securing the appointment at Harvard.[9]

Hemenway later remembered that Perry only got back to work on his Swanton chapter several years after obtaining his Harvard professorship. In the meantime, she had not only resumed publication of the *Gazetteer* but had also joined the Catholic Church. When she did finally receive a manuscript from Perry she was dismayed to discover that in this second draft he had changed what she referred to as "the Catholic historical part" into "a most bitter and hostile thing." The reasons for these changes are nowhere made clear, but when Hemenway suggested in a letter to Perry that he had been "a little hard on the poor Jesuits," his alarm was such that he traveled all the way from Cambridge to Burlington to ensure that she publish the chapter exactly as he wrote it.[10]

Hemenway reluctantly agreed to comply with his wishes but insisted that where he "had erred in historical statements through lack of better information" she would use her "editor's privilege," as she called it. "I would like to publish it," she told Perry, "but *with notes.*"[11]

After Hemenway mailed Perry's chapter to the Claremont Manufacturing Company (her printer for the second volume of the *Gazetteer*), the firm proceeded to lose the manuscript behind some papers in a safe. Then, in October 1872, before the printer recovered the chapter, Perry took ill with typhoid and died.

Upon hearing of her historian's premature death Hemenway decided to put off publishing the Swanton chapter—it appears at the end of the fourth volume—to give herself plenty of time to make her promised notes on Perry's essay "strong and pertinent." In the end she wrote a lengthy commentary, by far the longest she published anywhere in the *Gazetteer*.[12]

Perry's essay is divided into two parts. The first has nothing to do with either Jesuits or Indians, but discusses at length the possibility that English explorers, not French, were the first Europeans to set foot in what later would become Vermont. Perry's evidence was a piece of paper enclosed in a metal tube that was discovered one winter day in 1853 by two men who were shoveling sand for the Swanton Falls marble plant. The paper contained a note signed by John Graye and was dated November 1564. Graye wrote that he and four companions had come ashore three months earlier on the northeastern coast of North America. His companions had since perished and he himself was near death. Whether Perry saw the supposedly ancient piece of paper on which Graye's note was written or simply a copy of it is not clear from his account. He does, however, state that he learned of the discovery of the tube containing Graye's message directly from one of the men who had dug it up.[13]

Perry's determination to believe in the note's authenticity is demonstrated by his great effort to provide what he calls "strong presumptive evidence" to counter any possible objections. He concludes by admitting that positive proof may be wanting "to establish the genuineness of this manuscript," but insists that there are strong reasons to accept the document as authentic.[14]

Few today would doubt that Champlain was the first European to set foot on what is now Vermont soil, and somehow it seems out of character that a thorough and careful scientist such as John Bulkley Perry would be taken in by the John Graye story. But perhaps Perry didn't feel the need to prove his theory that Englishmen had been in Swanton in the mid-sixteenth century. Although he was an eager fact gatherer, particularly when it came to science, this essay of Perry's seems to revel in probability and hypothesis. Echoing Charles Darwin's approach to the theory of evolution, is it possible that Perry did not feel the need to prove anything? Was he rather attempting to argue his position by presenting a collection of facts and then leaving it up to his readers to interpret those facts? At the very least, Perry tells his readers in conclusion, "these supposed adventures and the time of their occurrence, serve to invest the early history of Swanton with a romance, which perhaps belongs to no other township in the state." And even if we are not satisfied that Graye himself existed, Perry concludes that at least we can be reasonably certain that countless others like him did.[15]

A darker explanation for the inclusion of this tale is that Perry's exposure to the beliefs among Harvard scientists such as Louis Agassiz in Nordic superiority had awakened in the one-time Swanton minister a hitherto dormant ethnic pride. In trying to prove Graye's earlier appearance, Perry presents a claim that the English had predated the French and that Champlain and his followers were thus interlopers, or at least second best.

Hemenway provides no editorial comment on this section of Perry's essay, but she later makes it clear that she gives little weight to the kind of "suppository evidence" that Perry relies on here and elsewhere in his history of Swanton. Nor would her own knowledge of, and sympathy with, the French have inclined her to believe a hypothetical story questioning their claim as the first Europeans in Vermont.

The second part of Perry's "Introductory Papers" on the

early Indian and French heritage of Swanton is in essence an overview of Vermont's Native American heritage. While he did not subscribe to the myth that Native Americans never lived in Vermont, he did portray the region as largely abandoned thanks to tribal warfare that raged for a century beginning in the mid-1500s. He claimed, too, that an earlier and relatively civilized tribe of Indians had inhabited the region at the time of Noah. By contrast, he dismissed the Abenaki as barbarians who gained "a subsistence living by fishing, hunting, and a rude species of husbandry" and made the far-fetched assertion that the corn and other crops planted by the Abenaki near their settlements "had mostly grown spontaneously."

According to Perry, the Abenaki were a naturally bellicose tribe, a fact attested to by the weaponry found near their graves. Then, during the colonial wars of the seventeenth and eighteenth centuries, the Jesuit missionaries encouraged a sympathy among the Abenaki toward the French, prompting these bloodthirsty "Red men," as he calls them, to build up alliances between various Indian tribes in southern New England and mount savage forays against the English settlements there. By his account, Queen Anne's War, which lasted from 1702 to 1713, "offered an extended field for Indian barbarities."[16]

As for the Jesuit missionaries, Perry says that he was unable to find much information on them. He suggests that the first were sent out by the French king about 1730 for the propagation of the faith among the heathen. While he is willing to credit these religious men with introducing the Abenaki to French culture, he doubts that they succeeded in persuading the Indians to make "any real commitment to Christianity, even though they took Christian names." He further claims that while the Abenaki became only nominal Catholics, they invariably sided with the French in the colonial wars. Thus, when the latter lost New France to the English in 1763, the Indians "were dispossessed of their lands and left without a home."[17]

Hemenway's treatment of Perry's history raises a number of interesting questions, most of them related to her disagreements with his findings. First of all, in defiance of Perry's wishes that his paper be printed exactly as he wrote it, Hemenway exerted her "editor's privilege" by lifting entire portions out of his essay and placing them in a separate section at the end labeled "Compiler's Notes." This rather unprofessional piece of editorship is compounded by another difficulty: The printed text of Hemenway's "Notes" is not as clear as it might be. Missing quotation marks and other typographical errors make it difficult to tell where Perry's own words, the words of his sources, and the editor's commentary begin and end.

Hemenway's principal quarrel with Perry's chapter was that he relied solely on English sources to recount what she considers a French story. "A historian," she tells her readers,

> must not know nationality, when he takes up his pen for another party or nation. He should be as true an historian when he essays to write their history, as for his own side when writing for that, give their facts as fully and explicitly, and where their history is unknown, or obscure, be as charitable in surmise or suppositions as he would upon the side where his sympathies are enlisted.

Perry's reliance on English sources was in Hemenway's mind the chief reason for his partiality; "he assumes the ground of an historian for Swanton, for its old Indian and French settlements while his knowledge, researches, and constructions seem mostly drawn from 'English' and colonial history—that is from the other and wrong side from this for which he is writing."[18]

As to Perry's statement that he "sought in vain for any definite information" respecting the Jesuit missionaries, including their names, Hemenway was quick to fault him for failing to consult certain French histories, particularly the multivolume *Jesuit Relations*, recounting the travels and explorations of the Jesuit missionaries in New France from the early sixteenth to the late seventeenth century. "We do not suppose that any of these names are lost," she told her readers. "The annals of the Jesuits can doubtless supply . . . all that is most important in their missions, true dates, and much interesting information in regard to the Indian nations." Even if Perry couldn't read French—which he could—histories were available in English, including one by the New England Protestant historian, Francis Parkman.[19]

According to Hemenway, Perry's failure to consult the French records led to numerous errors. Most notably, had he read his French history he would have learned that Canada was not, as he and many of his Protestant contemporaries believed, colonized for religious purposes but rather to advance the fur trade. Hemenway assures her readers that the decision of a seventeenth- or eighteenth-century Frenchman to come to Canada was no more motivated by missionary zeal than was the decision of the nineteenth-century Irish immigrant to settle in the United States. Both may indeed have been Roman Catholics, but both came to North America primarily for economic gain.[20] Critical as well of Perry's account of the Jesuit missions, Hemenway faults him for relying too heavily on the account of a Swedish naturalist, Peter Kalm, who traveled through the Missisquoi region in 1749. Hemenway questions Kalm's reliability as a witness, particularly his claim that the Jesuits said little about their religious work. How well could Kalm have known them, she asks? Because the priests saw him as a "naturalist" in religion as well as in science, they would have been reluctant, she felt, to speak to him "of the grand object of their lives," namely their mission to convert the Abenaki to Catholicism.[21]

Hemenway is equally dismissive of Perry's claim that the

Jesuit influence over the Missisquoi Indians was more political than religious. Acting as agents of the French king, the priests, Perry insisted, were determined to allow no friendly contact between the Indians and the English. He further suggests that the Missisquoi Abenaki took part in every bloodthirsty Indian attack on the English settlements. But, as Hemenway points out, he fails to substantiate this claim and such "suppository evidence" is "not allowable in courts," nor does it "weigh heavily in history." And even if these bellicose Indians did take part in raids on the English, did they behave any differently from the enemy? "Is the deadly embowelling of a bayonet-charge of a regiment," she asks her readers, "any more refined and Christian than a flourish of scalping knives?"[22]

Hemenway concedes that Perry may not have meant to portray the Missisquoi Indians as uniquely barbaric; he may simply have wanted to show them as competitive with what he describes as "the warlike cruel Huron, and the treacherous, bloody Iroquois." She contends further that the Abenaki's warlike spirit might have sprung as much from religious zeal as from the innate bloodthirstiness Perry ascribes to them. In this, she claims, they were no different from their enemies the English colonists, whose own will to fight had been instilled in them by their patriotic Massachusetts and Connecticut ministers. And yet Perry, in his sympathy with the English, had failed to grasp the similarities between the warriors of the two sides. "There have always been Christian soldiers," she writes, nor does it "usually make one unpatriotic to be a Christian." The very savagery of the Indians may actually have been heightened by what she calls "their perversion of the gospel." In other words, they had been led to believe that they were pleasing God by killing heretics. In this they were little different from the settlers of early New England.[23]

A further consequence of Perry's failure to give a clear presentation of the French side in the colonial wars is that he succeeds in making the English look like helpless victims rather than the warlike victors they in fact were. His editor wishes that "instead of leaving his savages and the French with the odium of being guilty of the most bloodshed," Perry might have questioned whether the English were not equally cruel.

To balance the image of Indian brutality, Hemenway provides her readers with a vivid and eloquent account of the massacre of the Abenaki in the village of St. Francis by Robert Rogers and his Rangers in 1759, an account that rightly paints a far less flattering picture of the English than the one popularized by Kenneth Roberts in *Northwest Passage*. "There was a night," Hemenway writes,

> our scouts were on the [war]path; the midnight moon and stars looked in stillness down upon a hundred, perhaps, silent wigwams, far away in Canada—the little "St. Francis Capitol," or village, where the women and children, the aged and the sick slept in supposed security: their men were on the war-path; not a warrior left behind to guard the helpless. How stealthily they come—that old Rogers and his scouts; not a twig must break; they are hunting Indians now; a reconnoitering spy has whispered the unconscious, helpless state, a ring is formed around that little Indian village, torch after torch silently applied till each wigwam rose up to light at once in flame. The infirm and the papoose perished in the flames within, the screeching squaws rushed at the doors of their wigwams, upon the bayonet, or were beaten to death by the breeches of the soldiers' guns.

But, as Hemenway queries, after describing this attack that today we would label almost genocidal,

> who ever charged it [the massacre] to the religion of Rogers or his band? Who amongst us would allow it fair to charge this barbarity of burning old men—too old to

fight, and defenseless women and children in the absence of all their warriors to the spirit of the religion generally professed in the colonies, and we fail to find it any more fair to charge the cruelty of French and Indian war-parties to their religion. We do not think there is much of the best spirit of any religion in any war; but it seems scant justice or charity to criticize on one side, and not as much on the other.[24]

In summary, Hemenway suggests that during the colonial wars both sides "doubtless with a terrible will shed what they could," and Perry would have done the English greater justice had he credited them "with having fought as hotly and well" as the French. At least let the English "claim the victory of conquerors," Hemenway writes, "and not the sympathy we give the conquered."[25]

Perry's exposure of his ignorance of not only French history but also of Roman Catholicism convinced Hemenway that she would never allow such a thing to happen again in the pages of her *Gazetteer*. "This is the first paper entered in this work," she tells her readers,

> where the writer has been allowed any criticism upon any religion but his own, and a privilege we hope to never be asked to extend again, it being the law of concord and equity for this history that it shall be for all parties and against none in religion and politics, etc., in which each are expected to write up their own records and to respect the same privilege allowed to others, avoiding all that may be, or seem like criticism upon others, in a work for the whole people, and not a partisan one.[26]

Thus for Hemenway the importance of Vermont's past was that it transcended all political and religious differences, binding its people together in a shared and admiring memory. Perry had provoked her by portraying the French and the Catholics in an unfavorable light, and she blamed this on his failure to do his homework. His neglect of the French and thus the Catholic side of the story touched a raw nerve in her. While a modern reader might prefer to learn that Hemenway's anger was provoked by Perry's insensitivity to the Abenaki, particularly his descriptions of them as barbaric and bloodthirsty, it is his bigoted picture of the Jesuits, whose religion also happens to be her own, which really offends her.

What Hemenway does not tell the readers of the *Gazetteer* is in what way she had found the original draft of Perry's essay much kinder to the French, particularly to the Jesuits, than the later published version. She presumably did this out of deference to Perry's wishes. But without a copy of the earlier version to compare with the later one there is no way of knowing whether he had in fact radically altered his portrayal of the Jesuits or whether Hemenway's conversion to Catholicism had sensitized her to his Protestant bigotry.

If Perry did make significant alterations to his history, his reasons for doing so are also a matter of conjecture. The move to Cambridge likely influenced him to alter his views toward Roman Catholics. In Swanton, with its large and well-established French population and its proximity to French Canada, Perry may have imbibed an understanding and sympathy for French culture and religion. In Cambridge and Boston, by contrast, he was exposed not only to Anglocentrism but also to the growing and deep suspicion toward all Roman Catholics fueled by the mounting tide of Irish immigrants pouring onto Boston's shores. Perry's ethnocentrism is further underscored in his account of the discovery of Graye's message in the lead tube, where he relies on "presumptive evidence" to suggest that English explorers had discovered the Missisquoi Valley well before the French.[27]

Perry's essay on the early Indian and French history of

Swanton finally made its way into print in 1882 as part of a lengthy supplement placed at the end of the fourth volume of the *Gazetteer*. Hemenway's critique, which follows, concludes with an assortment of excerpts from various Catholic histories of the Indian missions, providing names, dates, and facts that Perry had declared unobtainable.[28]

Hemenway's lengthy and forceful critique of Perry shows the degree to which her newfound religion had fortified her, enabling her to counter the American values and ideals reflected in his essay, particularly his ethnocentrism. It helped perhaps that Perry was dead and could not answer her charges. But Hemenway's Catholicism had heightened her marginality as a single woman professional. She was now a thorough outsider, and we can imagine the relish with which she vented her anger and frustration over the difficulties of her new position by taking this opportunity to censure the Protestant establishment. Furthermore, she had her facts lined up so she could topple Perry's "presumptive evidence" along with his Anglo-Saxon pride.

Having had her say and proved her Swanton historian wrong on nearly every count, Hemenway closes on a conciliatory note by asserting that "altogether, these papers of Mr. Perry are valuable, and the Catholic Church and the Jesuits are both indebted to him for having given to them the honor in this town of Swanton, of having erected the first Christian church probably in Vermont." In this way, she presumably hoped, harmony would be restored in the garden of the *Gazetteer*.[29]

Loss and Litigation

———•◦†◦†◦•———

We may not know any easy discouragement.

Abby Hemenway[1]

In 1867, when Abby Hemenway moved in with Lydia Meech, she had welcomed the arrangement as a convenience. Possessed at last of a comfortable room of her own in Burlington, she was free to devote long hours to editing her *Gazetteer*, to come and go as she pleased. But Hemenway's independence had its limits. Her landlady, she soon discovered, "preferred to hold her place at the head of her own household." As Judge Meech's wife, Lydia had been used to managing a large staff of servants who fed as many as forty people at mealtimes, and she chose to guard her new boarder very jealously. "The warmth of her partiality ripened my affections," Hemenway later wrote, showing her readiness to succumb to the older woman's charms.[2] As the months passed Hemenway was pulled ever more closely into the family circle. In 1869 DeWitt Clinton Clarke retired from his clerkship of the U.S. Senate and returned to Burlington to live. The Pearl Street household was now enlivened by the presence of this entertaining, genial man who claimed a wide circle of Protestant as well as Catholic friends.

This sociable time was destined to be shortlived. DeWitt had been home scarcely a year before he fell ill and died on August 31, 1870, suffering what were described at the time as "dropsical symptoms" with "severe inflammation and ulceration of the throat."[3] During his last illness DeWitt made Hemenway promise that she would never leave his mother. This proved to be an easy promise to keep.

By a sad coincidence, DeWitt's death occurred on the same day as that of Daniel Hemenway. Abby's father was then seventy-five years old, and family lore tells us that he spent his last years in deep mourning for his wife. But if Daniel turned to his eldest daughter for comfort, there is no record of it. The two seem never to have been particularly close, and Abby's move to Burlington only widened the gulf between them. Abby made no mention of Daniel's death in her surviving papers. All she recounts of this shared day of loss for herself and Lydia Meech is that from then onward "the sacred and precious attachment but deepened between us, and neither of us would from that day have consented to separation during her life." Bereft respectively of a father and a son, the two women were now all to one another.[4]

By making Abby Hemenway promise to remain, DeWitt was not only ensuring devoted care for his mother, but he was also hoping to protect her from the greed and malice of certain family connections, in particular Ezra Meech. Since her move to Burlington relations between Lydia and her stepson had not improved. If anything his stepmother's conversion to Catholicism only deepened Ezra's dislike of her and increased his efforts to defraud her of her widow's rights.

While the younger Meech son, Edgar, frequently called on Lydia, Hemenway remembered only two visits from Ezra during the years she lived in the Pearl Street house. Once he came long enough for dinner, but refused to sit with his stepmother after the meal was finished. The second visit occurred the winter after DeWitt's death. On this occasion, Ezra arrived by sleigh with his wife and daughter, but would not accompany them into the house. By Hemenway's account, Lydia Meech, "not fancying to be refused," sent Ezra's wife out after him three times before he finally relented and came in. Once in the parlor, however, Ezra declined a seat. Instead he walked nervously around the room for two minutes, all the while staring at his stepmother with "the eyes of a lynx." Then he left. When all three visitors had gone, Lydia Meech remarked on her stepson's strange behavior: "He was looking to see how much longer I would live," she told Hemenway. "What have I ever done to Ezra that he should look at me so?"[5]

Lydia Meech would live for another four years after DeWitt's death, and as her health deteriorated, her need for Hemenway's comforting and caring presence grew. In the last months of her life the older woman took an increasing interest in the *Gazetteer*, especially when Hemenway began working on the Rutland County volume. Lydia's native town, Shrewsbury, and Mount Holly, her first husband's birthplace, were both in that county. Like many old people, the past occupied her thoughts more than the present. She expressed a wish that Hemenway record her memories of the early history of Shrewsbury and something of her own childhood there.

This spate of interviews began in February 1873. As Hemenway tells it, Lydia compelled her to lay aside everything else "and turn in as her amanuensis, as we did, sitting by her bedside, till she had dictated to us, first, her 'Reminiscences of Shrewsbury' which she took a pride in furnishing, . . . and then of her family, and, lastly, her own private history, which she bequeathed to me—left to me and my discretion." When the widow finished recounting her life history, she admitted she had told it "as I would to a sister," declaring further that never before had she had "so much of a confidante . . . Two people cannot live together, so alone, so many years, and talk about the weather."[6]

Hemenway published the "Reminiscences of Shrewsbury" in the *Gazetteer*, assuring her readers that every item was from Lydia Meech's "own lips." The singular appeal of this oral history lies in its depiction of the humble frontier origins of a woman who would later grace the nation's capital as a brilliant and beautiful young congressman's wife. There was actually nothing new in this, because in her histories Abby Hemenway strove to include accounts of women who had distinguished themselves in a variety of ways. Not surprisingly, a good proportion of these women were the valiant wives of early settlers who braved bears, Indians, and Tories to protect their children. But tucked away in the hundreds of *Gazetteer* town histories are sketches of other notable Vermont women, including poets and teachers, doctors and midwives, missionaries and the founders of ladies' seminaries. Hemenway helped to rescue many of these individuals from oblivion by collecting their life stories herself.[7]

During the last two years of Lydia's life Hemenway spent more and more of her time caring for her. As the end neared Hemenway became so closely confined to "our dear old mother's sick room" that a cot was placed there for her use. Time and again over the course of these last months death seemed imminent, and a priest was called to give the dying woman the last sacraments.[8] Lydia Meech was eighty-eight years old, when, on September 29, 1874, the end finally came.

The loss for Hemenway was a devastating one, leaving her in some respects more bereft than she had been at the time of her own mother's death. "It always seems," Hemenway would write in 1878, "as if we had had two families, our father's that's gone now, and this gone now." For the eight years she had lived with Lydia Meech, Abby Hemenway had known love, companionship, and the security of a home. Now she was alone once again, and alone in a world that was, if anything, more wary than ever of the unattached spinster.[9]

In the decades following the Civil War, single women were both more numerous and more visible than earlier in the nineteenth century. Heavy casualties on and off the battlefield, combined with the failure of many surviving soldiers to return home, greatly reduced the number of eligible men in most communities, leaving not a few women husbandless. At the same time a widening of educational and career opportunities in these years promised more independence for those women who chose to stay single.

While some Americans viewed these changes as a healthy sign of women's advancement, others saw the growing number of independent spinsters as a threat to the social order. One New Englander, the Reverend John Todd, summed up the attitude of many when in 1867 he wrote that God had never intended woman to be independent and self-supporting. "Her support, her dignity, her beauty, her honor, and happiness," he maintained, "lie in her dependence as a wife, mother, and daughter. Any other theory is rebellious against God's law of the sexes, against marriage, which it assails in its fundamental principles, and against the family organization, the holiest thing that is left from Eden."[10]

In Abby Hemenway's case her uncomfortable position as a single woman living alone was not helped by her Catholicism, which erected a further social barrier between her and many of her neighbors. At the same time her intimate circle of fellow converts in Burlington was shrinking. Some, like Mrs. Meech, had died. Others, including William Hoyt and his wife, Anne, moved away.

Perhaps it was this sense of isolation that led Hemenway to pour her heart out to people she hadn't even met. Among her many correspondents was America's most eminent Catholic intellectual, Orestes Brownson. The two converts had been sharing views on religious and literary matters since 1873. But in a letter written six months after Lydia Meech's death Hemenway spoke candidly to Brownson of her "lonesomeness." She also complained of the inconvenience she had suffered while the Pearl Street house was being renovated. All March, she told him, carpenters, plasterers, and painters occupied the premises and she had been forced to live without a carpet for a whole month.[11]

While Abby Hemenway had lost her second family, she had not been left homeless. Shortly after her son DeWitt's death, Lydia Meech made a will leaving her companion a life interest in the Pearl Street house.[12] The renovations Hemenway described in her letter to Brownson were in expectation that one of her sisters and her husband might come and share the house with her. This, it turned out, was not to be. Nor was Hemenway given much time either to mourn her second mother's passing or to savor this promised security. Early in the new year, Ezra Meech, together with a number of Lydia's Shrewsbury relatives, filed an appeal in the Chittenden County Court suing Lydia Meech's estate for $3,950 in damages and contesting the dead woman's will.[13]

Three grounds were given for contesting the document. The first claimed that the will had been improperly executed, an objection that the judge quickly dismissed in the opening trial. A second and more serious charge described Lydia Meech as suffering from such severe physical and mental infirmity as to be wholly incapable of executing a valid will. The third charge was aimed directly at Hemenway, whom the contesters regarded as at best a meddling servant and at worst a parasite.[14] It claimed that Lydia had been subjected to "undue influence" from her companion and thus had not exercised her own "free and voluntary choice" in executing the will. A final objection to the instrument surfaced in the court arguments: The will

From the Gazetteer

* * *

Montgomery

from the *Vermont Record*

"The Lawyer and the Sawyer"

To fit up a village, with tackle for tillage,
  Jack Carter he took to the saw;
To pluck and to pillage the same little village,
  Tim Gordon he took to the law.
. . . .

[Volume II, page 469]

* * *

Westminster

by F. J. Fairbanks

"Apprehension of a thief"

[Example of how the early settlers had to take the law into their own hands.]

A traveler who had stopped at [William Goold's] tavern over night, found in the morning as he was about to start, that he had been relieved of a part of his load. In the absence of any detective police it was agreed to adopt the following shrewd plan: A rooster was placed under a large brass kettle, and each one present was to pass round and touch his nose to the kettle, and when the guilty one touched the kettle the rooster would crow. When they had all passed around and an examination was made of the noses, it was found that all but one had a black nose, and he was adjudged guilty of the theft.

[Volume V, Part 2, page 579]

specified that after Hemenway's death the house would pass to the Catholic Church.[15]

For the next four and a half years, while she continued to live in the Pearl Street house, Hemenway devoted a good portion of her time and energies to the ensuing court battle. Fortunately, she had the support of one of Vermont's most eminent lawyers, Edward John Phelps, who assured her from the start that it was her "moral and legal duty" as executrix to see that the will "was carried out." Hemenway's first action was to file a countersuit, claiming $5,000 against the estate for services rendered.[16]

The initial trial opened in the Burlington Probate Court on September 19, 1877. Despite the relatively small amount of property involved (some twelve to thirteen thousand dollars), eminent lawyers were marshaled on both sides and the case was followed with great public interest. Both Lydia Meech and Abby Hemenway were well-known figures in the city, and, according to the *Free Press*, many of their Protestant friends sided with their Catholic supporters in wishing "to see the will sustained." Mrs. Meech's family was divided on the issue, the newspaper informed its readers, "some being witnesses on one side and some on the other." Among those who refused to contest the will were Ezra Meech's brother, Edgar, and his family.[17] Hemenway later remembered how, on the first day of the trial, one of her three lawyers spoke ominously of the "awful weak looking jury," pointing out that they were "almost all young men who never sat on a case before." These fears were realized as the contesters' lawyer, in Hemenway's words, proceeded "to capture them [the jury] right up by foxy flattery. . . . He [the lawyer] made himself a 'boy' with them, and swooped up 'the boys' with him." In the end, despite the judge's charge that the will's contesters had insufficient evidence to support their case, the jury failed to reach a unanimous decision, going nine to three against the will. The case would have to be tried again.[18]

For the second trial, which opened the following April, Hemenway hired four lawyers to represent her. How she planned to pay for their services she does not say, but she was careful to note that this time the jury looked more promising. Nine were "good substantial men," and all were members of the Congregational Church. The *Free Press* gave an extensive report of this trial as well, writing at its close that the arguments "have all been unusually full and able, worthy of the best efforts of the speakers." Henry Ballard, counsel for the contestants, had spoken for more than four hours. Despite this barrage of eloquence, the jury once again failed to agree on a verdict, although this time a majority of eight favored the will.[19]

A third trial was expected in September 1878, and Hemenway decided that the time had come to tell her side of the story. What better way than by publishing her "memorial volume" for the Clarke family, a book she had begun to put together in the months following Lydia Meech's death. The lengthy reminiscences Lydia had dictated to her were already set in type, together with a hodgepodge of information about various Clarkes and Meeches. All Hemenway needed to add was an account of Lydia's death and the court battles that followed. Thus *The Clarke Papers*, though ostensibly a family history, was in fact written to bring a "happy end" to what Hemenway called "the will-warfare."[20]

In a review of *The Clarke Papers* the Burlington *Free Press* recommended the volume to DeWitt Clarke's "many old friends and acquaintances in Vermont," especially the more than two hundred pages devoted to his life, letters, and journals, which the editor promised would "vividly recall their genial and witty writer." The *Free Press* was less certain of Hemenway's wisdom in using the book to plead her case. "Opinions will differ," the review declared, as to the expediency of including a discussion of the legal controversy over Mrs. Meech's will.[21]

Whether or not publication of *The Clarke Papers* actually

contributed to the final settlement of Lydia Meech's will, in the end no further trial was held and in the early spring of 1879 the case was settled out of court in Hemenway's favor. But by this time she had spent so much money on lawyers and other expenses connected with the legal battle that she could no longer afford to keep the Pearl Street house. As she had written her friend Hiland Hall in September 1878, "*They cannot break the will*, thank God, but they may consume all its benefits to me in the process." Because Lydia Meech had designated the Catholic Church as the will's ultimate beneficiary, in July 1879 Hemenway gave the house and grounds over to Bishop Louis De Goesbriand, who in turn sold them to the Sisters of Mercy. For this Hemenway received a total of $8,500, but most if not all of this went to pay her litigation expenses.[22]

Fortunately, she was not forced to move out of the Pearl Street house immediately. Bishop De Goesbriand had no immediate use for the property when it was transferred to the diocese in July 1879. He also knew that his friend and parishioner had no other place to live. So, for the next year and a half she continued to call the Pearl Street house home, although she spent less and less time there. Meanwhile, De Goesbriand's generosity extended even further. At the time of the transfer of property, knowing that his friend had little or no money to live on, the bishop lent her the generous sum of $1,500, mortgaging some cathedral property to do so. The deed, dated July 18, 1879, stipulated that Hemenway was to receive $500 yearly for the next three years.[23]

In this period of Hemenway's life, as in others, the actual state of her finances is murky at best. She always complained of her straitened circumstances, particularly with reference to the *Gazetteer.* Yet after DeWitt Clinton Clarke's death she wrote of having sufficient cash both to pay taxes on the Pearl Street property and to lend Lydia Meech money.[24] In these years she also accumulated a sizable collection of valuable historical artifacts, books, pamphlets, and autographs. How

Hemenway paid for all this remains a mystery. While friends and family members, including Bishop De Goesbriand, and her sister Carrie's husband, did occasionally help her out with loans, the only other known source of funds would have come from the sales of her various books, including her three volumes of religious poetry. But the royalties from these works, if she did receive any, cannot have amounted to more than a few hundred dollars. Nor was Hemenway likely to have been paid much, if anything, for the occasional verses she published in *Ave Maria*. Even with her $1,500 loan from Bishop De Goesbriand, Hemenway's financial future was far from secure.

She had hardly put the Meech will troubles behind her before facing another crisis. This time the trouble was with her *Gazetteer*. By the late 1870s the work had reached such a state of financial instability that unless she found some major source of funding soon publication would cease.

These financial difficulties had been building for some time. Following the failure in the mid-1860s of J. Munsell (her printer in Albany for volume I) Hemenway had signed a contract with the Claremont Manufacturing Company. Her losses at the time were heavy, and by her account she had to take the best deal she could get. The exact terms of the arrangement with Claremont are not recoverable, but in a letter to the Vermont Historical Society's librarian, Marcus Gilman, Hemenway gave her version of the arrangement. Claremont "engaged first as silent partners," she told Gilman, "they to find capital, myself material, and to stand in as publisher with the public." Her responsibilities were to produce the necessary copy and obtain an agreed-upon number of subscriptions. She did not specify that number.[25]

Volume II, covering the histories of four counties— Franklin, Grande Isle, Lamoille, and Orange—was duly published in 1871, three years after volume I. This left five counties still to be done. Originally Hemenway had hoped the work could be completed in three volumes. But by the time the second was published she had accumulated enough material for the remaining town histories to fill two more 1,200-page volumes.[26] This escalating trend continued. By 1878 the total number of volumes had risen to five and finally, in 1882, to six.

How much was this mounting interest in the writing of local history in Vermont stimulated by the national celebration of the centennial? In 1872 the director of the U.S. Centennial Commission had urged each governor to have historical studies written of "the several communities" in their states.[27] While such official prodding was hardly necessary in Vermont, where the writing of local history was already well underway, the centennial celebration may have provided a further inducement for individual towns to contribute their histories to Hemenway's *Gazetteer* and encouraged her historians to produce lengthier, more detailed essays. Parenthetically, Hemenway said little herself about the centennial; although the preface of volume III is dated July 4, 1876, she makes no mention of the celebrations and commemorations taking place that day.

Of course, the prospect of longer histories meant more books, and this necessarily meant higher printing costs, at least over the long run. But the old problem of lagging subscriptions continued. In February 1870 Hemenway apologized to one of her historians for not paying him for his work, explaining that "as for money we have not yet sold enough to pay the enormous printing bills."[28] By the summer of 1871 her Claremont printers, in Hemenway's words, had become "sick of their own bargain—quarrelling ever with themselves." Anxious to ease the firm's worries and even more to see the work completed, she signed a new contract making Claremont the sole proprietor of volumes II and III. As she told it, the conditions under which she relinquished ownership were that "they [her Claremont printers] should promptly finish up volumes III and IV." These conditions, however, were not met.[29]

Some of the holdups that occurred were unavoidable. In the fall of 1872 a bad flood in the town of Claremont swept away much of the firm's property. As Hemenway put it, her printers "did not feel for a time like investing much prospectively in Vermont history."[30] In 1873 came the onset of a severe national depression, which would continue on and off for the next two decades. Massive railroad speculation had launched the crisis, causing business failures followed in turn by rising unemployment. The big cities were hardest hit, but Burlington also suffered and many workers lost their jobs. "The pressure on all trades has been so great," Hemenway wrote on July 14, 1874, that Claremont had called a halt to the printing of volume III the previous fall. Work had recently resumed, she noted, and books were expected in October. But delays continued for another two years. Not until early in 1877 did volume III finally appear.[31]

Meanwhile, hard times only made the selling of subscriptions more difficult. Vermonters were often willing to buy the issue or volume that contained the history of their town, but then showed little interest in keeping up their subscriptions. In 1877 Hemenway wrote of needing one thousand subscribers to keep the work alive but only having three hundred.[32] In an effort to bring in more money Hemenway and her printer offered to publish some of the longer town histories separately in pamphlet-sized booklets of twenty-five to fifty pages. If individual communities could pledge one hundred or more subscribers, she would print their histories at a cost of twenty-five to fifty cents. But this project, while successful in its own way, did not solve the problem of the *Gazetteer's* growing indebtedness.

Whether it was Hemenway's idea or the brainchild of one of her many antiquarian friends, state aid became the panacea for keeping the work alive. When the members of the Vermont

Historical Society gathered in Montpelier for their annual meeting on October 14, 1878, they passed a resolution calling for legislative support of the *Gazetteer* which read as follows:

> That this Society, recognizing the valuable services of Miss. A. M. Hemenway, as editor of the Vermont Historical Gazetteer, and appreciating the Gazeteer [sic] as a repository of historical information of very high value to the people of the State, respectfully recommends to the Legislature of Vermont to assist Miss Hemenway in the completion of her work by authorizing a subscription for copies of the Gazetteer on the part of the State, or in such other manner as their wisdom may direct.[33]

The biennial session of the legislature had already opened when this resolution was passed. Two days later, on October 16, Senator Loveland Munson of Manchester introduced a joint resolution in the Senate granting such aid. A *Free Press* article supporting the proposed resolution spelled out the principal reason why this aid was necessary: "any book which depends solely or largely for its sale upon a circulation confined to this State, cannot be made to pay expenses."[34]

While the joint resolution made its way through both houses that fall, Hemenway publicly defended her need for financial support. "All we ask of the Legislature," she explained in a letter to the *Free Press*, "is their vote that the State buy enough to pay the printing of the last two volumes." Without such aid, she wondered what might "become of the mass of historical material we have been so many years gathering—that many persons have expended so much labor on, in which much of interest in many towns has been garnered by men in their graves." She heightened the sense of crisis by describing how, in some instances, the heirs of deceased historians were clamoring for the return of their papers because they had not yet been published. "Shall we again scatter back all thus called for, to never again be gathered up? . . . We are hardly able to wait longer and resist this clamor. We must proceed if we would finish the work."[35]

Whether aided by Hemenway's pleas or not, the joint resolution was passed by the Senate on November 12 with only one dissenting voice and by a comfortable margin in the House eleven days later. The measure authorized the state librarian to "subscribe for and purchase twenty-five copies each of volumes One, Four and Five of said Gazetteer" (volumes II and III were owned by the Claremont Manufacturing Company). The joint resolution further authorized the state to underwrite $2 of the $6 cost of each volume to any town, organized public library, or individual wishing to purchase it.[36] As the *Free Press* was pleased to observe, "The indefatigable editor of this work has had better luck with the present Legislature than could have been anticipated."[37]

Support throughout Vermont at the 1879 March town meetings was less heartening. Only 24 communities in the whole state voted to spend town monies to purchase the *Gazetteer.* Another 18 towns did vote to furnish substitutes: representatives, town clerks, historians, or others designated by the town to take advantage of the discount. Over the ensuing weeks, 112 volumes were duly paid for and delivered. Accounts were then sent to the state auditor, who was to forward to Hemenway the balance of $2 owed on each volume.[38]

Two hundred and twenty-four dollars probably did not go far to meet the *Gazetteer's* debts, but in the end even this sum never materialized. In mid-July 1879 the Vermont state auditor announced that none of the five joint resolutions appropriating money at the last legislative session would be funded. Like other public and private laws they must be approved and signed by the governor. These had not been. No matter, declared the auditor, that this method of appropriating funds by joint resolution without the governor's signature had been employed in

Vermont for the past hundred years; this year the law would be obeyed as written.[39]

Hemenway appealed to Governor Redfield Proctor, but to no avail. While the Rutland businessman expressed sympathy for her plight, he said he could do nothing to help her. Wait for the next legislature, he told her, assuring her that her many friends in Vermont would again support her when the General Assembly convened in the fall of 1880.[40]

Hemenway's frustration and despair at this latest blow can only be imagined. In some respects this crisis in her life was not unlike the one she had faced in the mid-1860s when publication of the *Gazetteer* had halted for the duration of the Civil War. But Hemenway was older now (she turned fifty-one in October) and more isolated. Her housing situation was precarious at best, and the two people who had meant the most to her, her mother and Lydia Meech, were dead. With her personal and professional life in disarray, this aging, unmarried woman had one remaining refuge, the Catholic Church.

Exhausted and at her wit's end, Hemenway left Vermont in mid-January 1880, carrying with her for safekeeping an undisclosed amount of money and various articles, including a "silver set."[41] The funds presumably came from the final transfer of the Pearl Street property and the set of silver from Lydia Meech, a poignant reminder of better and happier times. Hemenway's destination was Notre Dame, Indiana, home of St. Mary's Academy—now St. Mary's College—where she had been hired to teach Latin for the spring term. Her duties were not onerous, and by late January she described getting "nicely rested."[42]

We know little about Hemenway's six months at St. Mary's except that by the end of her employment there she was seriously considering making this intellectually lively Catholic community her permanent home. As during her previous visit in 1865, she boarded with the Holy Cross sisters at St. Mary's

Convent. There she grew intimate with many of the nuns in the community, but their superior, Mother Angela Gillespie, became her special friend and guide. This gifted administrator had founded more than forty schools and colleges, hospitals, and asylums during her lifetime.[43] Her energy and skills, though differently directed, matched Hemenway's own. Above all, Mother Angela understood what it meant to be an ambitious, driven woman who saw work to be done and did it.

During these few months, then, Hemenway once again had a family, as well as the comfort of living in a community whose members all shared her religious faith. The appeal of such a life for a woman in her position was powerful. If she joined the order of the Holy Cross she would have a home and security, and her precarious existence as a single woman struggling to earn her keep would cease.

But for Hemenway the decision to make such a drastic change in her life cannot have been an easy one. If she joined the Sisters of the Holy Cross she could perhaps continue to teach, but at such a distance from Vermont that her historical labors would end. Also, the time-consuming work of editing her *Gazetteer* hardly squared with the total immersion in the religious life demanded of a novice. Had all the volumes been published few barriers would have stood in her way. As it was, she had obligations back home in Vermont. Town histories were written that she had promised to publish. Historical materials—documents, statistics—had been gathered that would be lost to history if she did not print them. The legislature was due to convene again that fall, and as Governor Proctor had suggested, the *Gazetteer's* many friends in Vermont would again support her effort to secure state aid. Hemenway owed it to the people of the Green Mountain State to finish the work.

In the end her decision to return to Vermont and complete her *Gazetteer* received the blessing of the priests and nuns at Notre Dame. Shortly before her departure, she signed an agreement with Father Edward Sorin, the president of Notre Dame College; Mother Angela Gillespie; and another Holy Cross sister, Mother Mary Ascension. This "business arrangement," as Hemenway called it, stipulated that she was "to go forth and try and finish" her history, and, when this was done, come back to Notre Dame. Meanwhile, the money and other items she had brought with her, including the "silver set," were to be kept safely for her until her return. At that time, if she decided to enter the religious life, they would serve as her dowry. But if she chose not to become a nun she was free to take back all she had left and depart.[44]

Hemenway's future was thus left open. Whether she ultimately chose the religious life or not, that option held out the promise of future security, particularly if legislative efforts to support her *Gazetteer* ultimately failed. In July, when she returned to Vermont, she knew at least that in Notre Dame she had both a home and a family she could call her own.

15

Keeping the Gazetteer Alive

———•◦◦◦◦•———

Only those who know the supremacy of the
intellectual life—the life which has a seed of
enobling thought and purpose within it—can
understand the grief of one who falls from serene
activity into the absorbing, soul-wasting struggle
with worldly annoyances.

George Eliot, Middlemarch[1]

By late July 1880 Hemenway was back in Burlington for a
"little sojourn," having made the long journey from Notre
Dame with Mother Angela Gillespie's railroad pass carrying
her free as far as Detroit. Although Hemenway no longer called
Burlington home, she had business as well as friends there and
needed to see her lawyer about an "attachment of the mortgage." Presumably one of her creditors was anxious to get his
hands on some of the money she had received from the final
transfer of the Meech property to the church.

During her stay in Burlington, Hemenway stored her trunk
with the Sisters of Mercy and spent several nights with the

Sacred Heart sisters in their convent on St. Joseph's Mount. Early on the morning of July 26 she went to confession to the same priest who had baptized her sixteen years earlier. Although she did not tell him of her conditional plan to join the Sisters of the Holy Cross—her "sweetest secret" as she called it—she was pleased when he advised her to "drop everything today, to henceforth give *only to Heaven every talent God has given you.*" She listened "silently and happily," and told him that that was just what she had agreed to do back in Notre Dame.[2]

While in Burlington, Hemenway also passed an afternoon in the studio of a local artist and fellow Catholic, Eliza Austin. Austin was then at work on a large painting of the Virgin Mary commissioned by a local church, and Hemenway took time to admire the tall, graceful Madonna in its Grecian drapery. Nothing gave her greater pleasure than talking with women artists and writers, and by her account she and Eliza had enjoyed "a dearly delightful, sweetly earnest visit." What particularly impressed Hemenway was the way her friend was able to combine her work as an artist with her calling as a Catholic. "The subject of religious vocation seemed as much to pervade her as her *art* vocation," she told Mother Angela.[3]

Despite her single-minded devotion to history, Hemenway was perhaps also lamenting the failure of her own ambitions as a religious poet. It had been nearly a decade since the appearance of the last of her three books on the Holy Family. *The House of Gold and the Saint of Nazareth. A Poetical Life of St. Joseph* was published in 1873. It had added little to the earlier volumes, and like its predecessor, *Rosa Immaculata*, suffered from what one reviewer described as jarring rhythms and a tendency to employ abstruse language.[4] In any case, Hemenway published no more religious poetry. By 1880 the *Gazetteer* was, as far as we know, her sole literary effort.

With no home to call her own that summer, she spent the weeks between her return from Notre Dame and the convening of the legislature in October visiting friends. Once her business in Burlington was completed, she took the train south to Whitehall, New York, a town just over the Vermont border on the southern end of Lake Champlain. Here she spent some weeks staying with two Catholic convert friends, Almon Hopson, a church architect, and his wife, Sarah. The Hopsons had been Hemenway's first Catholic godchildren, and they remained close friends to the end of her life.[5]

When she did return to Vermont in mid-October, Montpelier, not Burlington, became her home base. She was offered board and lodging in a convent run by the Sisters of the Immaculate Heart of Mary. All five nuns had recently moved from Burlington to the state capital to run the local parochial school. They invited Hemenway to stay with them for the duration of the legislative session.

The morning after her arrival, Hemenway walked over to the State House uneasy about what lay before her. Judging from her correspondence in these weeks, she was torn between an earnest desire to complete the *Gazetteer*—as everyone expected her to do—and a powerful longing for a home and rest from her arduous labors. As she admitted in a letter to Father Edward Sorin, the president of Notre Dame, if this second attempt to get aid from the legislature succeeded it would give her "two pretty hard years work."[6]

During her first day in Montpelier, Hemenway called first on the state geologist, Hiram A. Cutting, an old acquaintance. Cutting told her that she would easily get the same appropriation—passed by the legislature in 1878 but not funded—through both houses a second time. But when she stopped by to see Marcus Gilman, the historical society librarian, this friend was less sanguine. Apparently a representative of the Claremont Manufacturing Company had been in town trying to obtain for the firm a share of whatever state revenues the *Gazetteer* received. Gilman "saw at once," Hemenway told her friends at Notre Dame, that "we had been tampered with by

Claremont. He thought it would be easier and better" to get a new bill that would satisfy both parties.

Then Gilman cheered her up by telling her that the Montpelier representative, Hiram Huse, one of Hemenway's historians and a man of great influence in the legislature, had asked what he could do about her bill. Huse, who was also the state librarian, had supported her original bid for aid. When he learned that she was in town he invited her to come to the library the following afternoon so they could discuss "what is best to be done and how."[7]

Other early support came from the Vermont Historical Society, which, at its annual meeting on October 19, urgently recommended that the legislature vote to help fund the *Gazetteer*. At the same time, the Claremont Manufacturing Company continued to make trouble by insisting that they receive two-thirds, not one-half, of the monies obtained. The company representative, anxious to make what Hemenway called a "sharp bargain," hoped that with the help of a few powerful friends in the House and Senate, he could slip his own version of the bill through in a few days.[8]

But this ruse did not work. By mid-November, Hemenway could report that the Claremont representative had seen "his folly in retarding the work." Meanwhile, her bill was at last making its way through the legislature. "The house seems ripening well to receive it," she told her Notre Dame friends, but she feared that the "division of feeling and opinion in the Senate" might hinder its passage through both chambers and end in its defeat. She pronounced it "impassable [sic] to control the prolongation of matters that get entangled in the endless Legislature wheels within wheels—and all running so slow." One problem seemed to be that some senators wanted the remainder of the work completed in one volume, while others were agreeable to funding two more.[9]

During these weeks Hemenway spent a large portion of her time lobbying for the measure's passage. Thanks presumably to the kindness of Hiram Huse, she made the state library, then located in the capitol building, her headquarters. Every day from ten to noon and again from one to five she met with members of the House. Her scheme was to win support from individual representatives of Vermont's towns by promising them supplementary histories to be published in the last two volumes of the *Gazetteer*. She directed her attention primarily at legislators from towns in Addison and Bennington counties, whose histories, published in the first three numbers of the *Quarterly*, had been especially brief and only carried the story up to the Civil War.[10]

Hemenway began her conference with each member by discussing what writers might be secured to bring his community's history up to date in the supplement. "That is a great lever with the 8/11ths of the towns," she assured Father Sorin in a long letter describing her lobbying efforts. "When a man has picked his town board of writers he is going to vote to have the work completed." Meanwhile, she further heightened the member's interest by scribbling down as he talked a list of the "*subjects* to be brought down" in the supplementary essay—"long lists for each town."

The endless days spent in this fashion left Hemenway exhausted. "I come home so tired," she confessed to Father Sorin, "I have to lie right down for the hour before supper." Fortunately, her evenings were quiet. After supper at the convent she would read a little, and when the sisters had their recreation time she would listen to them talk "or tell them my little history of the day at the State House—who I have seen—what new towns booked."[11]

The weeks dragged on in this way until December 9, when Hemenway's appropriations bill was finally reported out of committee favorably. By this time a second, potentially serious obstacle to the measure's passage had arisen in the person of ex-Governor John B. Page of Rutland, whom Hemenway described as "a rich old banker" and "a sordid bigote" [sic].

"He opposes me, I am told and have no reason to doubt because he hates my religion," she informed her friends at Notre Dame. In Page's effort to get the third reading of Hemenway's bill refused he was seconded by a Windsor County acquaintance of hers, H. A. Fletcher of Cavendish. This "*rabid* Baptist," as Hemenway called him, had been a fellow member of the Ludlow Baptist Church and had once denounced her for abandoning the church of her youth.[12]

She was in the gallery that December afternoon listening to the spirited discussion of her bill, when she heard John Page make the erroneous claim that ex-Governor Hiland Hall had advised him not to sign the bill. Hemenway, who had recently received a letter of support from her friend Hall, knew this was an outright lie. Hall's letter was among her papers in the state library, and she slipped out of her seat as unobtrusively as possible to fetch it.

By Hemenway's account, in the interim, a House member and supporter of the bill, having heard Page's pronouncement, telegraphed Hall in Bennington. Hall's reply was immediate. No sooner had Hemenway returned to her seat in the gallery than the sergeant-at-arms, like the cavalry riding to the rescue, entered the legislative chamber to announce in a ringing voice that a telegram had been received from "his late *Excellency*," Governor Hall. In his message Hall denied outright ever having told Page not to sign the bill and assured the legislature that it would do Miss Hemenway "complete justice" by passing the measure. "This settled old Gov. Page for the time," Hemenway assured her Notre Dame friends, and when, on December 21st, the bill came up for a third reading, it passed in the House by a vote of 115 to 63. Two days later the Senate concurred with 17 members supporting the measure while 8 voted against it.[13] The bill, as finally passed, authorized the state librarian "to subscribe for twenty-five complete sets of Miss Hemenway's *Vermont Historical Gazetteer*, at four dollars per volume." In addition, each town, by a vote at town meeting, could obtain a subscription at a cost of two dollars per volume, or "furnish a substitute"—such as the town librarian—who would benefit from the same discount. The bill further stipulated that volumes IV and V would complete the *Gazetteer*, the first to be finished by the end of June 1882, and volume V in 1883. As Hemenway had written Father Sorin back in October, she had her work cut out for her.[14]

With state aid finally assured, her first job was to collect the unbound copies of volume I then in storage in Burlington and ready them for the bindery. Thanks to the appropriation, she had sold 266 books that might otherwise never have found buyers. But she had to pay for the binding herself at a cost of $1.00 per copy, and to meet this expense she needed to recall $250 of the money she had deposited at Notre Dame the previous summer.[15]

Hemenway's biggest task that winter of 1881 was to find a printer for her fourth volume. In 1878, George Grenville Benedict, the editor of the Burlington *Free Press*, had agreed to publish it. But that agreement had fallen through, perhaps because of the delay in state funding, or because she had failed to obtain a sufficient number of subscriptions. Fortunately, it didn't take Hemenway long to find a replacement. On February 23, 1881, Joseph Poland, the editor of the *Vermont Watchman and Journal*, a Montpelier newspaper, signed on as the printer for volume IV.[16]

Joseph Poland, a respected citizen of Montpelier, was also the editor of the *Vermont Chronicle* and a deacon of the Congregational Church. The *St. Albans Messenger* described him as "exceptionally free from the petty jealousies, . . . the rancor and unwarranted personal abuse which have prevailed too generally among the editors of the state." After many years spent enduring the sharp dealings of the Claremont Manufacturing Company, Hemenway must have felt that her *Gazetteer* was at last in good hands. And so it was, at least for the time being.[17]

Volume IV was originally intended to contain the histories of the last three counties: Washington, Windham, and Windsor. But sometime between the publication of volume III in 1877 and the appearance of volume IV in 1882 the whole work had expanded and only Washington, with supplements for Franklin, Caledonia, and Rutland County towns, would be found in this volume.

According to the schedule spelled out by the legislature in the 1880 appropriations bill, to receive state funding the fourth volume had to be in print by July 1882. This gave Hemenway a little more than a year to ready it for publication. Fortunately, she had completed editing a good number of the Washington County histories in the late 1860s.

Because the actual printing of volume IV did not begin until the late spring of 1881, Hemenway was able to make another visit to Notre Dame that winter. She stayed for several months, resting up for the season of toil that lay ahead. Once back in Montpelier, the editor of the *Gazetteer* went to work in rented rooms striving to meet a succession of printing deadlines.[18]

Joseph Poland began by publishing one-hundred-page sections of the volume in pamphlet form. These cost only fifty cents each and made it possible for individual towns to buy multiple copies of their own histories. The first of these pamphlets appeared in August 1881. It contained the complete histories of Barre and Berlin but broke off in the middle of the Cabot chapter. The second number completed the history of Cabot, continued with the histories of Calais and Fayston, and stopped in the middle of a sentence in the chapter on Marshfield. This rather disjointed but admittedly inexpensive approach was soon discontinued. The history of Montpelier was published on its own and thereafter only histories of the larger towns in Washington County seem to have been printed separately.[19]

For more than a year Hemenway worked unstintingly in

her rented room, getting manuscripts and copy ready for the printer. By April 1882 she had 1,000 pages of the volume completed and 245 more to go. To meet the fast-approaching July deadline she was editing 32 pages of unread manuscripts each day and reading proofs besides. She admitted to one of her friends at Notre Dame that she had few "even 'breathing moments.'"[20]

On June 13 Hemenway wrote Hiland Hall in Bennington to say that the last page of volume IV was set in type. "O how glad one feels to have a County done," she told him. But with the deadline for volume V only a year away, she had little time to rest. In her letter to Hall she informed him of her plan to include supplements for the town histories of Addison and Bennington Counties in the final two volumes. Much of that summer seems to have been spent working on these. Hall could expect to see her when she came to Bennington to "talk up her plans" with the leading writers in that town, a method she had "always found effective in kindling an interest in the work."[21]

By July 17 the fourth volume was in print in time to meet the legislative deadline. The centerpiece of this bulky book was the history of Montpelier, which took up 323 of its 1,245 pages and contained more than fifty illustrations, most of them portraits of eminent men. No other town history in the whole of the *Gazetteer* came close to taking up as much space as Montpelier's, and the reasons for its length are obvious; it enabled Hemenway to show her gratitude for the support she had received from the state government.[22] As she wrote on the book's dedication page, "this succeeding volume, with the history of the capital of the state in its bosom, will spontaneously be felt an offering happily due to the two legislatures [those of 1878 and 1880] who have thus preserved the history of the state." She concluded her dedication by describing herself as "proud and content at last to be a historiographer in Vermont." Thanks to support from the state government Abby Hemenway's dignity as editor of the *Gazetteer* had been restored.[23]

But the constraints put on her by the appropriations bill would take their toll. While the fourth volume did meet the publication deadline imposed by the 1880 legislature, the misspellings and typographical errors found on many of its pages betrayed the haste with which it was printed.[24] A review in the Burlington *Free Press*, while noting that "the proof-reading might have been more careful," was also ready to underscore the "difficulties and discouragements" under which the editor had worked. These would have "utterly daunted a person of less tenacity of purpose," the reviewer maintained. But under Abby Hemenway's editorship such "obstacles have only delayed not defeated the progress of the work, and it has now reached a stage, where its completion may be confidently expected."[25]

In late August 1882, Hemenway told Hiland Hall she had four unaccomplished things "most at heart," that her work would "never seem half done till I may see them done." These were to have the Windham and Windsor County histories published, together with the supplements for Addison and Bennington Counties. The manuscripts for Windham County were particularly rich and well written, she told Hall, adding that she intended to ask the legislature to let her have one more volume, "that I may at least do this as it should be done."[26]

Buoyed perhaps by her success in meeting the legislature's deadline for volume IV, Hemenway went back in the fall of 1882 to ask that the 1880 bill be amended to increase the number of volumes from five to six. She also asked for a freer hand in providing substitute subscribers for towns that voted to take the *Gazetteer* but failed to pay up. The bill that passed on November 28 granted both of these requests but insisted that the whole work should be completed by December 31, 1884.[27] This gave her a little more than two years to prepare two 1,200-page volumes. It was an impossible demand, particularly because obstacles continued to block her progress. Despite the optimism of the legislature, the editor of the *Free Press*, and, above all, Hemenway herself, volume IV of the *Vermont Historical Gazetteer* was the last to be published in her lifetime.

The next round of troubles began in the winter of 1882–83 when Hemenway discovered that several hundred copies of volume IV had missing pages and were thus defective. We only have her confusing account of this printing blunder, but its ramifications profoundly affected her future and that of the *Gazetteer*. The mistake occurred when volume IV was two-thirds printed and, more importantly, after Joseph Poland had sold his publishing business to William Prescott. This new owner, according to Hemenway, proceeded to run a tight ship.[28] Without hiring any new help, Prescott reduced the work week from six to five days. He also refused to adjust the workload. Thus the overtaxed printers quite naturally began making mistakes, and the most egregious was to omit eight to sixteen pages from more than four hundred copies of volume IV, or one-third of the total number printed. This was bad enough, but when the firm insisted, with Poland's backing, that Hemenway had to pay the wholesale price for all the volumes whether defective or not, she refused.[29]

The battle lines were drawn. We do not have Poland or Prescott's version of the story, but Hemenway by this time was already several hundred dollars in debt to the company for printing bills, and Prescott seems to have held Poland responsible for seeing that she paid up. True, it was Hemenway who owed Poland money, not the other way around, but he had also furnished a defective product. In letters describing the events of that winter and spring, she referred to the "wicked Mr. Poland," who had used her so fraudulently and "undertook to grab all I had worked on so hard for and had been successful in compiling."[30]

By Hemenway's account, early in March 1883, while she was out of town for a few weeks, Poland obtained a duplicate key to her office in Montpelier. One night he and a man identified only as Clement entered these rooms and took all the

Joseph Poland, editor of the *Vermont Watchman and Journal*,
who printed Volume IV of the *Vermont Historical Gazetteer*.
(From Volume IV of the *VHG*.)

copies of the fourth volume of the *Gazetteer* they could find. Poland then had an attachment (or mortgage) placed on the books.[31]

The official story of what took place that March night is rather different. Court records describe the deputy sheriff of Washington County, John L. Tuttle, as confiscating the books and storing them in the *Watchman and Journal's* bindery, belonging to J. D. Clark. To obtain their release Hemenway would have to pay Joseph Poland more than three hundred dollars. This was a foolish move on the part of both Poland and the court because without books to sell Hemenway had no income.

Hemenway, of course, was furious. She was also convinced, despite the rulings of the court to the contrary, that the confiscated books belonged to her. In response she filed a counter claim, protesting that Poland and his binder, J. D. Clark, had not fulfilled the terms of their contract with her, which included printing the books without omitting pages. Then, a few nights after her books were seized, Hemenway out of sheer desperation made an egregiously unwise move. As the court records describe it, on March 5, "without the consent of the said Joseph Poland, without the consent of said J. D. Clark, without the consent or knowledge of either," Abby Hemenway entered the bindery and removed the confiscated books.[32]

Meanwhile, the chancery suit filed by Poland against Hemenway had also been filed against Burgess Field, her sister Lydia's husband. Field too, apparently, held a mortgage for the newly printed volume IV. The whole business was getting messier and messier.[33]

The *Gazetteer's* mounting indebtedness, combined with Hemenway's unreasonable behavior toward Poland and the others to whom she owed money, did not improve her reputation as a responsible businesswoman. But, while we know the identity of some of her adversaries during these difficult months, we don't know who, among her many antiquarian friends, stood by her to offer advice and support. Nor do we know if she was willing to take counsel even when offered. Like a mother trying to preserve the life of a beloved child, she seemed ready to go to any lengths to save her *Gazetteer*.

In an effort to end the quarrel between Poland and Hemenway, on April 9, 1883, the Washington County Court submitted the case to a committee of arbitration consisting of William H. H. Bingham and M. E. Smilie. After studying the claims of both parties, the two referees concluded that Miss Hemenway owed Mr. Poland $344.62. They further stated that all copies of volume IV of the *Gazetteer*, currently in the possession of Poland, Clark, or Prescott, were the property of Abby Maria Hemenway. But these books were also subject to the lien placed on them, and not until her debt to Poland was paid would these volumes become "the absolute property of said Hemenway." Hemenway's debt to Poland remained unpaid until after her death, and she never regained possession of volume IV.[34]

Finally, the whole miserable experience drove the editor of the *Gazetteer* out of Montpelier and back to Ludlow. Hemenway's plan, because she could no longer afford to hire a printer, was to rent rooms and set up her own publishing establishment. Where she obtained the funds for this she does not say, but sometime before January 1884 she leased a large room in the Peabody Block on Ludlow's Main Street. Her young cousin, Alice Barton Piper, later described how the room was divided into three sections using "turkey red" curtains as partitions. The main room served as kitchen and printing shop with type cases, cupboards, a sink, and a stove. Both the "reception room," as Hemenway called it, and her bedroom displayed a few grand pieces of furniture, including a grandfather clock and a mahogany four-poster bed, which she had presumably inherited from Lydia Meech. Several old religious paintings adorned the walls.

In this makeshift setting Hemenway carried on her work, engaging relatives and friends to help her set type, a process she may have learned from her uncle Asa. Typesetters normally worked standing in front of a frame or stand that contained several cases of type. But Alice Piper, one of Hemenway's helpers, later remembered that her cousin didn't own such a piece of equipment. Instead she sat on the floor to set her type, "working night and day and scarcely eating in order to fulfill her contracts." Some of the younger cousins, Piper recalled, lacked a certain enthusiasm about working so hard for no pay. Not surprisingly, Hemenway found their attitude bewildering. How could anyone be concerned with financial betterment when there was such important work to be done in the world as publishing the *Vermont Historical Gazetteer?*[35]

For six weeks or so during the cold, snowy winter of 1884 Hemenway and her helpers made steady progress with volume V.

On Sundays she attended mass up the hill at the Church of the Annunciation, which had been built in 1876. Then, in late February, disaster struck again and Abby Hemenway met with what she called "the great accident" of her life. She was run over by a sleigh driven by George Bridges, the proprietor of Ludlow's only restaurant. The collarbone in Hemenway's right shoulder was broken, and for two months the arm she wrote with was in a sling. Worn out with work, and suffering from pneumonia at the time the accident occurred, she nearly died. But the ministrations of a doctor, paid for by George Bridges, brought at least a partial recovery. At the end of six weeks she was able "to use the pen considerably again by holding up our paper on a pasteboard."[36]

All this time work on the *Gazetteer* continued, with Hemenway directing her various helpers from her sickbed. When health and work permitted, she also entertained friends in her "reception room." She continued to hope that she would succeed in publishing volumes V and VI in time to meet the fast-approaching deadline. On April 29, 1884, she wrote Henry Sheldon, an antiquarian friend in Middlebury, that she was coming on "slowly but nicely" with volume V, using better paper and handsomer type. How she paid for this extravagance she did not say. "I do what I can," she told her Middlebury friend, "and in that find content."[37]

The new year arrived with much work left to be done on volume V and work scarcely begun on volume VI. In the end, Hemenway's earnest but largely futile efforts to meet her publishing commitments, combined with her ongoing legal battles with Joseph Poland, did little to improve her health. On April 23, 1885, she was ordered to appear in court in Montpelier in connection with her mounting debts. But by this time she may have been too ill to leave Ludlow. Although she didn't divulge the precise nature of her ailments, by her account they were severe enough to alarm her Ludlow doctor. In May, he warned her that, unless she stopped all work on the *Gazetteer* for at least four months and concentrated on taking care of herself, she would die. He advised her further that she would recover more quickly if she left home.[38]

Hemenway felt she had little choice but to comply with these orders. She closed up her printing shop in Ludlow, dismissed her young helpers, and left town. She went first to Brandon where her sisters Carrie and Lydia lived, and then to Whitehall to visit the Hopsons.[39]

She would turn fifty-seven in October, and uppermost in Hemenway's mind in these weeks was her own mortality. While staying in Whitehall with her Catholic friends she decided the time had come to make a will. Dated June 11, 1885, the document appointed Almon Hopson as her executor and directed him to pay her funeral expenses and all "just debts" from her estate. Any residue should be divided in two: one half to cover the costs of printing her own unpublished writings "either in poetry or prose," the other to be used for the benefit of the Catholic Church in Ludlow. Hemenway was ever the optimist, but the wonder is, given the extent of her financial liabilities, that she could imagine even the possibility of a residue.[40]

Finally, the will appointed Hopson to dispose of those manuscripts intended for publication in the *Gazetteer* according to Hemenway's explicit instructions. Unfortunately, these instructions were listed in a document separate from her will and no longer exist. Soon after the document was signed and given to Sarah Hopson for safe keeping, Hemenway left Whitehall. By the end of June, tempted by low railroad fares and the urging of friends in the Midwest, she was in Chicago. This thriving midwestern city would be her last home.[41]

16

Exile in Chicago

———•◦◊◦•———

I don't propose at all to give up the ship.

Abby Hemenway[1]

"Providence drifted me here," Hemenway told her Middlebury friend Henry Sheldon at the end of 1886 in a letter explaining her move to Chicago. She originally came to the city, she informed him, to sell her printing press and to visit friends. But having been there a few weeks she "concluded to send home to Ludlow" for her type cases "and to see what I could do with them here." She presumably had all her books and papers shipped to Chicago at the same time, including bound and unbound copies of the *Gazetteer* together with the manuscripts for the remaining two volumes.[2]

Thus, what began as a temporary sojourn became permanent. But how honest were Hemenway's stated reasons for going to Chicago? True, her doctor had ordered her to take a long rest, preferably away from Ludlow. She had friends in Chicago, and it was only a few hours by train from Notre Dame. But it was also a long way from Vermont, from Joseph Poland and her other creditors. A letter of Hemenway's dated soon after her arrival suggests that this distance was perhaps the most important reason she went west.

This letter, a confidential one, was addressed to Albert Hager, the librarian of the Chicago Historical Society and a longtime admirer of the *Gazetteer*. It gave a detailed account of Hemenway's difficulties with Poland, including his most recent demand: that she account for the whereabouts of every copy of volume IV, not omitting those delivered to her before the attachment, so that he could judge for himself whether they were under his lien or not.[3]

Hemenway, however, had no intention of telling Poland or the court about the one hundred unbound copies of volume IV that she had brought with her to Chicago. They were, as she told Hager, an important source of income, and what better way to keep them safe from her creditors than to carry them off to another state. Coming to the principal purpose of her letter she then asked Hager if he would be willing to store these volumes for her at the historical society. "It is indispensable for the completion of the work—that they be saved," she assured him, adding that she would pay for the storage with bound copies of the *Gazetteer*. Whether Hager acceded to her request or not, this letter makes it clear that Hemenway's reasons for coming to Chicago were not perhaps as innocent as she led Henry Sheldon to believe.[4]

Twenty years had passed since she had last seen this great midwestern metropolis. And, like everyone else who revisited Chicago after the devastation of the Great Fire of 1871, she found that a whole new city had risen up from the ashes of the old frontier town. Recovery had been both fast and spectacular. By the 1890s Chicago would boast the busiest and most modern downtown in the whole country.

After Hemenway's arrival in June 1885, she first found lodging in St. Joseph's Home, a Catholic residence for employed women at 409 South May Street. What her accommodations were like she did not say, but the residence contained a chapel, and thus allowed her the comfort of attending daily mass.

These quarters were home for the better part of a year, and as soon as her type cases, manuscripts, and other papers arrived from Ludlow, Hemenway was once again hard at work on her *Gazetteer*. After selling her press for $100 more in Chicago than she could have got for it in Vermont, she found herself a printer, the firm of Donahue and Henneberry on Wabash Avenue. As she told Henry Sheldon, the cost of printing was the same in Chicago as in Vermont and paper was cheaper. There were other benefits as well. "I can reach a class of Vermonters in the far west here that I c[oul]d not from Vermont," she informed him, noting further that volume I of the *Gazetteer* sold as well in Chicago as volume IV, "slowly, but now and then one."[5] She didn't mention the biggest advantage of publishing the *Gazetteer* in the West: Her reputation for indebtedness had not followed her there.

Hemenway's principal effort in these months was to publish pamphlet histories of various Windham and Windsor County towns, much as she had for Washington County. If she received orders for one hundred or more copies of an individual town history, Donahue and Henneberry would print them. In the meantime, she continued to edit her other manuscripts for volume V and set them into type. In June, shortly after her arrival in Chicago, she told Albert Hager that she had 548 pages of volume V completed. By the fall that number was up to 700, and she also had a promising number of orders for her pamphlet histories. All this, she hoped, would help reassure her supporters back home that she was still hard at work publishing the *Gazetteer*.[6]

While most of her labors in these months were directed to completing volume V, she was also planning to publish the first of her Windsor County histories, that of her mother's birthplace, Andover. As the hometown of the Barton family,

Andover held great sentimental value for Hemenway. But bringing out this history made financial sense as well. Andover's proximity to Ludlow and her many family connections there guaranteed a good subscription list. Publishing the history of Andover might actually bring in a little money.

Back in the 1870s, when she was still sanguine about a timely completion of the *Gazetteer*, she had corresponded at some length with Hiland Gutterson, Andover's historian, about the content of his chapter. After a hiatus of five years, their correspondence resumed in November 1885, when Hemenway wrote Gutterson that she was preparing to print his town's history in pamphlet form as soon as possible. Her letters to him in the ensuing months listed some of the items she wanted to include in his essay. Among these were sudden deaths and accidents. "All towns want these," she told him, adding that she would prefer to leave out "ordinary suicides." Murders, too, must be included, and as long as the crime was not "notorious" she wanted it described as briefly and simply as possible. She lamented that Ludlow had two murders on its record but was careful to point out that those apprehended had not been native-born. She also asked Gutterson for his opinion about including an incident involving some tramps who had visited Andover and upset the townsfolk. Hemenway apparently had little sympathy with these idle wanderers, assuring Gutterson that "at length they got their due." Finally, to ensure historical completeness, she asked for a list of all the old native-born, the original grantees.[7]

Printing problems continued to dog Hemenway even in Chicago. In a letter to Gutterson dated December 2, 1885, she told him that, thanks to a delay in printing the history of Westminster, she wouldn't be able to get Andover out much before Christmas. The previous day she had taken the cars downtown to Donahue and Henneberry to get what she supposed was "the last *form* to be printed of Westminster," only to discover that the firm had ruined ninety-seven pages. The

From the Gazetteer

* * *

St. Albans

by L. L. Dutcher

[This is a rare account in the *Gazetteer* of an execution. The victim in this case was an African American.]

In the year of 1820, the first and only execution in the county of Franklin took place in St. Albans. This was the hanging of Luther Virginia, for the murder of Rufus W. Jackson in the town of Highgate, Nov. 14, 1819. Virginia was a youngerly colored man of intemperate and dishonest habits. He had worked for Mr. Herrick, an innkeeper at Highgate Falls, and was convicted of stealing money from the till of the bar, and was sentenced to a term in the State's prison. After the expiration of his sentence, he settled in Canada near the line of Highgate. Sunday afternoon, November 14th, he came to Herricks', partially intoxicated and demanded liquor. This being denied him, he became quarrelsome and had some angry words with Jackson, who was present. He was finally expelled from the house and started, as was supposed, for home. Jackson, at sunset, started on horseback to go to the north part of the town, crossed the bridge over Mississquoi river and ascended the hill beyond, when he was knocked from his horse by Virginia, with a stake taken from the fence near by, and beaten to death. Virginia drew the lifeless body out of the road, and the riderless horse returned to the tavern. This created alarm for the safety of Jackson, and a party started off to search for him. The body was soon found and Virginia was captured before morning, at his home in Canada, and lodged in the jail at St. Albans. Jackson's watch was found secreted in his bed. He was convicted of wilfull murder at a special session of the Supreme Court, Dec. 13, 1819, and sentenced to be hung . . . [on] Jan. 14, 1820. . . . Virginia attended his own funeral service at the Court House, which was conducted by Rev. Phineas Culver, who preached a sermon from Genesis IX, 6, "Whoso sheddeth man's blood, by man shall his blood be shed." The execution was witnessed by an immense concorse of people.

[Volume II, page 298]

whole pamphlet would have to be reset, she told Gutterson, "a two or three days unlooked for delay." Further holdups followed, however, and the Andover history would not be published for another year.[8]

In the meantime, Hemenway was growing dissatisfied with St. Joseph's Home, wanting more comfortable and less expensive rooms in which to live and work—at least for the winter. To this end, sometime in the fall of 1885 she wrote one of her religious friends at St. Mary's, Mother Mary Ascension, to inquire if she might stay at Notre Dame. But Mother Ascension wrote back advising her to remain in Chicago and finish her history, leaving Hemenway little choice but to do as she was told. "If I have got to be [a] world's woman still," she told the Holy Cross sister, "I must indeed now put my old shoulder to the wheel," adding wistfully, "(How it be lonesome) May God keep my heart."

Somehow Hemenway would endure the winter in St. Joseph's Home. As she told Mother Ascension, she was comforted by the knowledge that her work was for the Blessed Mother Mary and that if she succeeded in completing the two remaining volumes of the *Gazetteer* she would end her life well. "I w[oul]d be too happy perhaps," she admitted, adopting the humble stance of a good daughter of the church, "but let our lot stay in His [God's] Hands."[9]

Then, sometime in the spring of 1886, she left St. Joseph's Home and moved into two small rented rooms on the second floor of a brick cottage at 29 Newberry Avenue. The front room with its overflowing bookcases she called her library. Here during the day she set type and at night edited manuscripts and wrote letters. The back room served as her living quarters. "It costs me no more than it would in Middlebury," she told Henry Sheldon, "as I am my own little house-keeper."[10]

Hemenway had hardly settled into her new home when the next in a series of tragic events took place. On May 25, 1886, a fire broke out on Wabash Avenue in downtown

Chicago, demolishing in an hour's time the entire block where Donahue and Henneberry was located. Consumed by the flames were 857 pages of volume V of the *Gazetteer*, 67 of which had been printed. In addition, all one hundred copies of the pamphlet history of Wardsboro were destroyed, as were another hundred partially printed histories of Brookline. In a letter to Hiland Gutterson, Hemenway estimated that she had lost "about $500 worth of work & stock, paper & types & all to be reset." There was, of course, no insurance.[11]

A less resolute person might have bowed to Fate at this juncture. But for Hemenway, what had begun as a four-year literary project had become a tenaciously held religious vocation. Like a great general in the field, she believed that the series of defeats that had plagued her editorship of the *Gazetteer* must only harden her determination to win the war. To her it must have seemed clear that God, by putting her through these trials, was insisting that she finish her history.

Certain, therefore, that she was doing the work of the Lord, Hemenway refused to give up. Instead she went to work immediately to recoup her losses. Not only did she have to reset all the type destroyed in the fire, she also had to find a new printer and acquaint the firm's workers with what she described as "the hardest of typographical work, a local and genealogical history filled with names." None of this, needless to say, could be done without money.[12]

One of Hemenway's fundraising schemes was to publish a little monthly entitled *Notes By the Path of the Gazetteer*, and she wasted no time bringing out the first number, which appeared within weeks of the disastrous fire. This eclectic twelve-page magazine, which she described as a "Benefit edition to the Vermont Historical Gazetteer for loss in the late henneberry [sic] fire," sold for twelve cents a copy and reflected its editor's increasingly eccentric taste and writing style. The centerpiece of each issue was a lengthy autobiographical essay describing in lively detail her early adventures as editor of the *Gazetteer*. But "The Path," as Hemenway explained in her first editorial, was also open to "every poet of the State for his verse, for selections from the best of our prose writers, and especially for the preservation of the fragments of history and biography that have and will escape even the profuse Gazetteer." She also managed to slip in several of her own poetic effusions here and there.[13]

"All walk amiably together in the garden of the Gazette[e]r; we think they will in the Path by the Gazette[e]r," the editor told the readers of the first number. "All religions shine therein and do not clash; politicians joke, rake all the nuts they can, but never quarrel, even our lawyers bring no fees against, but small ones to the Gazette[e]r."[14]

In addition to the prose and verse selections found in Hemenway's new magazine, each issue contained a paragraph or two on the "Status of the Gazetteer," as well as "Miss Hemenway's Index," which listed various items in her own collection that she hoped to sell. Among those mentioned are a "Henry Clay coat brush," and a William Henry Harrison handkerchief, the latter a souvenir of the 1840 presidential campaign. She later informed her readers that the coat brush had been sold to Mrs. Cornelia A. Miller of Waterloo, Iowa, who was known for possessing "quite a collection of bric-a-brac." She did not mention who bought the handkerchief.[15]

Hemenway invited "all Vermonters in Chicago and elsewhere" to subscribe to the *Notes* at twelve cents a copy. How many actually accepted this invitation she did not say, nor did she reveal how many copies of each number she printed. But whatever she earned from publishing the magazine, its ultimate value was not monetary. Rather, it allowed her to stay in touch with Vermont friends, family, and supporters and keep them apprised of the progress of her work. *Notes By the Path* also permitted the beleaguered editor of the *Gazetteer* to revisit her triumphant past, those early days when her persuasive skills had rallied men of influence throughout the Green Mountain State in support of her work.

The first issue of *Notes By the Path* came out in June 1886, and the numbers continued to appear with reasonable regularity for the better part of two years. In the meantime, Hemenway spent the bulk of her days resetting the pages she had lost in the Henneberry fire. At first she worked very fast and efficiently. By the end of 1886 she had nine hundred pages of Windham County in type together with one hundred pages for Windsor (the Andover history). Early in the new year she could boast that 250 copies of the Andover history were in print and that nearly half had been sold.[16]

Occasionally, on Sundays and holidays, Hemenway took a break from her labors. In May 1886 she shared a Sunday dinner with William Portus Baxter, a native of the Green Mountain State and a noted Chicago collector of Vermontiana. Particularly enjoyable was a Thanksgiving spent with her Catholic convert friend Eliza Allen Starr, whose small house and studio Hemenway had so envied when she visited Chicago in 1865. As Hemenway informed the readers of *Notes By the Path*, the guests at dinner with the "authoress-artist" hailed from Massachusetts, Venice, Iceland, Rhode Island, and Vermont.[17]

As the months passed, however, the unrelenting work and chronic lack of funds began once more to take their toll. By January 1888 Hemenway was plainly discouraged. Sales of her published volumes and pamphlets had slowed and she could no longer afford to hire a printer. Still, she was not ready to give up. Instead, she bought a small printing press and set about once again to do her own publishing, only this time without the help of her Ludlow friends and relatives.

In desperation she also launched a futile campaign to persuade the Vermont legislature to forgive her failure in meeting their deadline for publishing the remaining volumes of the *Gazetteer*. In July she wrote Henry Sheldon telling him of this plan and of her hope that the legislature of 1888 might be willing to reconfirm the appropriation of 1882. "I ask and trust you," she added further, "to see that your man for the Legislature understands the vote will come up."[18]

Hemenway had hoped to spend the summer setting all of volume V into type so that she could have something to show the legislature when it met that autumn. But an "ulcerated throat" accompanied by fever slowed her progress and forced her "to rest the oar a little," as she told Henry Sheldon. By early October she reported being "quite well for me again—w[oul]d be very well I believe if I did not have to work so continuously hard & under such a pressure of care."[19]

Meanwhile, ill health or no, Hemenway was still determined to have her proposed bill for support considered at the upcoming legislature. Not surprisingly, in view of her slow progress in printing the *Gazetteer*, she failed to generate much interest. But she wrote at least one assemblyman asking him to introduce such a measure, only to have him decline. She then tried to talk Henry Sheldon into finding someone "to see our bill admitted to the Legislature," but he turned her down as well, telling her that without another completed volume of the *Gazetteer* she stood little chance of further state support.[20]

The winter of 1888–89 was "long—weary and hard," and for a time Hemenway feared she might "drop" in her "historic traces." Fortunately, a reprieve came in the form of an offer from the Sister Principal of St. Francis Academy in nearby Joliet to teach a class in English literature for the spring term. She arrived at the school on March 24 and remained there until the end of June. As she informed Sheldon, her duties were light—only six hours of teaching a week. She also gave a number of lectures including three "Historical Descriptions" for "some ladies from the city." "Time has slipped by," she told him, adding that she was basking in the "delightful country air," and enjoying what she called her *"first vacation"* in almost four years.[21]

By July 1889 Hemenway was back in Chicago, hard at work once again on the *Gazetteer* and "some afraid," as she had confessed to Sheldon, "of breaking down there again." That summer she published the last number of *Notes By the Path.* No further issues would be forthcoming, she told her readers, "until the Gazetteer is finished." Meanwhile, she worked night and day on her history. Before the year was out she would be finished, she assured her Vermont friends with unfounded optimism.[22]

Hemenway's Chicago neighbors later remarked on her reclusiveness during these last months. When she left her apartment to buy milk or bread she took no notice of them or of her surroundings but "seemed to be eternally thinking and wrapped up in her own thoughts." She was last seen alive on Sunday, February 22, 1890, when she dined with the Smiths next door at 31 Newberry Street. Two days later Abby Maria Hemenway was found dead in her rooms of a stroke. She was sixty-one years old.[23]

∗ ∗ ∗ ∗ ∗

In the days immediately following Abby Hemenway's death, her brother Horace, then working as a railroad conductor in St. Louis, came to Chicago to carry his sister's body back to Ludlow. There, on Monday, March 3, a funeral mass was held in the Church of the Annunciation, followed by burial in Ludlow's Village Cemetery.

Notices of her death appeared in many of Vermont's newspapers. Nearly all spoke of her as a "remarkable," if "eccentric," woman and praised her work. Many of these accounts, however, were brief. As the Burlington *Free Press* observed, some years earlier Abby Hemenway had "been better known than any other woman in the state." This was no longer true. By moving to Chicago the editor of the *Gazetteer* had distanced herself from the people of Vermont. They remembered her, perhaps, as a woman who had produced a useful work of history for the state, but personally they dismissed her as an oddity. The myth of Abby Hemenway as an eccentric spinster who died in poverty in Chicago on the run from her creditors was taking hold.[24]

The longest and most intriguing notice of her death appeared in the Chicago *Tribune* on February 28. It, too, called her a "remarkable woman," claiming, quite accurately, that the "dream of her life" had been "to gather from the best-informed people in every section of the state a full account of the deeds and traditions of each county." But this same obituary implied that Hemenway was not as poor as her ascetic mode of dress and cramped living arrangements suggested. It even claimed that one of her sisters was married to a millionaire![25]

Of course, the actual state of Hemenway's finances was hardly as rosy as the *Tribune* suggested. While she was in possession of $700 in cash when she died, all this and more was owed to her creditors in Vermont, including Joseph Poland. On March 14, Franklin Denison, a Chicago lawyer employed by Poland to protect his interests, wrote another of her creditors, George Grenville Benedict (the publisher of the Burlington *Free Press*), describing the contents of Hemenway's estate. Apart from the $700 in cash, Denison estimated that there were about one thousand pounds of printed matter "ready to be bound up into the Gazetteer," many pamphlets and old books, as well as a collection of "original letters, nearly a thousand, from George Washington down, which are valuable." Because the cash was insufficient to pay Hemenway's considerable debts, Denison suggested that her creditors unite and bid for the mass of printed matter and take on the work of completing the *Gazetteer*. "I understand that you had trouble with Abby Hemenway," Denison concluded, "everybody did."[26]

Two days after this letter was written, William Portus Baxter, Hemenway's Chicago friend, visited her rooms accompanied by the administrator of her estate. The purpose of this visit was to look over her pamphlet histories and help arrange them. Baxter found fourteen Windham County towns printed and ready for the binder. In a letter to Henry Sheldon, he stated that it would be at least two months before any of Hemenway's possessions, including the pamphlets, could be moved and suggested that claims on her estate might tie up her assets for several years.[27]

Meanwhile, the task of publishing the *Gazetteer* fell to Hemenway's youngest sister, Carrie Page. A housewife, with few if any apparent qualifications for such editorial work, Carrie spent the better part of two years preparing volumes V and VI for the press. She worked out of her house in Brandon and soon discovered the magnitude of the task before her. Although one thousand pages or so for both volumes were already in print, and much of the type for the remainder of volume V had been set by Hemenway's own hands, a lot of work remained. Sections of the printed portion needed re-editing and resetting into type. A mass of historical material for the two volumes was waiting to be sorted through and readied for the press. Finally, commissioned contributions not yet sent in, including portraits and other illustrations, had to be secured and edited. All this work was to be done by a woman who, as far as we know, had little or no editorial or publishing experience.[28]

By the second anniversary of Hemenway's death, Carrie Page actually managed to bring volume V into print. In her preface, dated December 1891, she assured prospective readers that the work had been edited and published according to her sister's original plan. She admitted that while compiling and arranging the great mass of materials furnished by contributors she had been compelled "to omit some things the insertion of which would have swelled the volume to an unwieldy size." Carrie concluded by offering the book as a memorial to her sister, who had given the preservation of Vermont's history "the indefatigable labors of a life-time."[29]

By the time volume V appeared, Carrie had learned something of the difficulties and frustrations endured by her sister during her three decades as editor of the *Gazetteer*. Above all she had to confront the reality faced by Hemenway and most local historians that, while people might be willing enough to commend the writing of town histories, few were ready to back them financially.

The 1,249 pages of volume V are divided into three parts. The first contains the history of Brattleboro together with that of Cumberland County, which before 1781 included what are today Windham and Windsor and part of Orange Counties. Part 2 gives the histories of all but four of the remaining Windham County towns, which are found in part 3 along with the Bennington and Caledonia supplements.[30]

One senses Hemenway's presence less in this last published volume of the *Gazetteer*. The footnotes and other editorial insertions accompanying previously published town histories were less numerous here. When Hemenway did inject a comment, the motive was often nostalgic: to recall a fellow student or a favorite preceptress at Black River Academy, or to reflect on her teaching days in Londonderry over which time had "cast a soft halo." Loyal supporters of the *Gazetteer*, too, were occasionally singled out for special mention. One was William Czar Bradley, a noted citizen of Westminster, whom Hemenway had met in the early 1860s when she was launching her history. She could still remember "the charming countenance and figure of this grand old man, tall, large, rather-nobly developed, crowned with a hoary head, . . . one of our earliest and noblest friends in this enterprise." She recalled with particular gratitude that Bradley "always wrote to us on the reception of a new number, and these letters are treasures among those of the past correspondents of the work, many of whom are now in their graves." Such loyal friends had been few in Hemenway's last years.[31]

A marked difference between volume V and its predecessors is the abundance of genealogical information contained in the many family histories found in its pages. Frederick Robbins, the historian for Athens, claimed that his detailed account of James Shaffer's descendants was included for the benefit of future generations. "Not improbably," Robbins wrote, "years hence, this brief and simple narrative, trifling as it may seem in the day of its nativity, may be found copied into the genealogical records of many a family, who otherwise would have been unable to do so."[32]

Notices of this fifth volume of the *Gazetteer* in the Vermont press were few, yet another indication of Hemenway's waning fame in her home state. The *Free Press*, however, gave it a lengthy and favorable review, calling it "an exceedingly valuable addition to the series" and praising Carrie Page for her "perseverance and strength of purpose."[33]

Hemenway's sister had originally intended to publish both volume V and volume VI and thus complete the work. But Carrie suffered the same financial difficulties that had plagued Abby in her lifetime—lagging subscriptions. So great, in fact, were the monetary losses incurred in publishing volume V that she was forced to look for someone else to finance and publish the last volume.[34]

The firm Carrie Page contracted with in July 1893 was none other than Joel Munsell's Sons of Albany, New York, the same company that had published three of the early numbers of the *Quarterly Gazetteer* and also *Songs of the War*. Having secured Munsell's agreement to publish, Carrie mailed off the manuscript histories for eighteen Windsor County towns, fourteen cuts for portraits to be included in the volume, and a list of current subscribers. In return Munsell promised that the book would be in print as early as September.[35]

But the Albany printer also ran into difficulties funding the work and eventually sent all the manuscripts and other materials for volume VI to William Portus Baxter, who by this time was storing several trunks filled with Abby Hemenway's papers. Because no one else seemed to want them, Baxter held on to the trunks until his death in 1911, at which time they were forwarded to his niece Janette Baxter, who lived in Jackson Springs, North Carolina.

In the meantime, the Vermont Historical Society, presumably alerted by news of William Portus Baxter's death, finally took an interest in the fate of Abby Hemenway's papers. At their annual meeting in Montpelier in the fall of 1911 the members voted to obtain, if possible, possession of her "records and notes." A letter to this effect was duly mailed to Janette Baxter on November 22, but it arrived too late. The bad luck that had dogged the editor of the *Gazetteer* for most of her lifetime showed little sign of letting up after her death. On November 27, a fire destroyed the Baxter house, consuming all of Hemenway's papers in its wake.[36]

"The loss of the manuscript is a heavy one," observed a friend of the Vermont Historical Society, referring to the histories for the Windsor County volume. But the loss of the several trunks filled with Hemenway's papers was equally devastating. We can only imagine the amount of valuable historical and personal papers they contained.[37]

Epilogue

How Beautiful that they who are dead may
reappear in history.

Abby Hemenway[1]

In the years following Abby Hemenway's death, the *Vermont
Historical Gazetteer* came to be treasured less as a repository of local history than as a genealogical source. When an
index to the five volumes was finally published in 1923, its
compiler—the librarian of the Vermont Historical Society—
declared that the genealogical information contained in
Hemenway's work had "the widest interest to the general
reader." In an echo of this appraisal, Marion Hemenway, a
niece of Abby's, was told by the librarian of the Connecticut
Historical Library in Hartford that Miss Hemenway "was considered a wonder in genealogical circles and that her Gazetteers
were in growing demand."[2]

The *Gazetteer's* waning reputation as a source of local history in the early decades of the twentieth century matched that
of other antiquarian publications. New trends in the production
of town histories were part of the reason, as the sponsoring of

such works passed increasingly into the hands of commercial publishers who paid people to write them. This had the effect of undermining local sources of support.[3] But perhaps an even more important factor explaining the declining popularity of community historians such as Hemenway was the rise of a new professional class of historians who held positions in the country's universities. Under this academic influence the study of history was transformed into a disciplined and organized investigation of the meaning of the past, with its focus on national issues and events. By the late 1880s the age of the antiquarians was drawing to a close. The new class of professional scholars had little patience with what J. Franklin Jameson at the turn of the century called the "pettiness and sterility" of locally focused historical work.[4]

Abby Hemenway's *Gazetteer*, however, must be judged not by the criteria of twentieth-century historiography, but rather by the standards she set for herself. Her task as she saw it was to collect the stories of Vermont's towns, concentrating primarily on the early years of white settlement and the period of community building that followed. Above all she wanted these stories written down and preserved for posterity before they were forgotten.

Hemenway also preferred that her histories be collected and written by persons with an intimate knowledge of their communities, men and women who were familiar with the sources, especially with those individuals who had links to the early days of settlement. Thus, the hundreds of essays contained in the *Gazetteer* are necessarily uneven. In her later years as editor, Hemenway gave more explicit instructions to her town historians than she had at the start of her work. Whether this simply reflected an effort to produce more detailed and comprehensive essays or represented a change in her own views about history, or both, is difficult to gauge from the few directives that survive. In the end, however, no matter how explicit her instructions were, or how thoroughly she might edit the manuscripts sent to her, ultimately she was dependent on what her historians had to say.

The modern reader will find many of the published histories contained in the *Gazetteer* uncritical in their acceptance of a particular version of the past. This is especially true in the case of towns settled before the Revolution. In these communities few if any persons were still alive who could recall this earlier time. Thus the historians of these towns, lacking ready access to firsthand accounts of people and events, were dependent on already published works by such early chroniclers of the state's history as Ira Allen, Samuel Williams, and Zadock Thompson. At the same time we must remember that Hemenway, despite her lack of formal historical training, often cast a critical eye on the material sent to her. The examples described earlier of her editing of the histories of towns such as Panton and Swanton are evidence of this scrutiny. When she knew her historians had not gotten their facts straight, she did not hesitate to tell them so. Hemenway's critical powers sharpened as she grew more confident in her role as a Vermont historian, as demonstrated in her commentary on John Bulkley Perry's history of Swanton. Here her critique, especially of Perry's writing French history from English sources, is remarkably modern. So, too, is her own description of the English barbarity exhibited during Rogers' Raid on the Abenaki town of St. Francis. Here we might almost say that she anticipates the kind of revisionism heard from anti–Vietnam War activists in the 1970s.[5]

But Hemenway's importance transcends her discerning and questioning eye. Knowingly or unknowingly, she was one of the creators of the myth of Vermont as that state has come to be seen, not only by its residents but by many who have never even crossed its borders. A clear and direct line of descent runs from the *Gazetteer* of the nineteenth century through the writings of Dorothy Canfield Fisher to magazines such as *Vermont Life* in the twentieth century. The images put forth by these more recent publications build heavily on this vast storehouse of historical memory. As Ralph Nading Hill observed in 1950, the *Gazetteer* constitutes "the richest, most interesting and most valuable body of Vermont source material anywhere."[6] More recently, the Vermont historian John Duffy has suggested that students of Vermont history hang pictures of Abby Hemenway over their desks and thank the editor of the *Gazetteer* for her monumental work.[7]

Because Abby Hemenway was the preeminent nineteenth-century collector of Vermont source material, she played a vital role in molding what might be called the grand narrative of Vermont in the twentieth century. But it is important not to read Hemenway through spectacles tinted by the very vision of Vermont that she helped to create: as a storehouse of tradition, or as the last bastion of rural virtues in a changing world. If we do sentimentalize her work in this way we will miss a lot about her.

For Hemenway, in looking at Vermont's past, took a far more critical view of the component parts of that narrative than some of those who followed her. Her Vermont, after all, is not simply one of green meadows, red barns, golden leaves, and snow-white hills. She saw the seamy side as well, and knew, for example, that Vermont's heroes were not all paragons of virtue. In sum, a tension resides in Hemenway's work between "mythologizing" early Vermont and producing "the most reliable record of *facts* ever published."[8] If Hemenway never really resolved this tension between taking a critical and scientific approach to history and viewing the past as a source of pride, neither did many of her contemporaries, nor, for that matter, do scholars today. The morals that historians wish to draw from their work continue to influence their selection of facts and the way they order those facts.

There is yet another sense in which Hemenway's work can be counted as a success by modern standards, although she could not have foreseen this particular accomplishment. The rise of professional historiography in the late nineteenth and twentieth centuries—with its critical outlook, and its concentration on great themes of national importance—has led readers in the past to disparage the mere antiquarianism of histories like the *Gazetteer*. More recently she has come into her own. For example, a new interest in oral history has become notable. At the same time, movements such as feminism and the new social history seek to uncover in a variety of ways the pasts of those who left few or no conventional records—slaves, factory workers, women, and other people without a voice. Scholars in these fields have done much to make us appreciate sources that were overlooked earlier or brushed aside as unimportant. Hemenway's subjects, perhaps, are not people without a voice, for her historians saw to it that they were given one; but without her endeavors they might have remained silent, to the ultimate loss of those who cherish the past in all its diversity and richness.

In recent years respect for the singularity of the *Gazetteer* as a work of local history has been growing. Where else in the mass of published town histories in this country do you find so many firsthand accounts garnered directly from the people who participated in the events they describe? Or so many stories passed down by early settlers to their descendants? Where else, too, do you find so much material on the lives of women and their contributions to the history of their state?

Thus, while the *Gazetteer's* town histories focused almost solely on their communities' Anglo-Saxon Protestant heritage, Hemenway did not believe she was publishing for the elite. She wanted the history of even the smallest village included and insisted hers was a work "for the whole people." Nor would she have accepted the charge that she was biased against newcomers. As she saw it, the purpose of her work was to tell the story of the early white settlers of Vermont and their descendants, chronicling Vermont's "unique early history," as she put it, "and its progressive later history."[9] Because the vast majority of these white settlers had been Protestant Yankees, they quite naturally became the focus of the *Gazetteer's* town histories. While Native Americans do figure in the accounts of pioneer days, their presence is largely anecdotal and their portrayal not always flattering. As for the Irish, French Canadians, and other new ethnic groups that were swelling Vermont's urban population, the issue was not so much that these newcomers did not belong to Vermont as that they were not yet recognized as contributing to the state's heritage. Hemenway's Catholicism certainly increased her awareness of the burgeoning population of Irish and French Canadians, but beyond seeing them in church each Sunday, their lives would rarely have crossed with hers. Their customs and traditions were not yet a part of America's history.[10]

Abby Hemenway saw her history as uniting Vermonters, not dividing them. Each town in its individuality was part of a larger whole. In this way she nourished a communal pride. Towns, not the state, came first, and even the smallest, poorest community had something to contribute to the whole. The *Gazetteer* gave Vermonters a newfound pride in their local places and their local people.

Much as the *Vermont Historical Gazetteer* resembled other nineteenth-century local histories, but with marked differences, so, too, its editor was both a woman of her time and an outsider. Like other Victorians, she believed that women had a particular destiny determined by their sex as well as by their gendering, but she saw that destiny in broader terms than some. She believed strongly in the education of women and often added to her town histories an account of the local female academy, and in later years sometimes a list of female college graduates. But the women she claims to have admired the most are usually good homebodies. Like Abigail Dana Hemenway, they may write poetry, but their literary efforts invariably take second place to their families. A good example is Susanna Cram Jackson, a sentimental sketch of whom Hemenway added to the history of Dorset. "While woman's most pleasant cares filled well her hands, she yet found harmonious place for an occasional outburst of the poetical in her nature."[11] Here, as elsewhere in Hemenway's writings, such sentimentality stands in sharp contrast to her own behavior as the tough-minded editor of the *Gazetteer*.

Like Harriet Beecher Stowe, and other nineteenth-century literary women, Hemenway underscored the value of the cult of domesticity for others while largely eschewing it herself in her professional role as editor of the *Gazetteer*. In the same vein she sentimentalized home and family, including her own, while all the while leading a life that was only tangentially connected to the domestic realm. For a woman to live alone was considered improper, even scandalous. It also required resources Hemenway did not have. Yet we know that her dream as early as 1865 was to live—like her artist friend Eliza Starr in Chicago—in a cozy home of her own.

Still, a careful perusal of the *Gazetteer* shows that Hemenway was also proud of the emerging professional woman, especially teachers and doctors, biographies of whom are scattered through its pages. Hemenway made no mention, however, of the woman's rights movement. Even Clarina Howard Nichols, a prominent early Vermont advocate for female suffrage whom the editor of the *Gazetteer* surely knew of, is conspicuously absent from the history of Brattleboro.

Over the course of her own life Abby Hemenway neither conformed to the ideal of a home-bound, submissive daughter, nor did she openly rebel against the strictures imposed on her sex. Instead, she paid lip service to the pieties and sentimentalities of the Victorian age, while charting her own course.

From a very early age Abby Hemenway had possessed an acute sense of self. As a young girl she determined to develop all her faculties and put them to use. But this was a terrible problem for a mid-nineteenth-century woman. Social convention prescribed that the independence and freedom of mind and action enjoyed by the young, unmarried woman must be put aside once she married. To choose not to marry was to reject this convention and move into uncharted territory. While Hemenway appears to have made a conscious choice not to marry, nothing in the documentary record indicates that she was therefore uninterested in men or sex. Rather, she decided to remain single because she wanted to lead a professional life.

When Hemenway joined the Roman Catholic Church in the mid-1860s she was publicly declaring her difference from other people. At the same time her newfound faith enabled her to choose a system of beliefs that justified (as New England Protestantism did not) the worth of a single, chaste woman. It gave her a license to act in different ways and a justification for saying that in her history she was doing God's work, following a religious calling.

The problem was that Hemenway had created a life for herself that was not yet possible. For this reason her story, that of a professional woman determined to pursue her vocation in the face of any and all obstacles, had all the marks of incipient tragedy. At the start of her career as editor of the *Gazetteer* Hemenway's professional abilities, her sharp and well-organized mind, her persuasive powers, were evident to all who worked with her. In the early 1870s she was at the peak of her powers as an editor and historian. But then everything in her life began to fall apart. Lydia Meech died, money and legal troubles mounted, and always that pile of manuscripts waiting to be edited kept growing. Overwhelmed with work, she allowed careless mistakes and bad proofreading to mar the pages of her later town histories. By the 1880s, a shrill and desperate tone crept into her correspondence. Now a severe-looking woman in her fifties, Abby Hemenway was no longer the young, gifted editor, who in the 1860s had charmed everyone into doing her bidding, but rather a middle-aged, cranky spinster whom almost everyone found hard to work with. In these last difficult years Hemenway's growing sense of vocation was matched by an unreasonable, even martyrlike, sense of isolation. Her Catholic faith proved her only consolation. Even at the end of her life when illness, discouragement, and fatigue overwhelmed her, she struggled on, believing that "the Lord has had his purpose. . . . Let our lot stay in His Hands."[12]

More than twenty years after Abby Hemenway's death Vermont legislators, whose predecessors had been so reluctant to give its editor more than a few hundred dollars, voted to spend more than $12,000 simply to publish an index of her vast work. Perhaps the ultimate irony lies in the wording of the 1914 report of the Vermont Historical Society's librarian. Having described the *Gazetteer* as the greatest extant work on the founding fathers of Vermont, he then complained of the enormous difficulty of compiling an index to the *Gazetteer*, noting that it "has all along seemed too prodigious for any man to undertake." Yet it was one woman, Abby Maria Hemenway, who defied the incredulity of the Middlebury College faculty and compiled not only the history of Addison County but the history of every other county in the Green Mountain State.[13]

Notes

———◦◦◦◦◦◦◦◦◦———

List of Abbreviations Used in Notes

AM   *Ave Maria*

CP   Hemenway, *Clarke Papers*

FP   Burlington *Free Press*

HSM   Henry Sheldon Museum

MR   Hemenway, *Mystical Rose*

NBP   Hemenway, ed., *Notes By the Path of the Gazetteer*

P&P   Hemenway, ed., *Poets and Poetry of Vermont*

PAC   Province Archives Center

UNDA   University of Notre Dame Archives

SCUVM   Special Collections, University of Vermont

VH   *Vermont History*

VHG   Hemenway, ed., *Vermont Historical Gazetteer*

VHS   Vermont Historical Society

VQG   Hemenway, ed., *Vermont Quarterly Gazetteer*

Introduction

1. Abby Maria Hemenway, ed., *Notes By the Path of the Gazetteer*, 1 (July 1886): 17 (hereafter *NBP*).

2. Frederick P. Elwert, review of Brenda Morrissey, *Abby Hemenway's Vermont* in *Rutland Historical Quarterly Newsletter*, 3 (July 1973): 3.

3. Ralph Nading Hill, *Contrary Country: A Chronicle of Vermont* (New York: Rinehart & Co., 1950), 221.

4. *Poets and Poetry of Vermont* (Rutland: George A. Tuttle & Co., 1858); Rev. ed. (Boston: Brown, Taggard, & Chase, 1860); *Notes By the Path of the Gazetteer* (Chicago, 1886–1888); *The Mystical Rose, or, Mary of Nazareth, The Lily of the House of David* (New York: D. Appleton & Co., 1865); *Rosa Immaculata, or, the Tower of Ivory in the House of Anna and Joachim* (New York: P. O'Shea, 1867); *The House of Gold and the Saint of Nazareth. A Poetical Life of St. Joseph* (Baltimore: Kelly, Piet and Company, 1873).

5. Kevin Graffagnino, *Vermont in the Victorian Age: Continuity and Change in the Green Mountain State* (Bennington & Shelburne, Vt.: Vermont Heritage Press & Shelburne Museum, 1985), 25.

6. Marion P. Hemenway, "Abby Maria Hemenway," paper presented for the Daughters of the American Revolution, Ludlow, Vermont, 1917, copy in Brigham Index, Vermont Historical Society, Montpelier, Vt. (hereafter VHS).

7. George Eliot, *Middlemarch* (1871–1872; reprint, New York: The Modern Library, 1994), 1.

8. David Russo, *Keepers of Our Past: Local Historical Writing in the United States, 1820s–1930s* (New York: Greenwood Press, 1988), 131.

9. *NBP*, 2 (February/March 1888): 189.

Chapter 1

1. *NBP*, 1(July 1886): 20.

2. Joseph N. Harris, *History of Ludlow, Vermont* (Ludlow, 1949), 150.

3. Ruth A. Hemenway, "Genealogy of Harry E. Hemenway," courtesy David Hemenway; Harris, *History of Ludlow*, 179.

4. Marion Hemenway, "Abby Hemenway," 3–4.

5. Asa Barton to Hiland Gutterson, 21 March 1870, Andover Historical Society, Andover, Vt. (copy, VHS).

6. Frances Harriet Babb, "Abby Maria Hemenway (1828–1890), Historian, Anthologist, and Poet" (Master's thesis, University of Maine, 1939), 2–3; Hiland G. Gutterson, et al., *The Local History of Andover, Vermont* (Chicago: A. M. Hemenway, 1886), 31.

7. Gutterson, et al., *Local History of Andover*, 68.

8. Abby Maria Hemenway, ed., *Poets and Poetry of Vermont* (Rutland: George A. Tuttle and Co., 1858), 393–94 (hereafter *P&P*).

9. Gutterson, et al, *Local History of Andover*, 33; Asa Barton to Hiland Gutterson, 10 April 1870, Andover Historical Society, Andover, Vt.

10. Marion Hemenway, "Abby Hemenway," 7.

11. Clara Barton's memories of her "interesting, precise and intelligent grandmother Barton" is quoted in Laurel Thatcher Ulrich, *A Midwife's Tale: The Life of Martha Ballard, Based on Her Diary, 1785–1812* (New York: Random House, 1990), 11.

12. Daniel Hemenway to Abigail Barton, 22 January 1822 and 27 January 1822, courtesy David Hemenway.

13. Daniel Hemenway built the first house on the road leading to Weston in 1820. See Harris, *History of Ludlow*, 183.

14. Babb, "Abby Hemenway," 6.

15. Abigail Dana Hemenway, "The Miniature," in *P&P*, 395.

16. Quit Claim Deed, Ludlow land records, 27 April 1827. Babb, "Abby Hemenway," 7.

17. For the location of the various Barton and Hemenway houses see Harris, *History of Ludlow*, 175–183, and map, 168.

18. Ibid., 181.
19. Abby Maria Hemenway, ed., *Vermont Historical Gazetteer* (various publishers, 1860–1892), 3: 435 (hereafter *VHG*).
20. Harris, *History of Ludlow*, 70.
21. Marion Hemenway, "Abby Hemenway," 6.
22. Philip Greven, *The Protestant Temperament: Patterns of Child-Rearing, Religious Experience, and the Self in Early America* (New York: Alfred A. Knopf, 1977), 274.
23. *NBP*, 2 (January 1888): 177.
24. Ibid., 1 (December 1886): 91–92.
25. *P&P* (1858), 393–394.
26. Abby Hemenway speaks of her uncle Asa Barton's dislike of Baptist theology in *VHG*, vol. 3, p. 988.
27. *NBP*, 2 (May 1887): 3.
28. Abby Maria Hemenway (pseud. Marie Josephine), *The Mystical Rose: or, Mary of Nazareth* (New York: D. Appleton & Co., 1865), 18 (hereafter *MR*).
29. Marion Hemenway, "Abby Hemenway," 2; *NBP*, 2 (April 1888): 11.
30. For a discussion of widespread literacy in the upper Connecticut River Valley in the early nineteenth century see William J. Gilmore, *Reading Becomes a Necessity of Life: Material and Cultural Life in Rural New England, 1780–1835* (Knoxville: The University of Tennessee Press, 1989). The Chester and Andover libraries are mentioned on p. 456.
31. Asa Barton to Hiland Gutterson, 10 May 1871, Andover Historical Society, Andover, Vt. (copy, VHS). For a lengthier critical account of the Woodstock meeting, see Russell Streeter, *Mirror of Calvinistic Fanaticism, or Jedediah Burchard & Co. During a Protracted Meeting of Twenty-Six Days in Woodstock, Vermont* (Woodstock, Vt.: Nahum Haskell, 1835).
32. Randolph A. Roth, *The Democratic Dilemma: Religion, Reform, and the Social Order in the Connecticut River Valley of Vermont, 1791–1850* (New York: Cambridge University Press, 1987), 156–157.
33. *NBP*, 1 (December 1886/January 1887): 91.
34. Asa Barton to Hiland Gutterson, 16 April 1870, Andover Historical Society, Andover, Vt. (copy, VHS).
35. Barbara Chiolino, comp., *A Box of Letters Concerning the Vermont Family of Abby M. Hemenway* (c. 1978), iii.
36. This discussion of Abby Hemenway's relationship with the Bartons and particularly Asa Barton comes from Chiolino, comp., *Box of Letters*.
37. *VHG*, 1: 335.
38. Gutterson, et al., *Local History of Andover*, 27.
39. Marion Hemenway, "Abby Hemenway," 5.
40. Harris, *History of Ludlow*, 41–42; Gutterson, et al. *History of Andover*, 32–33; Luke 14.5 RSV.
41. Harris, *History of Ludlow*, 41–42; Gutterson, et al., *History of Andover*, 32–33.
42. Harris, *History of Ludlow*, 51–53.
43. Vermont lagged behind all the other states, except those in the South, in its "great deficiency of school apparatus." See George Gary Bush, *History of Education in Vermont* (Washington: Government Printing Office, 1900), 25.
44. Harris, *History of Ludlow*, 53.

Chapter 2

1. Quoted in Linda Kerber, *Toward an Intellectual History of Women* (Chapel Hill: University of North Carolina Press, 1997), 242.
2. Margaret K. Nelson, "Vermont Female Schoolteachers in the Nineteenth Century," *Vermont History*, 49 (Winter, 1981): 9–10 (hereafter *VH*). For information on women schoolteachers in Vermont and New England see also, Thomas Dublin, *Transforming Women's Work: New England Lives in the Industrial Revolution* (Ithaca, N.Y.: Cornell University Press, 1994), 205–227.

3. Nelson, "Vermont Female Schoolteachers," 25.

4. Nancy Cott, *The Bonds of Womanhood: "Woman's Sphere" in New England, 1780-1835* (New Haven: Yale University Press, 1977), 38.

5. *Chicago Tribune*, 28 February 1890, p. 3.

6. See "Book 1st of the Records of the Baptist Church of Ludlow," Baptist Church, Ludlow, Vt.

7. Ibid.; Harris, *History of Ludlow*, 32–33; T. Mace, Box of History and Genealogy of Ludlow, MSC, Box A23, VHS. The second church took the name of the Baptist Church of Ludlow in 1838 after the first church ceased to be recognized by the Woodstock Baptist Association in 1837. For a discussion of Baptist beliefs and those of other Calvinist churches in the Connecticut Valley during the 1830s and 1840s see Roth, *Democratic Dilemma*, 190–191.

8. Hemenway called the early books of *The Mystical Rose* the work of her "untried pen," suggesting that they comprised her first effort at writing poetry. Marion Hemenway confirms that Hemenway began writing this life of the Virgin Mary during her early teaching days. See Marion Hemenway, "Abby Hemenway," 10.

9. Abby Maria Hemenway (pseud: Marie Josephine), "Our First Annunciation Day," in *Ave Maria, a Catholic Journal*, 1 (1 May 1865): 4–5 (hereafter *AM*). Although the poem is unsigned, the dateline reads "Ludlow Vermont, 2nd Lent day, 1865." For the record of Abby Hemenway's baptism, see "Book 1st of Records of the Baptist Church of Ludlow."

10. Colleen McDannell suggests that for Protestants, Mary was emblematic of all mothers and not merely the mother of Jesus, and that they included Mary "among their visual images by emphasizing her maternal qualities and downplaying her mediating capacity." Colleen McDannell, *Material Christianity: Religion and Popular Culture in America* (New Haven: Yale University Press, 1995), 61.

11. Donal Ward, "Religious Enthusiasm in Vermont, 1761–1847" (Ph.D. diss., University of Notre Dame, 1980), 1-2, 166–167. Joe Citro, *Ghosts, Ghouls & Unsolved Mysteries* (Montpelier: *Vermont Life*, 1994), 173; Calvin Butler, "Mrs. Warner's Vision," unpublished manuscript, Henry Sheldon Museum, Middlebury, Vt. (hereafter HSM).

12. Roth, *Democratic Dilemma*, 217–218.

13. Karen Hansen, *A Very Social Time: Crafting Community in Antebellum New England* (Berkeley: University of California Press, 1994), 228; A[sa] S. Barton, *Miller Refuted By History* (Windsor, Vt: 1842).

14. *MR*, vii.

15. Ibid., 21–22.

16. Nancy Cott, *The Bonds of Womanhood*, 139–142.

17. "History of the Ladies' Benevolent Society of Ludlow," MSC-107, VHS.

18. Hemenway later mentioned Adaline Cobb as her first preceptress. Cobb taught at Black River Academy only during the spring term of 1847. See *History of Black River Academy As Seen Through Various Publications* (1972), 90. Hemenway is first listed in the *Catalogue of Officers and Students of Black River Academy, Ludlow, VT for the Spring, Summer, and Fall Terms, 1847* as one of 122 "ladies" in the English department.

19. *History of Black River Academy*, 21–23. The only mention of Abby Hemenway is as one of the "literary children" of BRA. Only her last name is given and that is misspelled, ibid., 108.

20. Ibid., 49.

21. George Gary Bush, *History of Education in Vermont* (Washington: Government Printing Office, 1900), 87.

22. *Middlebury College in the State of Vermont: General Catalogue* (Middlebury, Vt., 1950), 122; *History of Black River Academy*, 26, 35, 49, 50. For the rise in enrollment, see *Catalogue of Officers and Students* for the years 1847–1852.

23. *History of Black River Academy*, 51, 75. Thetford Academy, a coeducational school like Black River, also allowed its young women students to read their compositions from a public platform. See Mary B. Slade, *Thetford Academy's First Century* (Thetford, Vt., 1956), 99.

24. According to William Gilmore, "the only known mixed academy level instruction" conducted in the Windsor District was at Windsor in 1802-1805 and at Ludlow beginning in the mid-1830s, Gilmore, *Reading Becomes a Necessity*, 46.

25. *History of Black River Academy*, 30.

26. C. Robbins, biography of Abby Hemenway, in Abby Hemenway, ed., *VHG*, 6: vii.

27. *Catalogue of Officers and Students* (1847), 12.

28. Ibid. (1845–46), 14.

29. Gilmore, *Reading Becomes a Necessity*, 40.

30. Robbins, biography of Abby Hemenway.

31. *NBP*, 2 (April 1888): 214–215. In this recollection of her early reading in history Abby confesses that her mother did not share her enthusiasm for Sir William Edward Parry's works: *Journal of a Voyage for the Discovery of a north-west passage from the Atlantic to the Pacific; performed in the years, 1819–1820 in His Majesty's ships Hecla and Griper, under the orders of Captain William Edward Parry* (London: J. Murray, 1821); *Journal of a Second Voyage for the Discovery of a north-west passage from the Atlantic to the Pacific; performed in the years, 1821, 22, 23 in His Majesty's ships Fury and Hecla, under the order of Captain William Edward Parry* (London: J. Murray, 1824); *Journal of Third Voyage for the Discovery of a north-west passage from the Atlantic to the Pacific; performed in the years, 1824–25 in His Majesty's ships Fury and Hecla, under the orders of Captain William Edward Parry* (London: J. Murray, 1826).

32. Nina Baym, *American Women Writers and the Work of History, 1790–1860* (New Brunswick, N.J.: Rutgers University Press, 1995), 19.

33. *Catalogue of Officers and Students* (1847); Marion Hemenway, "Abby Hemenway," 7.

34. This optimism would be misplaced in the case of Ludlow, which actually saw its population decline slightly between 1850 and 1860.

35. Marion Hemenway, "Abby Hemenway," 7; Lee Chambers-Schiller, *Liberty A Better Husband: Single Women in America: The Generations of 1780–1840* (New Haven: Yale University Press, 1984), 125. Chambers-Schiller points out that such female reading circles played an important role in the informal education that inspired and encouraged nineteenth-century women in their drive for intellectual expansion. This was especially true for women who had received no advanced education.

36. Chiolino notes that Mrs. Washburn, Mrs. Robbins, and others were charter members of the Ladies' Association for Mental and Other Improvement. Chiolino, comp., *Box of Letters*, part 2, p.7.

37. Babb, "Abby Hemenway," 10. Chiolino describes the "Ladies Association for Mental and other Improvement," and the "Ladie's [sic] Society" who mounted the "Original Exhibitions" as one and the same organization; see Chiolino, comp., *Box of Letters*, part 1, p. 7.

38. A copy of the program for the 1851 "Original Exhibition" is in the collection of Rev. John McSweeney.

39. *VHG*, v. 5, part 2, p. 400. In the sixth volume of the *VHG*, which was never published, Hemenway planned to include a history of Ludlow written by her uncle Asa Barton. This history would presumably also have contained an account of Black River Academy.

40. Kathryn M. Kerns, "Farmer's Daughters: The Education of Women at Alfred Academy and University Before the Civil War," *History of Higher Education Annual* (1986), 11–12, 24. Kerns notes the lack of scholarship on coeducation at New England academies and blames it on an approach to higher education that "has taken the modern university as a model and searched for its antecedents in the past." This approach tends to undervalue the education acquired at small antebellum colleges and ignores completely the higher education men as well as women acquired at academies such as Black River, which flourished all over the Northeast in the years before the Civil War. Students of women's education have also ignored the coeducational academies, concentrating instead on the many female academies and seminaries that flourished at this time. One noted exception is William Gilmore's *Reading Becomes a Necessity of Life*, see especially, 42–47. T. D. S. Bassett notes that "the line between academies and colleges

did not become clear until completion of study at an academy became a requirement for college entrance." T. D. Seymour Bassett, *The Gods of the Hills: Piety and Society in Nineteenth-Century Vermont* (Montpelier: Vermont Historical Society, 2000), 179.

Chapter 3

1. *P&P* (1858), 95.
2. Abby Maria Hemenway, *Clarke Papers: Mrs. Meech and her Family* (Burlington, Vt., 1878), 18 (hereafter *CP*).
3. Hemenway does not give the parents' first names.
4. *CP*, 10–13.
5. Ibid., 13–14.
6. Ibid., 13; Caroll R. Tarbell, *History of Mount Holly, Vermont* (1987), 145. The summer teacher was paid $19.00 a term.
7. *CP*, 14.
8. Ibid.
9. Hemenway's name does not appear in the Black River Academy catalogues after 1852. In *VHG*, v. 5, part 3 (Londonderry), p. 24, there is an account of her teaching in this village in the mountains southeast of Ludlow in Windham County.
10. Dublin, *Transforming Women's Work*, 215.
11. Polly Welts Kaufman, *Women Teachers on the Frontier* (New Haven: Yale University Press, 1984), xxi.
12. Quoted in Graffagnino, *Vermont in the Victorian Age*, 107.
13. Lewis D. Stillwell, *Migration from Vermont* (Montpelier: Vermont Historical Society, 1948), 226; "Ludlow and Her Neighbors," *Special Souvenir Edition & Supplement of The Vermont Tribune* (Ludlow: E. H. Crane, 1899), 2.
14. Ralph Barton to ["Mrs. T."], 11 February 1852, in Chiolino, comp. *Box of Letters*, part 1, pp. 3–4.
15. Abigail Dana Hemenway, "The Californians," in "Poems of Abigail Dana Hemenway," unpublished manuscript, Fletcher Memorial Library, Ludlow, Vt.
16. Chiolino, comp., *Box of Letters*, part 2, p. 5.
17. Ralph Barton to Asa Barton, 14 November 1853, 13 March 1854, in ibid., part 1, pp. 21, 25.
18. William J. Gilmore-Lehne, "Reflections on Three Classics of Vermont History," *VH*, 59 (Fall, 1991): 235.
19. Kaufman, *Women Teachers on the Frontier*, 13–19.
20. In her first letter home from Michigan, Lucia Barton mentions that she is boarding with her aunt and uncle Hinkley. Lucia Barton to Asa Barton, [n.d.] September [1853], in Chiolino, comp., *Box of Letters*, part 2, pp. 6–8.
21. Ralph Barton to Asa Barton, 14 November 1853.
22. Kaufman, *Women Teachers on the Frontier*, 11.
23. For the decline of patriarchal authority in the antebellum Northeast see Chambers-Schiller, *Liberty a Better Husband*, 35.
24. *NBP*, 1 (July 1886): 20–21.
25. Stillwell, *Migration From Vermont*, 214, 226; Kaufman, *Women Teachers on the Frontier*, 23–24.
26. Lucia Barton to Asa Barton, [n.d.] September [1853].
27. Kaufman, *Women Teachers on the Frontier*, 26, 183–184.
28. Quoted in Michael Kammen, *Mystic Chords of Memory: The Transformation of Tradition in American Culture* (New York: Alfred A. Knopf, 1991), 51.
29. Lucia Barton to Asa Barton, [n.d.] September [1853].
30. Kaufman, *Women Teachers on the Frontier*, 27.
31. Lucia Barton and Abby Hemenway to Asa Barton, [n.d.] November [1853], in Chiolino, comp., *Box of Letters*, part 2, pp. 9–11.
32. [Abby Maria Hemenway] to [Elvira Hemenway], 8 October 1854, courtesy David Hemenway.
33. Ibid; Lucia Barton and Abby Hemenway to Asa Barton [n.d.] November [1853].

34. [Abby Hemenway] to [Elvira Hemenway], 8 October 1854.

35. Abby [Hemenway] to _____, Hopeville, 20 July 1855, Harold Rugg Collection, miscellaneous file #912, VHS.

36. Ibid. The quotation in Hemenway's letter, "I have bread that ye know not of," is from John, 4.32.

37. Carroll Smith-Rosenberg, "The Female World of Love and Ritual," in *Disorderly Conduct: Visions of Gender in Victorian America* (New York: Oxford University Press, 1985), 68.

38. *MR*, 29. Historians have described how the introspective revolution of the early nineteenth century encouraged the exploration of private feelings, the seeking out of friends to whom a woman could "unfold her whole heart." Cott, *Bonds of Womanhood*, 185–186; Chambers-Schiller, *Liberty a Better Husband*, 41–43.

Chapter 4

1. *P&P* (1858), 256.

2. Hemenway was publicly soliciting contributions for her book of Vermont poetry by early 1858. See her notice in St. Johnsbury *Caledonian*, 23 January 1858, p. 3.

3. In her later recollections of life in the Hemenway household in the late 1850s, Abby mentions that several younger members of the family were still living at home but she doesn't name them. See *NBP*, 2 (October 1887): 155. Much of this information about Abby Hemenway's siblings comes from Ruth A. Hemenway, "Genealogy of Harry E. Hemenway."

4. *MR*, 29.

5. Chambers-Schiller, *Liberty a Better Husband*, 2–27.

6. Ibid., 60.

7. Quoted in Bonnie G. Smith, *The Gender of History: Men, Women, and Historical Practice* (Cambridge: Harvard University Press, 1998), 42.

8. Joan D. Hedrick, *Harriet Beecher Stowe: A Life* (New York: Oxford University Press, 1994), 78–80.

9. Alice Cary, preface to *Clovernook*, in Judith Fetterley and Marjorie Pryse, eds., *American Women Regionalists* (New York: W.W. Norton & Company, 1992), 60.

10. For a discussion of the regional character of much of Vermont's nineteenth-century literature, see Arthur W. Biddle and Paul A. Eschholz, eds., *The Literature of Vermont: A Sampler* (Hanover, N.H.: University Press of New England, 1973), 5–10.

11. *P&P* (1858), iii-v.

12. Talk with folklorist Jane Beck, Vermont Folklife Center, Middlebury, Vt., 4 January 1994.

13. Ibid. See also Baym, *American Women Writers*, 68–69.

14. *P&P* (1858), iii; St. Johnsbury *Caledonian*, 23 January 1858, p. 3.

15. *VHG*, 3: 1189. Saunderson had served as pastor of the Congregational Church in Wallingford since 1852. Before that his ministry had been in Ludlow.

16. Ibid.; *NBP*, 1 (March 1887): 121; Biddle & Eschholz, eds., *Literature of Vermont*, 360; Babb, "Abby Hemenway," 26. Hemenway only gave the names of three of the men who served on her "examining committee" in *NBP*, but an autobiographical sketch of William Ford, in *VHG*, 3: 490, notes that he served on the committee, so he is presumably the fourth man. Paul Eschholz calls Julia Dorr an acknowledged literary critic. See *Rutland Historical Society Quarterly*, 4 (Summer 1974): 24.

17. For a biographical sketch of Dorr see Biddle and Eschholz, eds., *Literature of Vermont*, 360–61. For Botta, see Robert F. Marler, "Anne Charlotte Lynch Botta," *Notable American Women: A Biographical Dictionary* (Cambridge: Belknap Press of Harvard University Press, 1971), vol. 1, pp. 212–214. By the Civil War some eighty American women had published at least one volume of poetry. See Baym, *American Women Writers*, 69.

18. For brief sketches of the most most prominent nineteenth-century Vermont poets, see Walter J. Coates and Frederick Tupper, eds., *Vermont Verse: An Anthology* (Brattleboro, Vt.; Stephen Daye Press, 1931).

19. *VHG*, vol. 5, part 2, p. 712.

20. *P&P* (1858), 3–4.

21. William Ford, "Courage Pilgrim," ibid., 184.

22. Rhoda P. Tucker, "To an Autumn Bough," ibid., 39.

23. Ibid., 25.

24. Ibid., 393–400.

25. Abby Hemenway to the Reverend [Henry and Elizabeth] Saunderson, 11 September 1858, mss 8-858511, VHS.

26. *Bellows Falls Times*, 4 February 1859, p. 2; *NBP*, 1 (August 1886): 32. A copy of one of these illustrated presentation copies can be seen at Special Collections, Bailey/Howe Library, University of Vermont, Burlington (hereafter SCUVM).

27. *Middlebury Register*, 15 December 1858, p. 3; 22 December 1858, p. 1; Abby Maria Hemenway, ed., *Vermont Quarterly Gazetteer*, 1 (4 July 1860): back cover (hereafter *VQG*).

28. *Bellows Falls Times*, 4 February 1859, p. 2. While Ethan Allen is mentioned in numerous poems, he is the principal subject of only one, "Ethan Allen," by C. L. Goodell, *P&P* (1858), 132–137.

29. Letter to editor signed "Mansfield," *Bellows Falls Times*, 11 February 1859, p. 2.

30. *NBP*, 2 (December 1888): 246.

31. Abby Hemenway to Bernice Ames [n.d. 1861], Abby Hemenway Papers, SCUVM.

32. *Bellows Falls Times*, 11 February 1859, p. 2. Abby Hemenway to the end of her life believed this story, and was certain that "Ascutney" had been a proofreader for the *Times*, who had submitted "some twenty pages of his effusions," for inclusion in *P&P*, only to be rejected. She does not name this individual, however. See *NBP*, 2 (December 1888): 246.

33. *P&P* (1860), 454.

34. Coates and Tupper, eds., *Vermont Verse*, 248–49; Biddle and Eschholz, eds., *Literature of Vermont*, 45; *P&P* (1860), 29–30. An anthology of Vermont poetry published in 1872 also left out Rowley. See A. J. Sandborn, ed., *Green Mountain Poets* (Claremont, N.H., 1872). But *Literature of Vermont*, published in 1973, includes three poems of Rowley's.

35. *P&P* (1860), iii–iv.

36. These reviews are quoted on back cover of *VQG*, 1 (July 1860).

37. Quoted in Biddle and Eschholz, eds., *Literature of Vermont*, 8–9.

38. In a recent anthology of American verse, *American Poetry: An Anthology*, 2 vols. (The Library of America, 1993), only one Vermont poet, Carlos Wilcox, is included; see 1: 119–121. None of Abby's or Abigail Dana Hemenway's poems were included in later collections of Vermont poetry.

Chapter 5

1. *VHG*, 2: v.

2. Marion Hemenway, "Abby Hemenway," 2.

3. This and the following account of Hemenway's activities during the months following the publication of *P&P* is taken from her serialized autobiography in *NBP*, 1 (June 1886): 3.

4. Babb, "Abby Hemenway," 28; *NBP*, 1 (June 1886): 3–6.

5. Ibid., 6.

6. *VHG*, 1: iii; Daniel A. Metraux, "Early Vermont Historiography. The Career of Pliny H. White," *Vermont History News*, 43 (July–August, 1992): 63–66.

7. David Jaffee, *People of the Wachusett: Greater New England in History and Memory* (Ithaca: Cornell University Press, 1999), 5–6, 16–17.

8. David Hall, "Reassessing the Local History of New England," in *New England: A Bibliography of its History* (Boston: G. K. Hall & Co., 1981), 7: xxv–xxvii.

9. Quoted in ibid., 7: xix–xxi.

10. Russo, *Keepers of Our Past*, 38–39.

11. Zadock Thompson, ed., *A Gazetteer of the State of Vermont* (Montpelier, Vt.: E. P. Walton, 1824).

12. Samuel Swift, *History of the Town of Middlebury* (1859; reprint, Rutland, Vt: Charles E. Tuttle Company, 1971), 5.

13. *Middlebury Register*, 27 April 1859, p. 3. The statute passed by the General Assembly carried little force in its wording: "Any town at their annual March meeting, may authorize their selectmen to contract with some person to prepare and publish the early history of such town, at the expense of the town, under such restrictions and regulations as such towns shall provide." *Acts and Resolves Passed by the General Assembly of the State of Vermont* (1858), 53.

14. *P&P* (1858), 65–67.

15. *NBP*, 1 (June 1886), 6.

16. Dorothy Canfield Fisher, *The Vermont Tradition* (Boston: Little Brown and Company, 1953), 3.

17. For a discussion of early historical writing in Vermont, see Russo, *Keepers of Our Past*, 39–42.

18. Nina Baym, "At Home with History: History Books and Women's Sphere Before the Civil War," *Proceedings of the American Antiquarian Society*, vol. 101, part 2 (1992): 289. For a comprehensive study of antebellum women who studied and wrote history, see Baym, *American Women Writers*; Mary Kelley, "Designing a Past for the Present: Women Writing Women's History in Nineteenth-Century America," *Proceedings of the American Antiquarian Society* (1996): 315–346. Abby Hemenway is not included in either Baym's or Kelley's works, because these focus on antebellum women writers.

19. Quoted in Baym, *American Women Writers*, 94, 96.

20. *VHG*, 1: iii; *NBP*, 1 (June 1886): 6.

21. The following and only account of Hemenway's efforts to begin work collecting town histories for her *Gazetteer* is taken from *NBP*, 1 (July 1886): 15–17; 3 (August 1886): 30–32.

22. Ibid.

23. Russo, *Keepers of Our Past*, 57.

24. *NBP*, 1 (July 1886): 16.

25. Ibid., 1 (February/March, 1887): 107–109.

26. Frederick Rudolph, "Emma Hart Willard," *Notable American Women*, 2: 611. Middlebury College didn't admit women until 1883, and then mainly for economic reasons.

27. *NBP*, 1 (July 1886): 17.

28. Ibid., 1 (August 1886): 30-32. In fact the history of Orwell as published in the Addison County number of the *VQG* was not written by Judge Bottom. Nor is there a church history by Rufus Cushman. The very brief Orwell town history is unsigned and was most probably written by Hemenway herself. See *VHG*, 1: 73–77.

29. *Middlebury Register*, 31 December 1859, p. 2. Lady assistants for the four towns of Goshen, Hancock, Ripton, and Starksboro share the last name of their town's historian.

30. *NBP*, 1 (September 1886): 43–45.

31. Ibid., 1 (May 1887): 146–147. Rowland Robinson's son, the future novelist Rowland E. Robinson, was the author of the history of Ferrisburgh.

32. *NBP*, 1 (February/March 1887): 107–109.

33. In 1868 Eliakim Walton urged his fellow Vermonters to subscribe to the *Gazetteer*, and hoped that twenty thousand people would come forward. Hemenway would have been happy with ten thousand. *VQG* (3rd ed., 1868), vol. 1, back cover.

34. Babb, "Abby Hemenway," 32.

35. *NBP*, 1 (September 1886): 46–47.

36. Ibid., 1 (May 1887): 143.

37. Ibid., 1 (November 1886): 71.

38. *VHG*, 1: 106.

Chapter 6

1. *VHG*, 1: 495.

2. *NBP*, 2 (October 1887): 155.

3. *VHG*, 1: 106–107; J. Kevin Graffagnino, "The Vermont 'Story': Continuity and Change in Vermont Historiography," *VH*, 46 (Spring 1978): 77–99. Hemenway's history of Vergennes is, like other town histories that she wrote and/or collated herself, unattributed. Although she often gives herself away by using the editorial "we," it is difficult to be precise about how much of these chapters Hemenway actually composed herself. While some appear to be written entirely by her, others have numerous authors, including Hemenway. Still others are simply collations of materials sent to her by a town clerk. The vast majority of chapters in the *Gazetteer*, however, are attributed to a single named author.

4. Joyce Appleby, et al., *Telling the Truth About History* (New York: W. W. Norton and Company, 1994), 112–113.

5. Abby Hemenway to [John D.] Smith, 5 January 1860, Bixby Library, Vergennes, Vt. A description of the proposed *Gazetteer* can be found in the *Middlebury Register*, 7 December 1859, p. 2.

6. Babb, "Abby Hemenway," 28–29.

7. *NBP*, 2 (October 1887): 155.

8. David D. Van Tassel, *Recording America's Past: An Interpretation of the Development of Historical Studies in America, 1607-1884* (Chicago: University of Chicago Press, 1960), 53.

9. Abby Hemenway to [John D.] Smith, 31 May 1860, Bixby Library, Vergennes, Vt; *NBP*, 2 (January 1888): 178.

10. Abby Hemenway to [John D.] Smith, 31 May 1860; Babb, "Abby Hemenway," 35; *VQG*, 1 (April 1862): front cover.

11. Abby Hemenway to J[ohn D.]. Smith, 5 January 1860. For Smith's history of Panton, see *VHG*, 1: 77–84.

12. Abby Hemenway to [John D.] Smith, 31 May 1860.

13. J[ohn D.] Smith to Abby Hemenway, 4 June [1860], Bixby Library, Vergennes, Vt. Parts of this letter are torn away.

14. Abby Hemenway to J[ohn] D. Smith, 5 June 1860, Bixby Library, Vergennes, Vt.

15. *NBP*, 2 (October 1887): 155. The nature of Abigail Dana Hemenway's infirmity is not known.

16. Ibid., 166.

17. *VHG*, 1: 119–120.

18. Ibid., 1.

19. Ibid., 77.

20. These unattributed verses are found on the front cover of *VQG*, 1 (4 July 1860).

21. *VHG*, 1: 77.

22. Ibid., 50. A footnote in Smith's history of Panton directs readers to Swift's *History of Middlebury*, 88–89, for a fuller account than the one usually given of Benedict Arnold's supposed abandonment of his troops in Ferris Bay after the Battle of Valcour Island. See *VHG*, 1: 80.

23. Sources given for the Bridport history were Zadock Thompson, *A Gazetteer of the State of Vermont* (Montpelier, Vt.: E. P. Walton, 1824); Leonard Deming, *Catalogue of the Principal Officers of Vermont* (Middlebury, 1851); a manuscript copy of Josiah Goodhue, *History of the Town of Shoreham* (1861); and materials gathered for the editor by a Mrs. Olmstead, the wife of a Bridport clergyman. See *VHG*, 1: 16–18.

24. Ibid., 17–18.

25. According to David Russo, the lack of town records in Vermont was one reason why local historians such as Hemenway "relied heavily on the personal reminiscences of aged pioneers." Russo, *Keepers of Our Past*, 50.

26. *VHG*, 1: 34.

27. Abby Hemenway, "Reminiscences of Addison," ibid., 16.

28. *NBP*, 1 (February/March 1888): 188.

Chapter 7

1. Excerpt from Anne Lynch Botta's, "Ode," *VHG*, 1: 183.
2. *NBP*, 2 (April 1888): 200–201.
3. Ibid.
4. Babb, "Abby Hemenway," 36; *NBP*, 2 (April 1888): 200-202.
5. Ibid., 201.
6. Henry D. Hall, *Memoir of Honorable Hiland Hall* (Boston, 1887), 13; *NBP*, 1 (May 1887): 150. In 1868 Hiland Hall published his *Early History of Vermont*, which, according to Kevin Graffagnino, is "the most professional nineteenth-century statement of the traditional view of Vermont history." See Graffagnino, "The Vermont 'Story,'" 86.
7. *NBP*, 2 (January 1888): 179–180.
8. For an account of Hemenway's visit to the Hiland Halls in Bennington see ibid., 211–218.
9. Ibid., 2 (August 1888), 233. Hemenway's biography of the Jackson family of Dorset can be found in *VHG*, 1: 193–196. The particular interest of this sketch is the unusual amount of information it contains on the women of the family.
10. Abby Hemenway's account of her visit to the Reverend Frederick Wadleigh in Arlington can be found in *NBP*, 2 (August 1888): 234–235.
11. Ibid., 235.
12. Ibid., 2 (December 1888): 245.
13. *Historical Magazine*, 4 (June 1860): 350–351. For a discussion of the *Historical Magazine* as a promoter of a more critical spirit among American historians, see Van Tassel, *Recording America's Past*, 131–133.
14. Burlington Daily *Free Press*, 21 July 1860, p. 2 (hereafter *FP*); *Burlington Times* review is quoted on the back cover of *VHG*, vol. 1; *Middlebury Register*, 18 July 1860, p. 2.
15. B[enjamin] L[arrabee] to the editor, *Middlebury Register*, 17 October 1860, p. 1. Abby reprinted most of this letter in *VHG*, 1: 257–258.
16. Ibid., 255–256.
17. *VHG*, 1: 257; *NBP*, 1 (August 1886): 45.
18. *VQG*, 1 (April 1862): inside front cover. In a letter Hemenway wrote in January 1862 to John Bulkley Perry (her historian for the Franklin County town of Swanton) she said that, although Number 4 of the *Quarterly Gazetteer* "is in press at Albany," the publisher wouldn't release it until she had raised $400. Abby Hemenway to John Bulkley Perry, 29 January 1862, John Bulkley Perry Papers, SCUVM.
19. J[oel]. Munsell to Abby Hemenway, [n.d.], published in *VHG*, 1: 1096. See also Abby Hemenway to John Bulkley Perry, 29 January 1862.
20. *VQG*, 1 (October 1861): inside front cover.
21. Abby Hemenway to Henry Stevens, 25 July 1861; 7 October 1861, Stevens Papers, VHS.

Chapter 8

1. Oliver Wendell Holmes, "Voice of the Loyal North," in Abby Maria Hemenway, ed., *Songs of the War* (Albany, N.Y.: J. Munsell, 1863), 61.
2. *FP*, 8 October 1861, p.2.
3. Howard Coffin, *Full Duty: Vermonters in the Civil War* (Woodstock, Vt.: The Countryman Press, 1993), 22.
4. Ibid., 24. Hemenway's pride in Vermont's antislavery record is evident in her placement of the lines "Where breathes no castled lord or cabined slave" on the front cover of the first number of the *Quarterly Gazetteer*, see *VQG*, 1 (July 1860).
5. James M. McPherson, *Battle Cry of Freedom* (New York: Oxford University Press, 1988), 323; Harris, *History of Ludlow*, 151; Abby Hemenway to Henry Stevens, 7 October 1861, Stevens Papers, VHS.
6. Abby Hemenway to Cyrus M. Fisher, 1 January 1862, HSM.
7. *VHG*, 1: 857; Weston A. Cate, *Up & Doing: The Vermont Historical Society, 1838–1970* (Montpelier, Vt.: Vermont Historical Society, 1988), 7.
8. Abby Hemenway to Henry Stevens, 25 July 1861, Stevens Papers, VHS.

9. Abby Hemenway to Henry Stevens, 7 October 1861.

10. *VHG*, 4: 933; Abby Hemenway to John Bulkley Perry, 14 July 1862, Perry Papers, SCUVM. In this letter Hemenway describes a day spent copying material from Stevens's collection on Grand Isle. Unfortunately, much of Henry Stevens's valuable collection had perished in the Vermont State House fire of 1857. What remained (including the materials Hemenway used) is described in Thomas Goodwillie's sketch of him in *VHG*, 1: 282. Goodwillie himself made use of Stevens's maps and other documents, ibid., 296. Hemenway obtained from Stevens the valuable insight that few of the proprietors, or original landowners in Vermont's towns, actually settled there; see ibid., 857. Her indebtedness to him is mentioned also on page 1080.

11. Katherine M. Waterman to the editor, *FP*, 5 March 1940, p. 7.

12. *VHG*, 1: 1031. This description of Hemenway's visit to Maidstone is found in ibid., 1044–1045.

13. Abby Hemenway to Cyrus M. Fisher, 1 January 1862.

14. Abby Hemenway to John B[ulkley] Perry, 29 January 1862.

15. John Ufford to Abby Hemenway, July 7, 1862, in *VHG*, 2: 182.

16. The biography of John Ufford in the *Gazetteer* is by Mrs. G. H. Safford, ibid., 183. It describes Ufford as attempting to enlist in the fall of 1862, but because he wrote his history after being turned down, it seems more likely that he tried to enlist in the fall of 1861.

17. Harris, *History of Ludlow*, 155.

18. Coffin, *Full Duty*, 282; *VHG*, 1: 655.

19. Hemenway, ed., *Songs of the War*, 9. The style of "Send Them Home Tenderly" was, as Hemenway points out, modeled on the then-popular ballad, "The Bridge of Sighs," by Thomas Hood, an English poet.

20. Daniel Aaron, *The Unwritten War* (New York: Alfred A. Knopf, 1973), 149.

21. The author of this verse is not named. Hemenway intended to publish four or five sequels to *Songs of the War*, "at least a part for each year of the war, . . . for which I have much material—and may perhaps do when the history is finished." These sequels, however, were never published. See unpublished manuscript, misc. file #640, VHS.

22. *VHG*, 1: 249–250.

23. Ibid., 436–442; list of officers and volunteers, 443–452.

24. Hemenway, ed., *Songs of the War*, back cover; Abby Hemenway, broadside [January 1862], VHS; Abby Hemenway to [E. H.] St. John, 11 March 1862, courtesy Rev. John R. McSweeney.

25. Ibid.

26. Abby Hemenway to John Bulkley Perry, 9 June 1863, John Bulkley Perry Papers, SCUVM; *VHG*, 2: v–vi.

Chapter 9

1. Julia Smalley, *The Young Converts; or Memoirs of the Three Sisters, Debbie, Helen, and Anna Barlow* (Claremont N.H., 1868), 52. The Barlow family moved to St. Albans and all three sisters are buried there. *VHG*, 1: 366. A different version of this chapter was published earlier as "Abby Hemenway's Road to Rome," *VH*, 63 (Fall, 1995): 197–213.

2. Diary of William Henry Hoyt, 28 April 1864, SCUVM.

3. *MR*, vii–viii.

4. Ibid.; Hemenway, *Rosa Immaculata*, viii. Hemenway was not the only antebellum Protestant woman who cherished a devotion to the Virgin Mary before her conversion to Catholicism. Sophia Ripley, an 1848 convert from Transcendentalism and Unitarianism, wrote a cousin in 1846 that she had consecrated her school in the utopian Brook Farm community to "Our Blessed Mother." See Jenny Franchot, *Roads to Rome: The Antebellum Protestant Encounter with Catholicism* (Berkeley: University of California Press, 1994), 305.

5. "Statement of the [Catholic] Mission in the southern part of Vermont & of a part of New Hampshire under the Care of Reverend John B. Daly," in Bishop Fenwick's Journal, 17 December 1840, p. 240. The original of this manuscript is in the archives of the Diocese of Boston.

6. Harris, *History of Ludlow*, 117–119. "The Irish in Ludlow," Lucy Fletcher Chapter Daughters of the American Revolution, comp., *A Collection of Historical Essays of Ludlow, Vermont and Vicinity* (Ludlow, c.1940).

7. Bassett, *Gods of the Hills*, 86.

8. Roth, *Democratic Dilemma*, 273–275; Ralph Henry Gabriel, *The Course of American Democratic Thought* (New York: Ronald Press, 1940), 52.

9. Bassett, *Gods of the Hills*, 87.

10. Franchot, *Roads to Rome*, 281; Richard H. Clarke, "Our Converts," *American Catholic Quarterly Review*, 18 (July 1893): 511. A recent study of religion in nineteenth-century Vermont claims that only "a trickle of well-to-do, upper-class Vermonters converted to Catholicism." See Bassett, *Gods of the Hills*, 154.

11. See Abby Hemenway's inscription in volume I of the *VHG*, in Bishop Louis De Goesbriand's personal library, Vermont Diocesan Archives, Burlington, Vt. Hemenway family tradition tells us that Abby's conviction that Roman Catholicism was the only true religion came from her reading. See Marion Hemenway, "Abby Hemenway," 10.

12. Babb, "Abby Hemenway," 42; *VHG*, 1: 567.

13. Laurita Gibson, *Some Anglo-Catholic Converts to Catholicism Prior to 1829* (Washington, D.C.: Catholic University of America Press, 1943), 185–86. Fanny was only five years old when her father died in 1789. Her mother, Ethan's second wife, then married Dr. Jabez Penniman. Some accounts of Fanny Allen credit her with bringing numerous converts into the church, including American patients at the Hôtel-Dieu. Daniel Barber, the Episcopal minister who baptized her before she went off to school in Montreal, came into the church in 1816 through Fanny Allen's influence. He was followed by his wife, two children, his sister, and all her family. See Eleanor Simpson, "The Conservative Heresy: Yankees and the Reaction in Favor of Roman Catholics" (Ph.D. diss., University of Minnesota, 1974), 104.

14. This account of Fanny Allen's vision is taken from a children's column Abby wrote for the Catholic magazine *Ave Maria* in 1865 and 1866. See *AM*, 2 (12 May 1866): 303–304; 2 (30 June 1866): 415–416; 2 (7 July 1866): 429–430; 2 (14 July 1866): 445–447. For another account of Fanny Allen's vision see "Centenary of the Supposed Apparition of St. Joseph to Fanny Allen," *FP*, 10 September 1896.

15. *Memoires particuliers pour servir a l'histoire de l'eglise de l'Amerique du nord; vie de Mselle Mance et histoire de l'hôtel-Dieu de Villemarie en Canada*, vol. 3, part 2 (Paris, 1854), 294–303.

16. Abby Hemenway, *Fanny Allen, the First American Nun* (Boston: Thomas B. Noonan, [1878]), 6. Hemenway's French source was presumably *Memoires particuliers*. She refers her readers to this account in a note accompanying the sketch of Allen in the *Gazetteer*. Although the play's title calls Fanny Allen "the first American nun," she was not in fact the first Catholic woman in the United State to join a religious order.

17. Abby Hemenway, "An Hour in the St. Albans Cemeteries," *VHG*, 2: 365.

18. Roth, *Democratic Dilemma*, 279.

19. *VHG*, 1: 895–896. For other references in the *VHG* to division and dissension in the Protestant churches see "Joseph Hoag's Vision," 1: 740; the history of Stowe by M. N. Wilkins, 2: 713–714; and the history of Fletcher by Ben[jamin]. A. Kinsley, 2: 208-211.

20. Simpson, "Conservative Heresy," 25; Hemenway, *Fanny Allen*, 14.

21. Quoted in Simpson, "Conservative Heresy," 27.

22. Letter from Asa Barton to Lucia Barton, 23 July 1865, in Chiolino, comp., *Box of Letters*, part 2, p. 22.

23. Franchot, *Roads to Rome*, 305.

24. Simpson, "Conservative Heresy," 49; Sydney E. Ahlstrom, *A Religious History of the American People* (New Haven: Yale University Press, 1972), 622.

25. Louis De Goesbriand, *Catholic Memories of Vermont and New Hampshire* (Burlington: Louis De Goesbriand, 1886), 128–136; Simpson, "Conservative Heresy," 75; diary of William Henry Hoyt, 24 July 1846.

26. Smalley, *Young Converts*, 38–39; De Goesbriand, *Catholic Memories*, 131-133; Simpson, "Conservative Heresy," 76.

27. Hugh Marshall, *Orestes Brownson and the American Republic* (Washington, D.C.: Catholic University of America Press, 1971), 290–291.

28. A half dozen letters from Hemenway to Orestes Brownson dating from the mid-1870s survive. In one of these she admits to having been critical of his "former writings," which sought "to compromise or Americanize" the Catholic Church. Abby Hemenway to Orestes A. Brownson, 23 December 1874, Orestes A. Brownson Papers (hereafter CBRO), [I-4-f], University of Notre Dame Archives, Notre Dame, Indiana (hereafter UNDA).

29. Quoted from Brownson's *Convert* in Franchot, *Roads to Rome*, 337–338.

30. Abby Hemenway, "Our First Annunciation Day."

31. Christine M. Bochen, *The Journey to Rome: Conversion Literature by Nineteenth-Century American Catholics* (New York: Garland, 1988), 66-68. For descriptions of the conversion process, see also Franchot, *Roads to Rome*.

32. Hemenway, *Fanny Allen*, 51.

33. Sara Maitland, *A Big-Enough God: A Feminist's Search for a Joyful Theology* (New York: Henry Holt, 1995), 7.

34. Franchot, *Roads to Rome*, 280. For a discussion of Catholicism's romantic appeal for nineteenth-century Americans, see ibid., chap. 10.

35. Ibid., 307.

36. For the image of the Catholic church as "Holy Mother," see T. J. Jackson Lears, *No Place of Grace: Antimodernism and the Transformation of American Culture 1880–1920* (Chicago: University of Chicago Press, 1994), 197.

37. Chambers-Schiller, *Liberty a Better Husband*, 21, 24. In *The Young Converts* Debby Barlow describes her entry into the church as an act of defiant independence that puts the law of God above the law of parents. See Smalley, *Young Converts*, 14.

38. *MR*, 51.

39. Chambers-Schiller, *Liberty A Better Husband*, 52.

40. In one of her *Ave Maria* columns, Hemenway calls Burlington "that dearest old lake town . . . my other home." See *AM*, 2 (17 February 1866): 111.

41. Smalley, *Young Converts*, 41, 45.

42. Marion Hemenway, "Abby Hemenway," 10–11.

43. Book 1 of the records of the Ludlow, Vermont Baptist Church.

44. Babb, "Abby Hemenway," 43. David Hemenway, a descendant of Abby's brother Charles, is the source for the family's assessment of Abby as a "black sheep."

45. While there is no record of Daniel Hemenway's reaction to his daughter's decision to become a Catholic, in an era when women were not meant to make independent decisions, fathers and husbands were unlikely to approve of such strong-willed, and self-sufficient behavior from their womenfolk. See Simpson, "Conservative Heresy," 403.

46. Diary of William Henry Hoyt, 29 April 1864. In choosing to be baptized in a French church was Hemenway perhaps following in Fanny Allen's footsteps? For a description of the chapel, see Hemenway's column in *AM*, 2 (24 March 1866): 191.

47. Hemenway, *Fanny Allen*, 23.

48. Babb, "Abby Hemenway," 44.

Chapter 10

1. Hemenway, *Fanny Allen*, 51.

2. *AM*, 2 (7 July 1866): 430.

3. Ibid. Hemenway described an unnamed "rabid" Baptist who "hated me particularly for my secession from that church of my youth." See Abby Hemenway to Mother Angela

Gillespie, 8 December 1880, Edward Sorin Papers, Box 1881-B, Province Archives Center, Notre Dame, Ind. (hereafter PAC).

4. Abby Hemenway to Asa Barton, 27 January 1869, in Chiolino, comp., *Box of Letters*, 30–31.

5. Hemenway, *Fanny Allen*, 29.

6. Bassett, *Gods of the Hills*, 84.

7. Hemenway herself noted that the Vermont Catholic Diocese had "few Catholics but the very poor." See *AM*, 2 (17 February 1866): 111.

8. Quoted in Coffin, *Full Duty*, 325.

9. A copy of *The Mystical Rose* can be seen at the VHS. How Abby succeeded in finding a New York publisher for this book is not known. Nor do we have any information about numbers printed and sold.

10. *MR*, 6.

11. Marina Warner, *"Alone of All Her Sex": The Myth and Cult of the Virgin Mary* (New York: Vintage Books, 1983), 14–19. The sources Hemenway used for her life of the Virgin are cited in the footnotes and include Abbet Gerbert's *Lily of Israel*, Trombelli's *Life of St. Joachim and St. Anna*, and Sedelmayer's (or Seldmayr's) *Theologia Mariana*.

12. *MR*, 25.

13. Ibid., 51.

14. Ibid., 60.

15. Ibid., 73–74.

16. Ibid., 33–34. Hemenway refused to include stories about the Holy Family that went counter to accepted Catholic Church doctrine. For example, she dismissed any suggestion that Jesus had brothers and sisters because that would have denied that Mary was "a virgin-mother sanctified into Heaven forevermore." Ibid., 250. For an example of Hemenway's charge to her historians to include legendary lore in their town histories, see Abby Hemenway to [Charles C.] Abbott, 24 July 1871, Charles C. Abbott Papers, MSC 198, VHS.

17. *MR*, 280–285.

18. Babb, "Abby Hemenway," 89.

19. Ludlow Land Records, vol. 18, p. 318; vol. 19, p. 88, Town Clerk's office, Ludlow, Vt. On November 17, 1862 Abby Hemenway paid $600 for this piece of land. In September 1864 she sold the same piece of land for $970. Several sources suggest that Hemenway moved to Burlington as early as 1865, but I can find no reliable confirmation of this.

20. *AM*, 2 (22 December 1866): 812.

21. *VHG*, vol. 5, part 1, pp. 652–653. In a note preceding Stevens's sermon Hemenway writes, "How the people of Vermont received the ending of the war, is seen so clear in this sermon, we have included it as a descriptive chapter, fitting . . . for the entire State."

22. Chambers-Schiller, *Liberty a Better Husband*, 71.

23. Patrick Allitt, *Catholic Converts: British and American Intellectuals Turn to Rome* (Ithaca: Cornell University Press, 1997), 128.

24. For the Catholic Church's discomfort with unmarried laywomen, see Joseph G. Mannard, "'Maternity . . . of the Spirit': Nuns and Domesticity in Antebellum America," *U.S. Catholic Historian*, 5 (Summer/Fall 1986): 305–324.

25. According to Allitt, other women writers who converted to Catholicism in the nineteenth century saw the single life as a positive vocation, "providing an opportunity for work that would otherwise be denied to them." Allitt, *Catholic Converts*, 143.

26. *AM*, 1 (1 May 1865): 4–5.

27. Sister M. Madeleva, "Mother Angela Gillespie," *Notable American Women*, 2: 34; James K. Kenneally, *The History of American Catholic Women* (New York: Crossroad Publishing Co., 1990), 50.

28. Babb, "Abby Hemenway," 44. Babb apparently never read Hemenway's writings in *AM*. These make it clear that she spent nearly two months at Notre Dame and contributed poetry as well as a children's column to the magazine. Hemenway's "Dear Children," letters for *AM* begin publication on 30 September 1865, and run irregularly through December 1866.

29. Flora Louise Stanfield to [Daniel E. Hudson], 4 March 1890, X-3-K, Daniel E. Hudson Papers (CHUD), UNDA.

30. *AM*, 1 (30 September 1865): 319.

31. Ibid. (7 October 1865): 335.

32. Archibald J. Byrne, "Eliza Allen Starr," *Notable American Women*, 3: 350–351.

33. *AM*, 1 (30 September 1865): 367–368.

34. Ibid., 1 (2 December 1865): 463–464; (16 December 1865): 495.

35. Ibid. Hemenway does not say what her mother's illness was.

36. Newspaper clipping [n.d. 1866], courtesy David Hemenway.

37. Abby Maria Hemenway, "My Relic Box," *NBP*, 2 (January 1888): 177–78.

Chapter 11

1. *VHG*, 1: 747.

2. For descriptions of nineteenth-century Burlington see Ralph Nading Hill, *Lake Champlain, Key to Liberty* (Taftsville, Vt.: The Countryman Press, 1976), 231–233; T. D. Seymour Bassett, *The Growing Edge: Vermont Villages, 1840–1880* (Montpelier, Vt.: Vermont Historical Society, 1992).

3. Henry James, letter to *The Nation*, 12 August 1870, quoted in T. D. Seymour Bassett, *Outsiders Inside Vermont* (Canaan, N.H.: Phoenix Publishing, 1967), 89.

4. *CP*, 302.

5. Hemenway gives her residence as St. Joseph's Mount, another name for the location of the convent run by the Sisters of Providence. See *AM*, 2 (22 December 1866), 812.

6. A biography of Lydia Clarke Meech, including a lengthy memoir of her conversion to Catholicism, is found in *CP*, 251–284. Hemenway doesn't say when this first meeting with Lydia Meech occurred, but the latter's baptism on June 4, 1866 suggests the likelihood that it was sometime after that date. The information on Ezra Meech comes from Leonard Deming's *Catalogue of the Principal Officers of Vermont* (Middlebury, 1851).

7. Babb, "Abby Hemenway," 46–48.

8. *CP*, 20–23; DeWitt Clinton Clarke's obituary in *FP*, 1 September 1870, p. 3.

9. *CP*, 204; Babb, "Abby Hemenway," 47.

10. *CP*, 281–282.

11. Ibid., 302, 284.

12. For the layout and contents of Lydia Meech's house, see the inventory in Chittenden County Probate Court Records, Appraiser's Report, filed 22 October 1874.

13. *CP*, 302.

14. Franchot, *Roads to Rome*, 311. Julia Smalley wrote of her friendship with the Hoyts: "In *them* I feel as if I had found true friends . . . they *know what a person has to pass through in changing their religious creed*." Smalley, *Young Converts*, 58.

15. Both these accounts are in *VHG*, 2: 366.

16. Edward Hungerford, *Report on the Moral and Religious Condition of the Community* (Burlington, 1867), 29.

17. *FP*, 27 September 1867, p. 4; 30 September 1867, p. 4.

18. The Immaculate Conception of the Blessed Virgin was pronounced an official dogma of the Roman Catholic Church in 1854.

19. *FP*, 9 December 1867, p. 4.

20. Abby Hemenway to Carrie Hemenway, 22 March 1867, courtesy David Hemenway.

21. In a letter to E. H. St. John Hemenway claims that her publisher had kept her work in press for six years presumably waiting until she had the money to pay him. Abby Hemenway to E. H. St. John, 29 August 29 1877, courtesy Rev. John R. McSweeney.

22. Babb, "Abby Hemenway," 48. Lydia Meech owned no property until her son Dewitt Clarke died in 1870. After his death Hemenway claimed to have frequently loaned her friend money for taxes and other expenses. Where she obtained this money she doesn't say. See *CP*, 308.

23. The flyer or broadside, dated August 1868, is courtesy Rev. John R. McSweeney. Number 7 of the *VQG* has a publication date of 1867 but probably was not distributed until 1868.

A notice of the publication of volume I of the *Historical Gazetteer* in the *FP* on 22 August 1868, states that "it is some years now since the appearance of earlier issues," suggesting that number 7 of the *Quarterly* (which continued the histories of Chittenden County) had not been distributed until then. The *St. Albans Messenger*, in a notice of volume I, also mentions the long hiatus since the first six numbers had been issued. See *VHG*, 2: 1197.

24. The editor of the *Historical Magazine* had held out little hope for the future of the *Gazetteer* when he received early copies, remarking with prescience it was "too good to be profitable," though not "too good to be extremely useful and valuable." Quoted in *VHG*, 2: 1199.

25. *FP*, 22 August 1868, p. 4.

26. This and other favorable notices are published in, *VHG*, 2: 1197–1199.

27. Letter from Philip Battell to Abby Hemenway [n.d. c. 1868], in *VHG*, 2: 1200.

28. *Historical Magazine*, vol. 5 (second series), January 1869, pp. 94–95.

29. A copy of the Vermont Historical Society resolution of 1862 can be found in *VHG*, vol. 5, part 1, p. 186. Hemenway points out that this "was the first public notice of the work by an historical body."

30. Hemenway was not alone in thinking that hers was God's work. Nina Baym in her work on women historians describes them as sharing a "belief and pride in their extraordinary mission. . . . They saw themselves at work for women, for the nation, for God." See Baym, *American Women Writers and the Work of History*, 239.

Chapter 12

1. *VHG*, 1: 1070.

2. Meetings of the Vermont Historical Society were open to the public, and while there was no official restriction against women becoming members, the first woman was not elected until 1870. See Cate, *Up & Doing*, 17–18.

3. Abby Hemenway to Charles Reed, 5 January 1870, MSS 20, #112, VHS; Preface *VHG*, 2: v.

4. This undated letter from John M. Moore is printed on the inside front cover of the paperbound edition of *VHG*, vol. 2.

5. Ibid. Hemenway's response to Moore's letter is printed underneath it. The history of Rockingham is found in *VHG*, vol. 5, part 2, pp. 493–510.

6. See Amos Churchill's history of Hubbardton, prepared and arranged by E.H. St. John in *VHG*, 3: 756.

7. Ibid., 4: 979; 2: v.

8. This undated notice of volume I of the *VHG* is quoted in part in *VHG*, 2: 1197. Others in Vermont were impressed with Hemenway's strategy. Professor Joseph Torrey of the University of Vermont congratulated her on organizing "a regular campaign," insuring that her *Gazetteer* "cannot fail of being a standard work." Quoted in letter from Abby Hemenway to John B[ulkley] Perry, 29 January [18]62, John Bulkley Perry Papers, SCUVM.

9. Pliny White's history of Coventry is in *VHG*, 3: 136–160.

10. Ibid., 1: 553.

11. See editor's note following history of Wheelock, ibid., 433.

12. Ibid., 2: 455.

13. Faith L. Pepe, "Toward a History of Women in Vermont: An Essay and Bibliography," *VH*, 45 (Spring 1977): 70.

14. Wilkins, "History of Stowe," *VHG*, 1: 709. The history of Stowe fills seventy-three pages, the last twenty-two of which contain short biographies of all the soldiers from Stowe who fought in the Civil War.

15. Henry Clark, "Centennial Address, Delivered at Poultney, Vermont, 21 September 1861," *VHG*, 3: 980.

16. Ibid., 421.

17. For an excellent discussion of the differing agendas of the nineteenth-century antiquar-
ian and the twentieth-century social scientist as community historians, see Alan Taylor,
"The Advent and Triumph of the Community Study," *New England: A Bibliography of
Its History* (Boston: G. K. Hall & Co., 1989), xxxi–xlvii.

18. For a discussion of Harriet Beecher Stowe's part in the domestication of American literature, see Hedrick, *Harriet Beecher Stowe*.

19. *VHG*, 3: 138, 141, 142, 148.

20. I am indebted to Betty Bandel for the suggestion that the histories of the newer, smaller
towns are the richest. See her review of Brenda Morrissey, *Abby Hemenway's Vermont:
Unique Portrait of a State*, in *VH*, 41 (Fall 1973): 237–239. In a notice of volume II of
the *Gazetteer*, Hemenway's historian for Franklin County, George F. Houghton, noted
with surprise and pleasure the richness of the town histories from those more recently
settled counties which he had "supposed to be almost without histories. . . . We feel it
most emphatically the history of the people by the people." See *VHG*, vol. 4, back matter.

21. Sylvanus Nye's papers on the Berlin history are in the VHS.

22. Nye's history of Berlin is in *VHG*, 4: 53–74.

23. Ibid., 2: 1027.

24. Nye Papers, VHS.

25. Russo, *Keepers of Our Past*, 50.

26. Tamara Hareven, "The Search for Generational Memory," in David K. Dunaway and
Willa K. Baum, eds., *Oral History, An Interdisciplinary Anthology* (Walnut Creek,
Calif.: Altamira Press, 1996), 247–248.

27. Charles T. Morrissey, "Why Call It 'Oral History'? Searching for Early Usage of a Generic
Term," *Oral History Review* (1980): 20–22.

28. *VHG*, 3: 1145.

29. Harry H. Dewey to Sylvanus Nye, 30 January 1873; 11 February 1873, Nye Papers, VHS.

30. These two documents are in the Charles Abbott Papers, VHS.

31. For a biographical sketch of Abbott, see *VHG*, 4: 911–912.

32. Abby Hemenway to [Charles C.] Abbott, 24 July 1871, Abbott Papers, VHS.

33. Ibid.

34. *VHG*, 4: 887, 898–900. Hemenway apparently felt less free to tamper with Daniel
Thompson's wolf-hunt story, which she printed verbatim. See Nye papers, VHS.

35. *NBP*, 1 (June 1886): 7.

36. Abby Hemenway to John B[ulkley Perry], 29 January 1862.

Chapter 13

1. *VHG*, 4: 977.

2. Biographical sketch of John Bulkley Perry from the *Congregational Quarterly* reprinted in
VHG, 4: 986. For a modern assessment of Perry as a geologist see Kevin T. Dann, "John
Bulkley Perry and the 'Taconic Question,'" *Earth Sciences History*: 3 (1984): 153–159.
Dann suggests that Perry's extreme humility, the nature and timing of his geological
publications, his theological preoccupations, and his death at an early age, all contributed to his being overlooked as a major contributor to the Taconic controversy. For
a discussion of Perry's religious modernism, see Bassett, *Gods of the Hills*, 906–909.

3. *VHG*, 4: 933. Letter from Abby Hemenway to John Bulkley Perry, 29 January [1862], John
Bulkley Perry Papers, SCUVM.

4. Ibid. Perry's history of the Patriote War can be found in *VHG*, 4: 1073–1077. Other
accounts of this war can also be found in ibid., 2: 266, 298–300.

5. There seems to be a discrepancy here between Hemenway's account of when she received
this chapter and the date at the end of the essay, which is 1868. *VHG*, 2: 88.

6. John B. Perry, "The Natural History of the Counties, Chittenden, Lamoille, Franklin, and
Grand-Isle," ibid., 2: 21–88.

7. Abby Hemenway to Orestes Brownson, 11 November 1873, Brownson Papers, [I-4-f], UNDA; Abby Hemenway to John Bulkley Perry, 29 January [1862].

8. See John Bulkley Perry, "Book of Clippings and Notes," John Bulkley Perry Papers, UVM. In a letter of appointment from Charles W. Eliot, president of Harvard, to Perry dated 14 March 1870 his title is given as "University Lecturer in Geology," ibid.

9. Dann, "John Bulkley Perry," 157.

10. Abby Hemenway to Orestes Brownson, 11 November 1873.

11. Ibid. In her letter to Brownson, Hemenway asked him if he would read Perry's essay and her commentary. Whether Brownson ever did this is not known. Hemenway's notes appear at the end of Perry's essay, see *VHG*, 4: 975–983. Although Perry's published essay in the *Gazetteer* ends with the close of the American Revolution in 1783, an unpublished manuscript covering the years from 1783 to 1793 is contained in the John Bulkley Perry papers, SCUVM.

12. Abby Hemenway to Orestes Brownson, 11 November 1873.

13. For Perry's discussion of the John Graye manuscript see *VHG*, 4: 934–941.

14. Ibid., 940. The story of John Graye has long fascinated Vermonters. Recent versions can be found in Cora Cheney's *Vermont, The State with the Storybook Past* (Shelburne, Vt: The New England Press, 1979), 12–14; and Joe Citro's "The Mystery of the Graye Area," in *Green Mountain Ghosts*, 215–217. Ralph Nading Hill concludes that the story is most likely a hoax. Ralph Nading Hill, "John Graye," *Vermont Life* (Spring 1966), 53–55.

15. This interpretation of Perry's account of the John Graye story was suggested to me by reading Paul Croce's *Science and Religion in the Era of William James: The Eclipse of Certainty, 1820-1880* (Chapel Hill: University of North Carolina Press, 1995), a book that maintains that truth and falsity were central concerns of nineteenth-century American culture.

16. *VHG*, 4: 950.

17. Ibid., 961.

18. Ibid., 976.

19. Ibid., 980. For an English translation of *Jesuit Relations* see Reuben E. Thwaite, ed., *The Jesuit Relations and Allied Documents: Travels and Explorations of the Jesuit Missionaries in New France 1610-1791*, 73 vols. (Cleveland: Burrows Brothers Co., 1896-1901). According to Kevin Dann, beginning in 1860 Perry carried on an extensive correspondence with the noted geologist Jules Marcou in French. See Dann, "John Bulkley Perry," 154.

20. *VHG*, 4: 978.

21. Ibid., 975.

22. Ibid., 975–977.

23. Ibid., 975, 977. Note that the long paragraph on page 975 that begins "And where the second points are . . ." appears to be all a quote from Peter Kalm's *Travels in North America*. Quotation marks should be inserted after "permit the English to come amongst them." The remainder of the paragraph is by Hemenway. For a twentieth-century translation of Kalm, see Adolph B. Benson, ed., *The America of 1750; Peter Kalm's Travels in North America* (N.Y.: Wilson\Erickson, Inc., 1937).

24. *VHG*, 4: 977–978. Hemenway does not give her source for this version of Rogers' Raid, but it is obviously not taken from Roberts Rogers's own account, the source used until recently by Kenneth Roberts and others. Rogers's account implies that he massacred all the villagers, not just the women, children, and old men described in Hemenway's version. This would suggest that Hemenway had access to French as well as English accounts of the incident. See William A. Haviland and Marjory W. Power, *The Original Vermonters: Native Inhabitants, Past and Present* (Hanover, N.H.: University Press of New England, 1994), 236–237.

25. *VHG*, 4: 976–977.

26. Ibid., 979. As early as 1862 Hemenway had instructed her town historians to have their church histories written by the pastors of those churches whenever possible. See Abby Hemenway to C. C. Torrey, 12 February 1862, courtesy Mary D. Torrey.

27. *VHG*, 4: 934–941.

28. The sources for these excerpts include John Gilmary Shea, *History of the Catholic Missions among the Indian Tribes of the United States* (New York: P. J. Kenedy, c. 1854); Pierre-Francois-Xavier de Charlevoix, *History and General Description of New France*, 6 vols. (New York: J. G. Shea, 1866–1872).

29. *VHG*, 4: 983.

Chapter 14

1. *CP*, 308.

2. Ibid., 49, 302–303.

3. *FP*, 1 September 1870, p. 3.

4. Ibid.; *CP*, 302–303.

5. Ibid., 304-305.

6. Ibid., 53.

7. *VHG*, 3: 1133. Hemenway's sketches of women are often placed at the end of her town histories.

8. Abby Hemenway to Orestes Brownson, 15 May 1874, Orestes A. Brownson Papers, [I-4-f], CBRO, UNDA. See also appraisal of Lydia Meech property in Chittenden County Probate Court.

9. *CP*, 309–310.

10. Chambers-Schiller, *Liberty a Better Husband*, 190–91.

11. Abby Hemenway to Orestes Brownson, 26 April 1875, Brownson Papers, [I-4-f], CBRO, UNDA.

12. *CP*, 303. DeWitt Clinton Clarke died intestate, thus his Meech cousins, once Lydia herself died, would inherit the Pearl Street house in Burlington.

13. The damages were to the Meech property in Shelburne which Ezra claimed had deteriorated since his stepmother had moved to Burlington. See "Application for Appeal and Declaration" filed 17 July 1875 in the Lydia Meech Estate Papers, Chittenden County Probate Court, Burlington, Vt.

14. This is implied in the judge's charge to the jury at the conclusion of the first trial. See *FP*, 28 September 1877, p. 3.

15. An announcement of the original appeal is contained in the *FP*, 6 October 1875, p. 6. Grounds for contesting the Meech will were spelled out in the *FP*, 19 September 1877, p. 5. The anti-Catholic views of the contesters are implied in the judge's charge to the jury in the first trial. See *FP*, 28 Sept 1877, p. 3. Hemenway notes that the lawyer for the contesters "put his lever against" the possibility that the Catholic Church might "receive some little benefit from this will by and by." *CP*, 306.

16. Ibid., 204.

17. *FP*, 28 September 1877, p. 3; *CP*, 306.

18. Ibid., 307.

19. Ibid.; *FP*, 16 April 1878, p. 3.

20. *CP*, 311. *The Clarke Papers* had in fact largely been set in type in 1875. All that Hemenway added in 1878 were the concluding pages dealing with the court case. Abby Hemenway to Orestes Brownson, 26 April 1875, Brownson Papers, [I-4-f], CBRO, UNDA.

21. *FP*, 14 Sept 1878, p. 3.

22. Abby Hemenway to Hiland Hall, 6 Sept 1878, courtesy Rev. John R. McSweeney; Babb, "Abby Hemenway," 52.

23. Copy of mortgage deed signed by Louis De Goesbriand, 18 July 1879, Diocesan Archives, Burlington, Vt. The information that cathedral property was mortgaged to make the loan was given to me by the late William Goss, archivist for the Diocese of Burlington.

24. *CP*, 303.

25. Abby Hemenway to Marcus Gilman, 28 June 1877, mss 20 #112, VHS.

26. *VHG*, 2: v–vi.

27. Russo, *Keepers of Our Past*, 79.

28. Abby Hemenway to Hiland Gutterson, 1 February 1870, courtesy Florence Plumb.

29. Abby Hemenway to Marcus Gilman, 28 June 1877.

30. *VHG*, 3: v.

31. Abby Hemenway to [?], 14 July 1874, courtesy Donald B. Johnstone.

32. Abby Hemenway to Marcus Gilman, 28 June 1877.

33. *FP*, 18 October 1878, p. 3.

34. *Journal of the Senate of the State of Vermont, Biennial Session 1878* (Rutland: Tuttle & Co., 1879), 54; *FP*, 19 October 1878, p. 3.

35. Abby Hemenway to editor, *FP*, 31 October 1878, p. 2.

36. *The Journal of the House of the State of Vermont, Biennial Session, 1878* (Rutland: Tuttle & Co., 1879), 117.

37. *FP*, 23 November 1878, p. 3. According to Michael Kammen, there was a powerful presumption in both Europe and the United States that "government bore virtually no responsibility for matters of collective memory." Kammen, *Mystic Chords of Memory*, 54.

38. *VHG*, 4: 1193.

39. *FP*, 16 July 1879, p. 3. In a letter to Volney Vaughn, the historian for Middlesex, Hemenway writes that "for the first time our State Auditor last year questioned the legality of appropriations unless *signed* by the Governor. Heretofore it has not been the practice to ask any signature for appropriations given by joint resolution of both house." Abby Hemenway to Volney Vaughn, 26 January 1880, courtesy Ruth Cozzens.

40. *VHG*, 4: 1193–94.

41. Hemenway writes that she is being sued for "attachment of a mortgage" in Abby Hemenway to Mother Angela Gillespie, 26 July 1880, Sorin Papers, Folder 27, PAC.

42. Abby Hemenway to Volney Vaughn, 26 January 1880.

43. Madeleva, "Angela Gillespie."

44. Abby Hemenway to Mother [Mary] Ascension, 12 November 1885, Sorin ERA Papers, folder 29, PAC.

Chapter 15

1. George Eliot, *Middlemarch*, 702.

2. Abby Hemenway to Mother Angela Gillespie, 26 July 1880. In 1874 the Sisters of Mercy of Manchester, New Hampshire, came to Burlington to run the parochial school that had previously been operated by the Sisters of Providence.

3. Ibid.

4. *AM*, 3 (19 October 1867), 667.

5. Abby Hemenway to Father Edward Sorin, 13 October 1880, Sorin Papers, Box 6-1880-B, PAC.

6. Abby Hemenway to Father Edward Sorin [n.d. after 19 October 1880], Sorin Papers, Box 1, fold. 11, PAC.

7. Abby Hemenway to Edward F. Sorin, 13 October 1880. Hiram Huse wrote an essay on the Vermont State Library for the *Gazetteer*, *VHG*, 4: 324.

8. Abby Hemenway to Father Edward Sorin, 15 November 1880, Sorin Papers, Box 6-1880-B, PAC. The text of the Vermont Historical Society resolution can be found in *Proceedings of the Vermont Historical Society, 19 October 1880* (Rutland, 1880), xviii. See also *FP*, 22 October 1880, p. 3. No record survives of the Claremont Manufacturing Company's proposed bill.

9. Abby Hemenway to Father Edward Sorin, 15 November 1880.

10. Until 1965 each town in Vermont was represented in the legislature by one House member.

11. Abby Hemenway to Father Edward Sorin, 15 November 1880.

12. Abby Hemenway to Mother Angela Gillespie, 8 [January] 1880, Sorin Papers, Box 1881-B, PAC.

13. Abby Hemenway to Mother Angela Gillespie, 8-13 [December 1880], Sorin Papers, Box 1881-B, PAC; *FP*, 23 December 1880, p. 3; *Journal of the Vermont Senate, 1880*, 375.

14. *Acts and Resolves Passed by the General Assembly of the State of Vermont at the Sixth Biennial Session, 1880* (Rutland: Tuttle & Co., 1881), 120; Abby Hemenway to Father Edward Sorin, 13 October 1880.

15. Abby Hemenway to Father Edward Sorin, 10 January 1881, Sorin Papers, Box 1881-B, PAC.

16. Abby Hemenway to Hiland Hall, 6 September 1878; *VHG*, 4: 218, 599; Chancery Records of Washington County Court, State of Vermont, vol. 10, p. 353.

17. Jacob G. Ullery, *Men of Vermont: An Illustrated Biographical History of Vermonters and Sons of Vermont* (Brattleboro, Vt.: Transcript Publishing Co., 1894), 321–322.

18. In a letter to Henry Sheldon, Hemenway describes renting rooms from a woman in Montpelier but does not identify her or the location of her house. Abby Hemenway to [Henry Sheldon], 12 January 1883, HSM.

19. *VHG*, vol. 4 (August, 1881), (October, 1881). The only examples I found of these separately published numbers of volume IV of the *Gazetteer* are courtesy Rev. John R. McSweeney. Along with the history of Montpelier, Northfield and Waterbury are the other Washington County towns whose histories were published separately by Joseph Poland.

20. Abby Hemenway to James F. Edwards, [30 April 1882], XI-I-b, James F. Edwards Papers, CEDW, UNDA.

21. Abby Hemenway to Hiland Hall, 13 June 1882, Hiland Hall Papers, Park-McCullough House, North Bennington, Vt.

22. The histories of Burlington and Rutland, the two largest towns in the state, take up 268 and 111 pages respectively in the *VHG*.

23. *VHG*, 4: iii.

24. See for example the many typographical errors in the "compiler's notes" following John Bulkley Perry's essay on the early Indian and French history of Swanton, *VHG*, 4: 975–980.

25. *FP*, 3 August 1882, p. 3.

26. Abby Hemenway to Hiland Hall, 25 August 1882, Park-McCullough House, North Bennington, Vt.

27. *Acts and Resolves Passed by the General Assembly of the State of Vermont at the Seventh Biennial Session, 1882* (Rutland: Tuttle & Co., 1883), 261.

28. Ullery, *Men of Vermont*, 322. *Walton's Vermont Register and Business Directory* for 1883 lists W. W. Prescott, not Joseph Poland, as the publisher of the *Watchman and Journal*.

29. Abby Hemenway to Albert E. Hager, 2 August 1883, Chicago Historical Society Letterbook, box 39, pp. 76, 77, Chicago Historical Society, Chicago, Ill.

30. Abby Hemenway to Mother [Mary] Ascension, 12 November 1885, Sorin ERA Papers, folder 29, PAC; Abby Hemenway to Henry Sheldon, 16 February 1884, HSM.

31. Abby Hemenway to [Albert E.] Hager, [27] June 1885, Chicago Historical Society Letterbook, box 59, pp. 31–38, Chicago Historical Society, Chicago, Ill. It is not clear whether the rooms Poland and Clement entered were in Hemenway's boarding place or some other location. Hemenway does not give Clement's first name.

32. Quoted in Babb from Chancery Records of Washington County Court, State of Vermont, vol. 10, p. 353. I have had to rely on her for this account since the original court records have been destroyed and the film copies are mostly illegible. Babb, "Abby Hemenway," 55–56. There is no record of how Hemenway gained entrance to the bindery.

33. Ibid.

34. Quoted in Babb, "Abby Hemenway," 56.

35. Alice Piper's recollections of her cousin Abby Hemenway's printing establishment in Ludlow are found in Babb, "Abby Hemenway," 57–58.

36. Abby Hemenway to Henry Sheldon, 29 April 1884, HSM.

37. Babb, "Abby Hemenway," 57; Abby Hemenway to Henry Sheldon, 29 April 1884.

38. At the time of her death in 1890 Hemenway owed money to others in addition to Joseph Poland, including George Grenville Benedict and Samuel Farnam, the printer for the

Claremont Manufacturing Company who owned volumes II and III of the *VHG*. See letter from Franklin Denison to George Grenville Benedict, 14 March 1890, Benedict Papers, SCUVM.

39. Frances Babb asserts that Hemenway had left Ludlow by April 23, 1885, the date when she was expected to appear in court, claiming that she was pursued by the threat of fore-closure. Babb, "Abby Hemenway," 68.

40. From a copy of Abby Hemenway's will, courtesy of David Hemenway.

41. Abby Hemenway to Henry Sheldon, 30 December 1886, HSM.

Chapter 16

1. Abby Hemenway to [Albert E.] Hager, [27] June 1885, Chicago Historical Society Letterbook, box 59, p. 32, Chicago, Ill.

2. Abby Hemenway to Henry Sheldon, 30 December 1886, HSM.

3. Abby Hemenway to [Albert E.] Hager, [27] June 1885. A sketch of Hemenway by Mrs. E. C. Robbins in *VHG*, 5: vii–viii, says that she went to Chicago because friends had made it sound like a better place to finish the *Gazetteer*. I am presuming that this second chancery suit is the reason Abby was asked to appear in court on April 23, 1885.

4. Abby Hemenway to [Albert E.] Hager, [27] June 1885.

5. Abby Hemenway to Henry Sheldon, 30 December 1886, HSM.

6. Abby Hemenway to Mother [Mary] Ascension, 12 November, 1885; Abby Hemenway to [Albert E.] Hager, [27] June 1885.

7. Abby Hemenway to [Hiland Gutterson], [n.d., October 1886], courtesy Florence Plumb; fragment of letter to same, [n.d., summer or fall 1888], courtesy Florence Plumb.

8. Abby Hemenway to Hiland Gutterson, 2 December 1885, courtesy Florence Plumb.

9. Abby Hemenway to Mother [Mary] Ascension, 12 November 1885.

10. Babb, "Abby Hemenway," 60; Abby Hemenway to Henry Sheldon, 30 December 1886.

11. Babb, "Abby Hemenway," 60; *NBP*, 1 (June 1886): 10; flyer for *NBP*; Abby Hemenway to Hiland Gutterson, 6 August 1886, courtesy Florence Plumb.

12. *VHG*, vol. 5, part 2, p. 405.

13. *NBP*, 1 (June 1886): 7.

14. Ibid., 7.

15. Ibid., 1 (September 1886): 51, 80.

16. Ibid., 1 (December/January 1887): 91.

17. William Portus Baxter to Henry Sheldon, 18 May 1886, HSM; *NBP*, 1 (November 1886): 76.

18. Abby Hemenway to Henry Sheldon, 9 July 1888, HSM.

19. Abby Hemenway to Henry Sheldon, 8 October 1888, HSM.

20. Ibid. In a later letter Hemenway indicates that Henry Sheldon had advised her to "have the Vt. Hist. Gaz. ready in Season," if she wanted further help from the Vermont leg-islature. Abby Hemenway to Henry Sheldon, 29 June 1889, HSM.

21. Ibid.

22. Ibid.; *NBP*, 2 (June 1889): 281–282.

23. Obituary for Abby Hemenway, Chicago *Tribune*, 28 February 1890, p. 3.

24. *FP*, 3 March 1890, p. 3.

25. Chicago *Tribune*, 28 February 1890, p. 3. This article describes Abby as having a number of wealthy siblings and goes on at some length about the "rare collection" of antique jewelry found in Abby's rooms at the time of her death. Where the rumors of Hemenway wealth come from we don't know. But the jewels were almost certainly part of her inheritance from Lydia Meech.

26. Franklin Denison to George Grenville Benedict, 14 March 1890. The other creditor Denison mentioned is Roswell Farnham. He really meant Samuel L. Farnam of White River Junction, part owner of the Claremont Manufacturing Company, who owned vol-umes II and III of the *Gazetteer*. See Babb, "Abby Hemenway," 72.

27. William Portus Baxter to Henry Sheldon, 14 and 16 March 1890, HSM.

28. *FP*, 30 June 1892, p. 4.

29. *VHG*, 5: vi.

30. The pagination in volume V is very erratic. Some page numbers are missing. In other cases individual towns, such as Guilford, are set off with their own pagination. This is probably because these towns were originally printed as separate pamphlets.

31. *VHG*, vol. 5, part 2, p. 611; Londonderry history in ibid., part 3 (Londonderry), p. 25.

32. Ibid., vol. 5, part 2, p. 364.

33. *FP*, 30 June 1892, p. 4.

34. Julia A. Pierce to editor *Middlebury Register*, 19 January 1912, p. 1.

35. Joel Munsell's Sons to [Carrie Page], 17 July 1893, misc. file #640, VHS.

36. Pierce to the editor, *Middlebury Register*, 19 January 1912.

37. *Proceedings of the Vermont Historical Society for the Years 1913–1914*, 52–53.

Epilogue

1. *VHG*, vol. 5, part 2, p. 270.

2. Marion Hemenway, "Abby Hemenway," 13.

3. Hall, "Reassessing the Local History of New England," xxx.

4. Peter Novick, *That Noble Dream: The 'Objectivity Question' and the American Historical Profession* (New York: Cambridge University Press, 1988), 73.

5. David Van Tassel points out that a critical spirit was present in the field of local history in the mid-nineteenth century and actively promoted by the *Historical Magazine*. With the demise of this journal in 1875 this critical spirit faded from local history writing. Van Tassel, *Recording America's Past*, 131–133, 161–169.

6. Hill, *Contrary Country*, 220.

7. John Duffy to author, 15 September 2000.

8. See chapter 6, pp. 115–166.

9. *VHG*, vol. 2, title page.

10. It should be noted that the histories of towns with Roman Catholic parishes published in volumes II–V do usually contain a paragraph or two of Catholic history, most of them contributed by Bishop De Goesbriand. Also, Abby was probably unaware of the many people of Native American ancestry living in Vermont. Until recently most descendants of the Abenaki and other tribes preferred to keep their ethnic identity to themselves.

11. *VHG*, 1: 193.

12. Abby Hemenway to Mother [Mary] Ascension, 12 November 1885.

13. *Proceedings of the Vermont Historical Society for the Years 1913–1914*, 52–53.

Select Bibliography

Publications of Abby Maria Hemenway

Hemenway, Abby Maria. *Clarke Papers: Mrs. Meech and her Family*. Burlington, Vt., 1878.

_____. [Marie Josephine, pseud.]. *Fanny Allen, The First American Nun*. Boston: Thomas B. Noonan & Company, [1878].

_____. [Marie Josephine, pseud.]. *The House of Gold and the Saint of Nazareth. A Poetical Life of St. Joseph*. Baltimore: Kelly, Piet & Company, 1873.

_____. [Marie Josephine, pseud.]. "Loretto Leaves, or Imaginary Origins of the Litany of the Blessed Virgin," *Ave Maria: A Catholic Journal Devoted to the Honor of the Blessed Virgin*, 3 (23 March 1867): 139–140; (8 June 1867): 356–358; (15 June 1867): 371–373; 4 (7 March 1868): 150–153.

_____. [Marie Josephine, pseud.]. *The Mystical Rose, or, Mary of Nazareth, the Lily of the House of David*. New York: D. Appleton & Co., 1865.

_____. [Marie Josephine, pseud.]. *Rosa Immaculata, or, the Tower of Ivory, in the House of Anna and Joachim*. New York: P. O'Shea, 1867.

_____, ed. *Notes By the Path of the Gazetteer* (1886–1889). Miss Hemenway of the Gazetteer, publisher, Chicago, Ill.

_____, ed. *Poets and Poetry of Vermont*. Rutland: George A. Tuttle & Co., 1858.

_____, ed. *Poets and Poetry of Vermont*. Rev. ed. Boston: Brown, Taggard & Chase, 1860.

_____, ed. *Songs of the War*. Albany, N.Y.: J. Munsell, 1863.

_____, ed. *Vermont Historical Gazetteer*,
vol. 1. Addison, Bennington, Caledonia, Chittenden, Essex Counties. Burlington: 1867;
vol. 2. Franklin, Grande Isle, Lamoille, Orange Counties. Burlington: 1871;
vol. 3. Orleans, Rutland Counties. Claremont N.H.: Claremont Manufacturing Co., 1877;
vol. 4. Washington County; also Swanton, Groton, Hubbardton, Berlin. Montpelier: Vermont Watchman & State Journal Press, 1882;
vol. 5. Windham County; also Sutton, Bennington, Brandon. Mrs. Carrie H. Page, 1891.

_____, ed. *Vermont Quarterly Gazetteer*, vol. 1, nos. 1–11 (1860–1867).

Manuscript Collections

Small collections of Abby Maria Hemenway's letters and other unpublished manuscripts can be found at the following libraries:

Special Collections. Bailey/Howe Library. University of Vermont. Burlington, Vt.
Vermont Historical Society. Montpelier, Vt.
Henry Sheldon Museum. Middlebury, Vt.
Bixby Library, Vergennes, Vt.
Park-McCullough House, North Bennington, Vt.
Chicago Historical Society. Chicago, Ill.
Province Archives Center. Notre Dame, Ind.
University of Notre Dame Archives. Notre Dame, Ind.

Books

Aaron, Daniel. *The Unwritten War*. New York: Alfred A. Knopf, 1973.

Ahlstrom, Sydney E. *A Religious History of the American People*. New Haven: Yale University Press, 1972.

Allit, Patrick. *Catholic Converts: British and American Intellectuals Turn to Rome*. Ithaca, N.Y.: Cornell University Press, 1997.

Appleby, Joyce, et al. *Telling the Truth About History*. New York: W. W. Norton and Company, 1994.

Bassett, T. D. Seymour. *The Gods of the Hills: Piety and Society in Nineteenth-Century Vermont*. Montpelier, Vt.: Vermont Historical Society, 2000.

_____. *The Growing Edge: Vermont Villages, 1840–1880*. Montpelier: Vermont Historical Society, 1992.

Baym, Nina. *American Women Writers and the Work of History, 1790–1860*. New Brunswick, N.J.: Rutgers University Press, 1995.

Biddle, Arthur W., and Paul A. Eschholz, eds. *The Literature of Vermont: A Sampler*. Hanover, N.H.: University Press of New England, 1973.

Bochen, Christine M. *The Journey To Rome: Conversion Literature by Nineteenth-Century American Catholics*. New York: Garland, 1988.

Cate, Weston A. *Up & Doing: The Vermont Historical Society, 1838–1970*. Montpelier, Vt.: Vermont Historical Society, 1988.

Chambers-Schiller, Lee. *Liberty A Better Husband: Single Women in America: The Generations of 1780–1840*. New Haven: Yale University Press, 1984.

Chilolino, Barbara, comp. *A Box of Letters Concerning the Vermont Family of Abby M. Hemenway*. Barbara Chiolino: 1978.

Coates, Walter J., and Frederick Tupper, eds. *Vermont Verse: An Anthology*. Brattleboro, Vt.: Stephen Daye Press, 1931.

Coffin, Howard. *Full Duty: Vermonters in the Civil War*. Woodstock, Vt.: The Countryman Press, 1993.

Cott, Nancy. *The Bonds of Womanhood: "Woman's Sphere" in New England, 1780–1835*. New Haven: Yale University Press, 1977.

Croce, Paul. *Science and Religion in the Era of William James: The Eclipse of Certainty, 1820–1880*. Chapel Hill: University of North Carolina Press, 1995.

De Goesbriand, Louis. *Catholic Memories of Vermont and New Hampshire.* Burlington: Louis De Goesbriand, 1886.

Dublin, Thomas. *Transforming Women's Work: New England Lives in the Industrial Revolution.* Ithaca, N.Y.: Cornell University Press, 1994.

Epstein, Barbara Leslie. *The Politics of Domesticity: Women, Evangelism, and Temperance in Nineteenth-Century America.* Middletown, Ct.: Wesleyan University Press, 1981.

Fisher, Dorothy Canfield. *The Vermont Tradition.* Boston: Little Brown and Company, 1953.

Franchot, Jenny. *Roads to Rome: The Antebellum Protestant Encounter with Catholicism.* Berkeley: University of California Press, 1994.

Gibson, Laurita. *Some Anglo-Catholic Converts to Catholicism Prior to 1829.* Washington, D.C.: Catholic University of America Press, 1943.

Gilmore, William J. *Reading Becomes a Necessity of Life: Material and Cultural Life in Rural New England, 1780–1835.* Knoxville: The University of Tennessee Press, 1989.

Graffagnino, J. Kevin. *Vermont in the Victorian Age: Continuity and Change in the Green Mountain State.* Bennington and Shelburne, Vt.: Vermont Heritage Press and Shelburne Museum, 1985.

Greven, Philip. *The Protestant Temperament: Patterns of Child-Rearing, Religious Experience, and the Self in Early America.* New York: Alfred A. Knopf, 1977.

Gutterson, Hiland G., et al. *The Local History of Andover, Vermont.* Chicago: A. M. Hemenway, 1886.

Hansen, Karen. *A Very Social Time: Crafting Community in Antebellum New England.* Berkeley: University of California Press, 1994.

Harris, Joseph N. *History of Ludlow Vermont.* Ludlow, 1949.

Hatch, Nathan O. *The Democratization of American Christianity.* New Haven: Yale University Press, 1989.

Haviland, William A., and Marjory W. Power, *The Original Vermonters: Native Inhabitants, Past and Present.* Hanover, N.H.: University Press of New England, 1994.

Hedrick, Joan D. *Harriet Beecher Stowe: A Life.* New York: Oxford University Press, 1994.

Hill, Ralph Nading. *Contrary Country: A Chronicle of Vermont.* New York: Rinehart & Co., 1950.

――――. *Lake Champlain, Key to Liberty.* Taftsville, Vt.: The Countryman Press, 1976.

History of Black River Academy As Seen Through Various Publications. 1972.

Jaffee, David. *People of the Wachusett: Greater New England in History and Memory.* Ithaca, N.Y.: Cornell University Press, 1999.

Juster, Susan. *Disorderly Women: Sexual Politics and Evangelicalism in Revolutionary New England.* Ithaca, N.Y.: Cornell University Press, 1994.

Kammen, Michael. *Mystic Chords of Memory: The Transformation of Tradition in American Culture.* New York: Alfred A. Knopf, 1991.

Kaufman, Polly Welts. *Women Teachers on the Frontier.* New Haven: Yale University Press, 1984.

Kenneally, James K. *The History of American Catholic Women.* New York: Crossroad Publishing Co., 1990.

Kerber, Linda. *Toward an Intellectual History of Women.* Chapel Hill: University of North Carolina Press, 1997.

Lears, T. J. Jackson. *No Place of Grace: Antimodernism and the Transformation of American Culture, 1880–1920*. Chicago: University of Chicago Press, 1994.

Marshall, Hugh. *Orestes Brownson and the American Republic*. Washington, D.C.: Catholic University of America Press, 1971.

McDannell, Colleen. *Material Christianity: Religion and Popular Culture in America*. New Haven: Yale University Press, 1995.

McLoughlin, William G. *New England Dissent, 1630–1883: The Baptists and the Separation of Church and State*. Cambridge: Harvard University Press, 1971.

McPherson, James M. *Battle Cry of Freedom*. New York: Oxford University Press, 1988.

Memoires particuliers pour servir a l'histoire de l'eglise de l'Amerique du nord; vie de Mselle. Mance et histoire de l'hôtel-Dieu de Villemarie en Canada. Paris, 1854.

Morrissey, Brenda. *Abby Hemenway's Vermont: Unique Portrait of a State*. Brattleboro, Vt.: The Stephen Greene Press, 1972.

Muller, H. Nicholas, III. *From Ferment to Fatigue?, 1870–1900: A New Look at the Neglected Winter of Vermont*. Burlington, Vt.: Center for Research on Vermont, 1984.

Novick, Peter. *That Noble Dream: The "Objectivity Question" and the American Historical Profession*. New York: Cambridge University Press, 1988.

Rabinowitz, Richard. *The Spiritual Self in Everyday Life: The Transformation of Personal Religious Expierience in Nineteenth-Century New England*. Boston: Northeastern University Press, 1989.

Roth, Randolph A. *The Democratic Dilemma: Religion, Reform, and the Social Order in the Connecticut River Valley of Vermont, 1791–1850*. New York: Cambridge University Press, 1987.

Russo, David. *Keepers of Our Past: Local Historical Writing in the United States, 1820s–1930s*. New York: Greenwood Press, 1988.

Smalley, Julia. *The Young Converts; or Memoirs of the Three Sisters, Debbie, Helen, and Anna Barlow*. Claremont, N.H., 1868.

Smith, Bonnie G. *The Gender of History: Men, Women, and Historical Practice*. Cambridge: Harvard University Press, 1998.

Smith-Rosenberg, Carroll. *Disorderly Conduct: Visions of Gender in Victorian America*. New York: Oxford University Press, 1985.

Stillwell, Lewis D. *Migration from Vermont*. Montpelier, Vt.: Vermont Historical Society, 1948.

Thompson, Zadock. *A Gazetteer of the State of Vermont*. Montpelier, Vt.: E. P. Walton, 1824.

Thwaite, Reuben E., ed. *The Jesuit Relations and Allied Documents: Travels and Explorations of the Jesuit Missionaries in New France 1610-1791*. Cleveland: Burrows Brothers Co., 1896 1901.

Van Tassel, David D. *Recording America's Past: An Interpretation of the Development of Historical Studies in America, 1607–1884*. Chicago: University of Chicago Press, 1960.

Ward, Donal. *Religious Enthusiasm in Vermont, 1761–1847*. Ann Arbor, Mich.: University Microfilms International, 1985.

Warner, Marina. *"Alone of All Her Sex": The Myth and Cult of the Virgin Mary*. New York: Vintage Books, 1983.

Williams, Samuel. *The Natural and Civil History of Vermont*. Burlington, Vt., 1809, 2nd edition.

Articles

Baym, Nina. "At Home with History: History Books and Women's Sphere Before the Civil War." *Proceedings of the American Antiquarian Society*, vol. 101, part 2 (1992): 275–295.

Clifford, Deborah P. "Abby Hemenway's Road to Rome." *Vermont History*, 63 (Fall, 1995): 197–213.

Cott, Nancy. "Passionlessness: An Interpretation of Victorian Sexual Ideology, 1790–1850." *Signs*, 4 (Winter 1978): 219–236.

Dann, Kevin T. "John Bulkley Perry and the 'Taconic Question.'" *Journal of the History of the Earth Sciences Society*, 3 (no. 2): 153–159.

Gilmore-Lehne, William J. "Reflections on Three Classics of Vermont History." *Vermont History*, 59 (Fall 1991): 227–249.

Graffagnino, J. Kevin. "The Vermont 'Story': Continuity and Change in Vermont Historiography." *Vermont History*, 46 (Spring 1978): 77–99.

Greene, Janet. "The Woman Who Told Everything." *Vermont Life*, 15 (Winter 1960): 27–31.

Hall, David. "Reassessing the Local History of New England." In *New England: A Bibliography of its History*, xix–xxxi. Boston: G. K. Hall & Co., 1981.

Hareven, Tamara. "The Search for Generational Memory." In David K. Dunaway and Willa K. Baum, eds., *Oral History, An Interdisciplinary Anthology*, 241–256. Walnut Creek, Calif.: Altamira Press, 1996.

Hill, Ralph Nading. "John Graye." *Vermont Life* (Spring 1966): 53–55.

Kelley, Mary. "Designing a Past for the Present: Women Writing Women's History in Nineteenth-Century America." *Proceedings of the American Antiquarian Society* (1996): 315–346.

Kerns, Kathryn M. "Farmer's Daughters: The Education of Women at Alfred Academy and University Before the Civil War." *History of Higher Education Annual*, 6 (1986): 11–28.

Metraux, Daniel A. "Early Vermont Historiography: The Career of Pliny H. White." *Vermont History News*, 43 (July–August 1992): 63–66.

Morrissey, Charles T. "Why Call It 'Oral History'? Searching for Early Usage of a Generic Term." *Oral History Review* (1980): 20–48.

Nelson, Margaret K. "Vermont Female Schoolteachers in the Nineteenth Century." *Vermont History*, 49 (Winter 1981): 5–30.

Pepe, Faith L. "Toward a History of Women in Vermont: An Essay and Bibliography." *Vermont History*, 45 (Spring 1977): 69–101.

Roth, Randolph A. "Why Are We Still Vermonters? Vermont's Identity Crisis and the Founding of the Vermont Historical Society." *Vermont History*, 59 (Fall 1991), 197–211.

Sicherman, Barbara. "Reading and Ambition: M. Carey Thomas and Female Heroism." *American Quarterly*, 45 (March 1993): 73–103.

Sklar, Kathryn Kish. "American Female Historians in Context, 1770–1930." *Feminist Studies*, 3 (1975–76): 171–184.

Taylor, Alan. "The Advent and Triumph of the Community Study." *New England: A Bibliography of Its History*, xxxi–xlvii. Boston: G. K. Hall & Co., 1989.

Unpublished Material

Babb, Frances Harriet. "Abby Maria Hemenway (1828-1890), Historian, Anthologist, and Poet." Master's thesis, Unversity of Maine, 1939.

Hemenway, Marion P. "Abby Maria Hemenway." Paper presented for the Daughters of the American Revolution, Ludlow, Vermont, 1917. Copy in Brigham Index, Vermont Historical Society, Montpelier, Vt.

Hemenway, Ruth A. "Genealogy of Harry E. Hemenway." Courtesy David Hemenway.

Mace, T. Box of History and Genealogy of Ludlow. MSC, Box A23, Vermont Historical Society, Montpelier, Vt.

Simpson, Eleanor. "The Conservative Heresy: Yankees and the Reaction in Favor of Roman Catholics." Ph.D. diss., University of Minnesota, 1974.

Index